Gender and Management

women's worlds congress 2014 india

Other titles in this series...

Gender Violence
Rekha Pande and Sita Vanka (eds.)

Gender and History
Rekha Pande (ed.)

Gender and Work: International Perspectives
Sita Vanka, Rekha Pande and Bharat Kumar Chillakuri (eds.)

Gender and Structural Violence
Rekha Pande and Sita Vanka (eds.)

Gender, Law and Health
Sita Vanka and Rekha Pande (eds.)

Gender and Management

International Perspectives

Editor

SITA VANKA

RAWAT PUBLICATIONS

Jaipur • New Delhi • Bangalore • Guwahati • Kolkata

ISBN 978-81-316-0886-9

Published by
Prem Rawat for **Rawat Publications**
Satyam Apts, Sector 3, Jawahar Nagar, Jaipur 302 004 (India)
Phone: 0141 265 1748 / 7006 Fax: 0141 265 1748
E-mail: info@rawatbooks.com
Website: www.rawatbooks.com

New Delhi Office
4858/24, Ansari Road, Daryaganj, New Delhi 110 002
Phone: 011 2326 3290

Also at *Bangalore, Guwahati* and *Kolkata*

Printed at Chaman Enterprises, New Delhi

Contents

The Prologue

Gender could be understood as a construct, which enables men and women to conduct themselves in a characteristic style and helps them understand their respective roles in family and society. The business world and management is no exception to this fact. Researchers have constantly studied the effect of gender on management and business but the dynamic changes in the business environment leaves a gap leading to a paucity of perspectives on the role of gender in management.

Taking clue from research, an attempt was made to discuss, deliberate and present multiple perspectives from various parts of the world in the Worlds Women's World Congress–2014 conducted at the University of Hyderabad. Academics, researchers, NGOs and organizations working for gender justice participated and presented their perspective in a six-day Congress held at the university focusing on *Gender in a Changing World.* The conference deliberated on an agenda for global gender policies and strategies, laying down a road map for gender-just society, gendered budgeting to empower women and engagement with the industry to create awareness on gender issues and network with the stakeholders for engendered solutions. WWC was a significant event of the university, where a galaxy of 1,000 speakers spread across 850 panels and paper presentations from different parts of the world, including Brazil, USA, UK, France, Germany, Korea, Nepal, Bangladesh, Canada, Israel, and across India participated in the conference.

Varied themes such as *Gender and Culture, Gender and History, Gender and Management, Gender and Violence, Gender and Digital Divide, Gender and Globalization, Gender and Work, Gender and Law, Gender and Science, Gender and Health, etc.* were discussed and deliberated during the six-day event. The programme was structured in plenaries, presentation of papers, workshops, panels, discussions, along with informal interaction and networking along with exhibitions. The Congress had a varied participant profile. There were researchers, scholars, government officials and policy-makers, NGOs, students, company representatives, feminists and many more who were interested in making positive contributions towards the cause of women's welfare and empowerment across the world, and becoming more useful to their own communities. Overall, the 12th Women's World Congress was aimed at each and every one interested in the creation of a gender just society and provided unlimited resources and opportunities to interact with prominent leaders in the field of gender and women's studies, so as to greatly expand on the global network of scholars and professionals.

Since it is a worldwide perspective on gender in a changing society, *Gender and Management* was one of the themes, where a number of papers were presented. These perspectives were brought together in a volume showcasing the best practices, success stories, research papers from across the world. The contributors of this volume have covered a wide variety of subjects encompassing important issues on *Gender and Management*, which broadly included educational management, enterprise management, healthcare, employment, and labour issues in the manufacturing and service sectors in the form of research articles, case studies and success stories.

Empowerment of women was the focus, for which the authors highlighted the development at the grassroots level with a case from Uganda. Grassroots democracy leading to women empowerment was also highlighted from a study in Kerala, India. The communication revolution has provided various ways of improving the social status of women. The role of mass media in women empowerment from a gender lens was discussed by some researchers. Public employment and gender wage gap have also been studied by authors. While scholars examined manufacturing of jobs for women from a Canadian perspective, the others critically looked at a cross country analysis of the gender wage gap in India. The role of women in engineering labour market along with an analysis of public employment programmes in India were also highlighted.

The role of women in enterprise management is a significant dimension of *Gender and Management.* The journey of women entrepreneurs from the north eastern region and Odisha in India was also depicted in the form of a case study and a research study. Since the role of women in entrepreneurship is in its infancy, scholars have attempted to provide a conceptual framework in the management of small and medium enterprises. The social cognitive factors influencing the relationship on the physical activity of Spanish students from a gender perspective was discussed to understand gender inequalities in the participation rates of men and women. Similarly, the role of emotional intelligence and values across gender in India depicting the psycho-socio-cultural heritage formed part of studies in the Indian context.

The gender division of domestic and child work in dual earner families were examined by some authors. Similarly, case studies of tribal villages in Madhya Pradesh, India, looked at female participation in the family economy. There is an increasing evidence worldwide enabling sustainable gender equitable outcomes of development interventions across the world. Gender transformative approaches in nutrition and livelihood interventions were focused with examples from Bangladesh. Disaster management is a part of human development process and hence, coping strategies assumes significance in such situations. The impact of natural disasters on the coping strategies of women in central Himalayas, India, was analysed empirically by the researchers.

The prevalence of glass ceiling as a societal phenomenon and overcoming the same with case studies on Indian women in corporate India was also highlighted by some studies. Similarly, the information revolution and ICT has enabled women to participate in new ways that redefined the traditional roles that they have been playing. Thus, studies on the role of women in the information age received attention from an Indian perspective. Economic empowerment of women in a changing world assumes significance in the current context. Micro-finance as a path towards women's empowerment was studied from the Mexican perspective. Similarly, the role of self-help groups in enhancing the capabilities of women with a case study in India was also attempted by scholars.

This book primarily aims at a compendium of articles and literature to the professionals, scholars and researchers on issues relating to gender and management. More specifically, the book seeks to include views of the experts on the gender issues and experiences of women from a multi-stakeholder perspective – policy-maker, managers, academics and beneficiaries in the process of management from different parts of the world. The theme is contemporary and includes issues, perspectives, approaches, research studies/frameworks and emerging patterns relating to gender and management from across the world in a lucid way. The volume provides an excellent opportunity for all those interested to update their knowledge on the concept, processes, issues, emerging paradigms on Gender and Management from a multidimensional cross country perspective.

I place on record a deep sense of gratitude to a number of people, who have directly or indirectly helped me in the completion of this volume. An event of the magnitude of the WWC–2014 and compiling the papers presented in the form a volume would not have been possible without the help and assistance of scores of people involved in it. The then Vice-Chancellor, Professor Ramakrishna Ramaswamy, and the administration of the University of Hyderabad merits mention for their support and encouragement in academic endeavours. I am thankful to the authors of the scholarly papers for patiently awaiting the completion of this volume. More particularly, the help, effort, time and editorial assistance of Dr. Bharat Kumar Chillakuri, Client Account Manager at Deloitte, for his support in the finalization of this volume is acknowledged wholeheartedly. The enduring support of my family has always enthused me in turning my dreams into reality. Thanks are also due to Rawat Publications and the team of professional editors for their cooperation, excellent editing and the formatting of the work.

Sita Vanka
Editor

Contributors

Harriet Nannyonga, Board Member, Maama Watali Development Association, Uganda.

Susan Namulindwa, Founder and Director, Maama Watali Development Association, Uganda.

Lydia Muyingo, Researcher, Maama Watali Development Association, Uganda.

Jayasree Paul, Assistant Professor, Department of Economics, Director of Collegiate Education, Kerala.

June Corman, Department of Sociology, Brock University, Ontario, Canada.

Ann Duffy, Department of Sociology, Brock University, Ontario, Canada.

Norene Pupo, Department of Sociology, York University, Ontario, Canada.

Manju Singh, Professor, Symbiosis International University, Pune, India.

Agrima Singh, Post Graduate Student, Symbiosis International University, Pune, India.

Namrata Singha Roy, Scientific Officer, International Crops Research Institute for Semi-Arid Tropics (ICRISAT), Hyderabad, India.

Ishita Mukhopadhyay, Professor, Department of Labour Economics, University of Calcutta, Kolkata, India.

Seema Singh, Associate Professor, Department of Economics, Delhi Technological University, Delhi, India.

Claret P.E. Mendonca, Research Scholar, School of Management, National Institute of Technology Karnataka, India.

A.H. Sequeira, Professor and Head, School of Management, National Institute of Technology Karnataka, India.

Mitoo Das, Assistant Professor, Faculty of Anthropology School of Social Sciences, IGNOU, New Delhi, India.

Arpita Kumari Mishra, Project Coordinator, Oxfam India, Odisha, India.

Sita Vanka, Professor, School of Management Studies, Hyderabad, India.

Ramneet Kaur, Research Scholar, Department of Political Science, University of Delhi, Delhi, India.

Neelu Rawat, Assistant Professor, Department of Sociology and Social Work, Dr. Harisingh Gour Vishwavidalaya, Sagar, M.P, India.

Ramona Ridolfi, Gender Manager, Helen Keller International, Dhaka, Bangladesh.

Meredith Jackson-de Graffenried, Technical Advisor, Helen Keller International, Dhaka, Bangladesh.

Marie Sophie Sandberg Pettersson, Gender Advisor and Programme Analyst, EEP, Dhaka, Bangladesh.

Faria Shabnam, Nutrition Coordinator and Gender Focal Point, EEP, Dhaka, Bangladesh.

Paula Kantor, Senior Scientist, Gender, World Fish, Cairo, Egypt.

Afrina Choudhury, Gender Specialist, World Fish, Dhaka Bangladesh, Egypt.

Annpurna Nautiyal, Professor, Department of Political Science, HNB Garhwal University, Srinagar Garhwal, Uttarakhand, India.

R.K. Maikhuri, Senior Scientist, GP Pant Institute of Himalayan Environment and Development, Srinagar Garhwal, Uttarakhand, India.

Bulan Pal, Senior Manager, Marketing, GODREJ and BOYCE MFG CO LTD, India.

Anindita Paul, Assistant Professor, IT and Systems, IIM Kozhikode, Kerala, India.

Soma Nandi, Associate Professor, Department of Education, East Calcutta Girls College, Kolkata, India.

Sri Mrinmoy Roy, Research Scholar, Department of Education, University of Calcutta.

Elena Ramírez-Rico, Department of Physical Education, University Complutence of Madrid, Spain.

Emilia Fernández-García, Department of Physical Education, University Complutence of Madrid, Spain.

Tripti Kumari, Research Scholar, Department of Geography, Benaras Hindu University, Varanasi, India.

Alicia Girón, Researcher and Tutor, Economic Research Institute, National Autonomous University of Mexico, Mexico City.

Anita Jagota, Associate Professor, School of Life Sciences, University of Hyderabad, Hyderabad, India.

Navya Jannu, Research Scholar, Civil Law, Someville College, Oxford University, United Kingdom.

Suchitra Boro, Research Scholar, Centre for Women Studies, University of Hyderabad, Hyderabad, India.

1

Empowerment of Women at Grassroots as a Local Development Reorientation Impetus

The Case of Maama Watali in Uganda

HARRIET NANNYONGA, SUSAN NAMULINDWA AND LYDIA MUYINGO

Abstract

The level of women's participation in prioritizing community development focus varies across regions. Based on the self-gathered field observations and informal feedback from two locations (Luweero and Nyenga) involving an indigenous organization, Maama Watali Development Association, this paper demonstrates how the increased participation of local women is contributing to defining and a reorientation in socio-economic development policy focus in a rapidly changing Uganda. The paper demonstrates that once focus is placed on empowerment of local women, there is not only a change in gender roles but also more crucially a change in the focus of development policy priorities and ultimately the allocation of financial and other resources. Empowered women didn't only talk but made the leap to action by undertaking specific activities including: library, health-promotion, credit for agricultural-related activities, soliciting funding for cooking stoves, and history documentation. Women's burgeoning activities caught the attention of the local male-dominated leadership who were then influenced and wanted to be associated with the practical outcomes reinforcing the argument that success attracts support. Males, who had previously ignored the women, are now listening more closely and turning to these outcomes as key information resources, exploring the possibility of allocating additional resources, and for policy prioritization and guidance. In addition, the women's activism has contributed to identification and development of leaders who are then in turn serving as role models within the community. The combined effect is that the goal of achieving full participatory democracy at the grassroot level becomes increasingly important and achievable.

Keywords

Maama Watali Development Association, Uganda, Luweero-Triangle, Nyenga, women's empowerment, gender balance

Introduction

Rationalizing Women's Issues in Policy-Making

Practitioners of and advocates for women's empowerment and gender balance believe that for a community to develop and flourish, it must pay equal attention to issues that are a priority for enhancing the welfare of all genders. The case for gender balance is reinforced by collections of anecdotal and empirical evidence which demonstrates that if focus is placed on everyone's circumstances and concerns then improvement in welfare of the general public occurs. Pursuing such a gender-balance approach enables a community to tap the unique talents of each individual while at the same time addressing the challenges that may be faced by specific sections of the populace.

History has documented many failures and consequences inherent in trying to maintain the status quo of a male-dominated society and a decision-making structure that marginalizes women. Many potential and actual shortcomings arise out of a community, institution or nation that takes a gender-biased approach. Key among these is that economic activity and community progress is hindered. Furthermore, there is not only a growth in resentment from the marginalized individuals but a direct constraint is put on their participation in the socio-economic development of all. It is, therefore, very important that the issue of women's marginalization is addressed and that women's participation is enhanced in the policy making process. Paying attention to gender would improve the formulation and implementation of and benefit from rational resource-based models of development and thereby enhance the resulting practical output within the community.

Although the participation of local women in defining development priorities varies across regions, an emerging pattern is that as females become more vocal, they are making steady gains in the level of influence on defining policy. However, even as the advocacy for gender balance and prioritizing women's concerns is increasing across the world, in some places like Uganda, the level of influence women have in formulating policy is still low. Hence, any mechanism through which this gender balance can be further increased and maintained for the long-term should be sought and this paper contributes to that quest.

Initiatives that Focus on Gender Balance in Policy-making

Women around the world have tried to reorient development policy focus so that formulation and allocation of resources reflects that women make up about 51 per cent of the population, 70 per cent of the poorest of the poor, and hold less than 20 per cent of elected positions (OECD, 2008; WEforum, 2012; *Business Week*, 2012). At the local, regional and global level, different types of initiatives have been undertaken in order to highlight the effect of ignoring gender balance issues and/or to correct these omissions. Among these initiatives are:

- International Women's Year (IWY), 1975

- United Nations Decade for Women, (1976 to 1985)
- International Women's Year Day, 8 March of each year
- Convention on the Elimination of All Forms of Discrimination against Women (CEDAW)

A prominent feature of 1985 Third World Conference of Women, held in Nairobi, was that during the proceedings, member countries set the goal of 'removal of legislated gender discrimination in the national laws by the year 2000'. This was point of pride in the conference's final communiqué. Almost one-and-a half decade after the goal was set in this momentous meeting, it would be prudent to: (a) pause and examine what, if any, kind of progress has been made on the national laws and regulations; (b) evaluate what difference such official goals have made in the lives of ordinary marginalized women on the ground; (c) examine if the official declarations to empower women have led to tangible and permanent change in the prioritization of policy made at all levels of the government and more importantly in the allocation of scare resources, and (d) ponder what these milestones represent today, what role have they played over time, and how much have they been used to promote women's empowerment and work towards the goals they were set up to achieve.

Uganda's Official Attempts towards Gender Balance and Women's Empowerment

Uganda as a nation is still characterized by a lack of equitable gender balance in its policy formulation and implementation. However, there are a number specific steps Uganda has taken to address gender balance as a nation and has signed onto goals and initiatives proposed by influential global organizations that attempt to change the dynamics of women's role. Uganda is a signatory to the UN's Millennium Development Goals, International Women's Year, International Women's Day and other related declarations. It has set up a framework for gender-streamlining through the creation of the Ministry of Gender, Labour and Social Development. Through its official education policy, the government representatives have repeatedly pronounced the need to focus on the education of girls citing the common adage that 'to educate a woman means to educate a community'. One commitment to this is the implementation of universal access to primary education for all children irrespective of gender (UNICEF, 2013). Uganda has officially taken up the issues of eliminating female genital mutilation, sexual and gender-based violence, and promoting sexual and reproductive health. It passed the Female Genital Mutilation Act of 2009 and Domestic Violence Act of 2010.

Uganda has made some progress towards the goal for gender equity. However, the implementation of most initiatives still falls short of the goals set therein. When compared to the world and to other African nations on the issue of addressing gender disparity, Uganda gets an average 'grade'. One can speculate that in spite of these commitments, the gender imbalance still persists and falls short of the set goals because of long-term cultural and political systemic gender imbalance that is ingrained within the family and community norms. Societies resist change because of the people who 'stand to lose' with the progress. In addition, although addressing gender imbalance may be a point of interest among some in national leadership, it is not a key priority for a government that is also trying to devise ways to reduce the glaring poverty and lack of basic needs. Furthermore, while commitment to addressing gender imbalance has been made on paper and is proclaimed by the leadership, it is also true that not an adequate amount of resources has been committed to support the actual implementation of these goals.

Therefore, additional follow-up needs to be made to examine the efforts the nation has made towards achieving gender equity or directed at changing the role that women play and see how much of the rhetoric has been put in practice. A more sensitive but crucial determination needs to be made about how these gender equity efforts have in fact been exploited by women in the higher socio-economic echelons while ignoring the marginalized women. If there are efforts that have focused on the extremely marginalized women in Uganda and abroad, then these need to be identified and explained how these have affected resources distribution.

Clearly huge gender disparities still exist in Uganda and especially with respect to the socio-economic progress. Results of the 2011 Uganda Demographic Health Survey (UDHS, 2011) highlighted that:

- Women earn only less than 30 per cent of the agricultural incomes yet they contribute 80 per cent of agricultural labour.
- Economic progress of rural women is limited by a high illiteracy rate estimated at an average of 66 per cent and low set of skills that constrain their ability to earn high regular incomes (i.e. most are engaged in the less predictable informal sector).
- Lower levels of incomes of women lead to gender inequities, increase their economic dependency and vulnerability within and outside of the household and thereby constrain their contribution to their personal, community, and national development.
- Women's decision-making power is also limited and this is especially pronounced in the areas of healthcare, reproductive rights, education, legal and property-ownership rights. Only three in 10 women utilize modern family planning methods and at least 6,000 women die each year as a result of complications from child birth and pregnancy. In addition, sexual and gender-based violence is still prevalent with 43 per cent reporting that they have been victims of physical violence and 28 per cent have suffered sexual violence.

In order to remove these gender disparities, structural and cultural changes need to be made and this can only be achieved if there is a long-term guarantee of resources committed for this goal and this is a accompanied by constant vigilance to monitor the scale, magnitude and pace of progress. Quantifying and affirming the transition or progress requires designing appropriate signals/indicators of this change and constructing and refining a framework to support this nuanced and long-term trend.

Analytical Framework

Developing the Analytical Framework

The preliminary step is to properly gather empirical evidence about the changes that have been taking place through informal talks with people who have either been practitioners or have lived in the area for some time. In order to attain a better representation of what has really happened in the community on-the-ground efforts are made to use a combination of social indicators and anecdotal evidence. Extra care is taken to separate 'mythical' history from facts and to avoid blindly accepting the tendency of local politicians of making theoretical or outlandish claims of changes which remained on the policy papers and were never implemented. Transitions cited must be tangible and demonstrable beyond just speeches and promises made by politicians/policy-makers as part of a media public relations exercise that in reality leaves marginalized women in the same status quo. Of course, success brings support ... politicians may be influenced by the 'glow' of the changes and see the longer-term advantages of being affiliated with a constituency that prioritizes gender-focused issues as guide to their voting choices. Hence, in the next section, attempts are made to construct the general empirical parameters/framework under which one can judge that there is a tangible change in the process. Can one identify notable changes of women's voices being treasured or rejected and that a diverse cross-section of women can achieve traction in the various political/social/economic spheres.

Working Definition of Parameters, Indicators and Signals of Development Policy Orientation

Based on personal experience and review of literature in the field, the paper suggests that some of the indicators and signals that can be used to demonstrate on-the-ground empowerment of women, changes in gender balance and tangible orientation of the development policy and priorities include:

- *Policy Characteristics:* Goals, number, frequency, and quality/content of gender-balanced policies that are formulated, passed and implemented by the decision-makers.
- *Operational Participants/Beneficiaries:* Demographic composition of the intended and hands-on beneficiaries/participants during policy formulation and implementation.
- *Trends in Socio-Economic Diversity:* Quantifiable (magnitude, speed) transition in the socio-economic status of the participants/beneficiaries and especially those who were previously living at the margins.
- *Resource Allocation:* Financial and material resources designated to implementing the policy is a tangible demonstration of commitment to the goals.
- *Knowledge Fusion:* Public pronouncements and sensitization of goals and achievements to enlighten the general public and other key stakeholders.
- *Duration:* Tangible long-term guarantees of policy retention reflected in how long and deep change is ingrained and streamlined into routine activities.
- *Role Models and Leaders:* Ability to create strong female role models who are able to join and challenge the current leadership structure and set the course of changes.

These working definitions formed the basis for collecting the empirical evidence.

Empirical Evidence and Lessons Learned from Maama Watali

Empirical evidence, generated by field observations by the authors, is used as a case study. Based on the history and activities of an indigenous organization called Maama Watali Development Association (MWDA), the study demonstrates how MWDA's presence in the community and its focus on empowerment of local grassroots women, has led to some notable changes in gender balance of power in a community where women previously had little or no say in defining local policy priorities, policy formulation and very little resource commitments.

History of Maama Watali Development Association

Founded in 2007, in the post-conflict location of Luweero in Uganda, Maama Watali Development Association has been officially registered by the government of Uganda since 2009. By its charter, it is a community-based organization whose mission is to provide a sustainable safety net, and holistic socio-economic services for young people and women who exist at the margins of the social-economic environment, so that they can attain independence as individuals. It provides direct services which include residential, microcredit, community information resource centre (library) and skills development to orphaned youth (especially girls) who are no longer eligible to be wards of the state or private orphanages or who have been excluded from receiving care from extended-family households. The hope is that with adequate socio-economic services to youth and women living at the margins of communities. They can start to reverse their unacceptably low standards of living, improve their prospects for future success as adults, and make a strong positive contribution to community advancement.

Profiles of Key Participants in Maama Watali's Grassroots Empowerment Reorientation Development Focus

One of the challenges of working in rural areas of a developing country is the lack of resources to collect and maintain reliable data by administrative arms of government. As a result, it is difficult to find reliable data that can indicate the difference/evolution between apriori and current state and to accurately identify trends. This has been the case with Luweero administration. Hence, any judgments made about changing trends in the participation levels of local government officials is based on the observation of the nature and frequency of interaction that these officials started and continued to have with MWDA. Overall, the trend was positive with more local leaders showing up and seeking information from the organization and then inviting MWDA's leadership and representative to make presentations during policy formulation forums. With respect to the female beneficiaries of Maama Watali's development initiatives, the participation rate is always increasing with female beneficiaries spreading the benefits of participation by word of mouth to more girls and women who in turn show up and request to be included in the programme.

Characteristics of Community Served by Maama Watali

Luweero Triangle is located in the central region of Uganda with an estimated population of over half a million people, growing at a rate of 2.3 per cent per year (GoU, 2013). Although there are no formally drawn boundaries to designate

Luweero Triangle, the term refers to an area in the north of Uganda's capital city Kampala, in which the 1981 to 1986 guerrilla war was started by Yoweri Mueseveni's then rebel group known as the National Resistance Movement (NRA). Geographically, Luweero Triangle includes a collection of the central-western districts – Mubende, Nakaseke, Kiboga, Wakiso, Kyankwanzi, Mityana, Luweero, and Nakasongola. During the civil war from 1981 to 1986, thousands of civilians were killed, displaced, homes and farms were completely destroyed – some have referred to it as the 'Killing Field of Uganda'. Before this war, the Luweero Triangle was one of the most productive farming regions in Uganda. Massive population displacement and the forced conscription of youth into the war resulted in the loss of able-bodied young and middle-aged workforce that is vital to agricultural production. Not only was the infrastructure devastated, but additionally, the smooth inter-generational transfer of agricultural production knowledge was interrupted and a sense of disillusionment set in among those left behind. The Luweero Triangle has yet to fully recover from this situation even though many people have returned to their land.

The Luweero Triangle was also impacted by the HIV/AIDS pandemic. The first known cases of HIV in Uganda are reported to have been discovered here in 1982 during the war (Basaza, Kaija and Ochola-Odongo, 2002). This situation has made socio-economic recovery very difficult. The incidence of this disease was also more prevalent amongst the most productive group of the population. Youth population accounts for over 78 per cent of the total population but most are unemployed and unsuccessfully attempt to seek employment in urban areas (Ahaibwe and Mbowa, 2014; UBoS, 2013; Bwambale, 2013; World Population Review, 2014). As a result of the twin challenges of the civil war and the HIV/AIDS pandemic, occurring on top of the general poverty levels in the nation, this community has a significant number of its resident classified as living at the margins.

Profile of Maama Watali's Beneficiaries

Maama Watali Development Association's target clientele or beneficiaries are young people who live at the margins of the society with a special focus on girls. Primarily these include young adults who are aged between 12 and 25 years. Priority is given to those who have been orphaned at early age and are either no longer eligible to be wards of the orphanages and/or those who lack adequate support from extended families. In those instances where weak family support is extended to young people, services are provided to the principal fostering relative in a bid to strengthen the family structure or safety net. Maama Watali is also focused on the empowerment of rural women and devotes resources to marginalized young women who are diverse in their personal histories, capabilities/talents, and are exposed to different opportunities to succeed. This support is in for education, micro credit, healthcare, and residence information communication technology and skills development.

Direct Opportunities through which Maama Watali has Empowered Women at the Grassroots

Operating in two locations (Luweero and Nyenga) Maama Watali consulted some current and potential clientele and sought their input about what they believe would be best relevant to improving their socio-economic welfare. Feedback from the youth and women identified that addressing the following issues is more important in their quest to change and improve their individual and collective circumstances education, micro-credit, agricultural production, reliable cooking fuels, communication infrastructure, health, youth employment, nutrition, waste disposal and resolving prior traumas inflicted by political strive and civil wars. As a result, Maama Watali was set up and is operating a number of programmes:

- *Women's Grassroots Mobilization and Empowerment Sensitization Programme:* Focuses on mobilizing women living at the margins so that they can play a strong role in changing their dire conditions and claim ownership of the programmes that are put in place to effect that change. It specifically teaches basic human rights with an emphasis on women's rights and trains local women to undertake political organization at the grassroots and encourages them to run for office to become key decision-makers. Furthermore, it enables women to examine long-standing cultural norms to determine which need to change if the marginalization and exploitation of women is to reduce or disappear. The programmes sensitize local leaders about the role they can play in improving the lives of women and streamlining these into regular policy at all levels of the community.
- *Youth Residential Programme:* Premises in Luweero Town serve as a temporary home for youth-in-transition (including HIV-positive youth and orphans) for an average stay of 4 to 6 months. During this time, a resident, aged 13 to 24 years, is provided with basic needs skills development lessons, and guidance about how they can start on a new path to improve their life condition. The long-term plan is to design a Maama Watali Youth Village which would include constructing a multiple-use training and residential facility that provides comprehensive services to the beneficiaries. Overall the comprehensive programme would reflect the concept of 'mother' and answer the question: what does the role of a mother mean? It would demonstrate that no child should be without a mother (whether biological or adopted mother) because absence causes a loss of anchor and compass.
- *Microfinance Programme:* Started in July 2011, using funds granted by icAfrica, provides working capital in form of micro loans (US $ 30 to 80) to the youth-in-transition and women living at the margins of the society. The financial investment is meant to grow the already existing businesses or to start new businesses for which beneficiaries possess or are ready to gain the necessary talent. Borrowers have to repay the loan in 12 installments.
- *Arts and Crafts Programme:* Involves young women learning to make arts and crafts pieces. Women from the local community are recruited and encouraged to come and share their skills of craft-making with the young people. Some instructors share skills as a secondary result of being clients/beneficiaries of the micro credit loan programme who have agreed to mentor the youth-in-transition. Craft products are taken to be sold in Canada and USA.

- *Maama Watali Information Resource Centre (MWIRC):* Grew out of a desire to form a public library that members of the community (especially the youth) could use. In 2011, mobilization for resources and material comprising the library collection commenced. Contributions came from ordinary people in and around Kanata Ottawa and from the members of The Rotary Club of Ottawa-Stittsville in Canada. In January 2012, preparation on premises began in Luweero and this was followed by set up of materials shipped in from Canada. After cross-collaboration with different partners, the goal of forming a community library was expanded to convert it to a community Information Resource Centre. The scope of the institution increased so that it can now serve as an integrated community information centre that focused jointly on the basic duties of public library and combines this with advanced information dissemination and utilization. MWIRC will utilize computer information technology and traditional methods to promote access to high quality and timely information by members of the community. Information availability will be increased through increased access to books and other printed educational materials, multimedia products, and especially through providing electronic links to networks that produce and use educational, output production, distribution and marketing materials. As a complement to increasing physical access to information, the centre will serve as a central point through which relevant and cost-effective literacy activities will be identified, refined and implemented. The centre will also have a component to increase typing skills for the local population as well as a training point for children and adults about how to use computer information technology.

Maama Watali was able to design and implement its programmes by recognizing and taking advantage of some of the opportunities presented to it. However, it is clear that there is still a need for additional leadership in MWDA that would be surely focused on responding to these opportunities.

Opportunities that Maama Watali Tapped in Implementing the Women's Grassroots Empowerment, Mobilization and Outreach

A number of factors on the ground made the start and expansion of the empowerment possible and some of these are:

- *Committed Human Resources:* MWDA was lucky that at each step of the way, a crucial number of players came into the process and made a real difference or a turning point. Apart from the diverse knowledge-base and talents they brought to bear, many had a significant level of empathy towards those who are marginalized and were therefore determined to do all they can to help as circumstances demanded of them.
- *Local Opinion Leaders Clarity:* A number of the local leaders with whom the staff of MWDA interacted were quick to recognize the potential that the opportunities being offered represented. When needed, these people were able to step in as stakeholders and help the organization to address the bureaucratic hurdles.

- *Partnerships:* MWDA does not work in isolation but rather seeks out and engages dependable domestic and international partnership. Partners include researchers, government sectors, businesses, educators, the media, national and international development workers, volunteers, community leaders, community service organizations, parents and children themselves. Partnerships are sought and nurtured at every level from the individual, family, school, parish, sub-county, district, right up to the international level.
- *Group and Club Formation:* This strategy is based on the concept of formation of self-help groups to undertake collective action. MWDA relies on this as one of sustainability strategies, to ensure that the impact of its projects survives for a long time. During the project life, these groups are empowered through training sessions aimed at building their capacity to carry out manageable and sustainable project activities. Collective action plays a crucial part in relation to the clientele's education, healthcare, career development and support in partnership.
- *Peer Education:* Developed and used to promote participation in the socio-economic development initiatives. MWDA uses key tenets of this approach to engage young Ugandans and overseas volunteers, who are trained and deployed as Volunteer Peer Educators (VPEs). It is especially vital for sensitization of potential clientele, soliciting initial participation from individuals, and increasing project outreach throughout the community.
- *Community Involvement and Participation:* MWDA recognizes that sustainable socio-economic development cannot be achieved without the active participation of the community members. The community members generally define cultural norms, and parameters for attitudinal change in which children must live and be nurtured. In addition, community values are a crucial factor in determining the acceptable community standards and in ranking priority development areas. More crucial to the success of MWDA, community values influence whether or not any proposed change/intervention will be supported by the intended clientele and what level of outreach, success and sustainability, a given programme/project will attain. Discussions of cultural norms which are potentially unhealthy or contributing to child vulnerability are identified and a plan is designed to eliminate them. Furthermore, at every stage of the programme development and implementation, the organization actively engages community leaders, parents, community workers, teachers and traditional leaders to determine the best way forward.
- *Knowledge-Sharing:* Traditional and modern knowledge about improving socio-economic standards is shared across households, communities and even across the globe. Use of information communication technology has hastened the rate of knowledge-sharing and has helped MWDA to break down bottlenecks that slow or block the flow of information.
- *Replication:* Once a technique has been proven to work it then it is modified if necessary and transferred to other areas to be implemented.

Challenges Maama Watali Faces During Implementation of Empowerment

The challenges MWDA has faced in empowering women and influencing the orientation of development include:

- Logistical and Bureaucratic Bottlenecks: The main challenge faced during the initial stages of forming the public library component of Maama Watali Information Resource Centre (MWIRC) were the Ugandan Government logistical and bureaucratic delays and inconsistence in the processing policy for the materials as they were transported from Ottawa to Luweero.
- Resources and Materials: Because most programmes are being designed from scratch and are designated to be implemented among communities with high poverty levels, resource availability is a frequent challenge. For example, modernizing the collection of reading materials continues to be a work in progress as efforts are made to build and accumulate the content of the library component of MWIRC.
- Community Doubts and Apathy: Based on previous experiences, there is a lack of trust of the potential beneficiaries as to how long MWDA's programmes will last. Suspicion results from the abandonment from prior organizations, implementing programmes in the area, who packed up and left at the first sign of the challenges inherent in operating in a post-conflict area. One must also keep in mind the concept that just like individuals, a society can suffer from post-traumatic stress disorder.
- Demographic Shocks: The HIV pandemic led to a loss of the most productive force. In addition to this are wounds, inflicted by a long civil war, such as loss of life, destroyed families, deteriorated infrastructure, lack of intergenerational knowledge transfer of crucial agricultural and other production techniques.
- Resentment built up due to the abandonment by the current government that used this area as a staging point to start anti-government activities and a civil war and yet has not made a significant level of investment to replace what the community lost.
- Systemic Governance-Hindering issues such as corruption, the fact that mid-level staff is inadequately trained for their level of activity and/or have no incentive for high performance results in an under-performing bureaucracy.

Matching Maama Watali's Progress to the Working Definition of Parameters, Indicators and Signals of Development Policy Orientation

One can detect that there is start of a reorientation of development policy, at the grassroots, to take into account women's priorities and gender balance issues. The indicators that this reorientation is most probably occurring are in the following areas:

- Increased number of opinion leaders who are sensitized to and are more loudly advocating for gender equity. These advocates are in turn undertaking mentioning for ordinary people (especially young women) so that they too can take up decision-making positions, a matter of routine across most levels of the local government.

- Allocation of financial and other material resources towards women's empowerment has increased.
- Improvement of Communication within the General Community: This is seen through increased public service announcements. There is also a notable reduction in self-consciousness and resistance when discussing issues pertaining to gender balance and empowerment – topics that were previously taboo in this male-dominated society.
- Institution Building: Creating strong durable institutions, like Uganda Women's Finance Trust Limited (UWFT), The Council for Economic Empowerment for Women of Africa – Uganda (CEEWA), Women's Empowerment in Agriculture Index (WEAI), Ministry of Gender, that are primarily focused on promoting and/or implementing these gender equity issues (WOUGNET, 2014). These institutions create a permanent long-term platform which will not be affected by changes in government leadership,
- National-Level Advocacy: Incorporating these issues among the national priority list and policy definition raises awareness and also enables allocation of resources.

Moving Forward

Clearly there are challenges imposed on Maama Watali and similar organizations focused on women's empowerment that hinders their ability to smoothly move forward.

Best Practices that Maama Watali Recommends

Based on its experience in Uganda that Maama Watali has had, the following are suggestions of practical ideas and lessons learned:

- Partnerships are crucial in designing, modifying, refining and implementation of activities to promote gender balance and women's empowerment. As more individuals and organizations understood and observed what MWRIC is trying to achieve as a transformative force within the community, many sought out a chance to participate in an interdisciplinary and multi-facet approach to achieve the overall objective. Maama Watali has the following academic institutions as potential partners: University of Ottawa, Ontario, Canada; University of Edmonton, AB, Canada; Carleton University, Ottawa, Canada; North Carolina State University, United States; Makerere University, Uganda; and Mutesa I University in Uganda. Furthermore, the project has the following partner organizations: Maama Watali Foundation in Canada, Buganda Kingdom; Rotary Club of Ottawa-Stittsville in Canada, Uganda Rotary Club; icAfrica in Canada and Women's Initiative in Development and Para-legal Association (WIDPA) in Uganda. Scholars, researchers, subject-matter experts and practitioners associated with these institutions will train the youth in best practices in sustainable agriculture, food security, nutrition, gender issues, maternal and child health and overall family health. In addition, the partners will access and clarify the conditions on the ground as well as develop a sustainable communication network to get continuous input from the target population. Scholars from Canada have conducted field assessment as part of the programme evaluation, as preliminary steps towards developing a base-line for future actions.

- Diversity of talent and professional qualifications is important when a solution to the problem requires an integrated approach. The professional team is notable for its diversity of subject matter disciplines, including African Studies, Agriculture, Medicine, Nutrition, Water Resources, Public Health, Communication, Animal Husbandry, Information Technology, Community Development, Gender Studies, Business and Project Management, and Maternal Health.
- Local buy-in from the community and key opinion leaders: Initial community buy-in is represented by the fact that the local leadership has endorsed the project and is ready to mobilize other stakeholders to facilitate individual participation and smooth implementation. These partner organizations will provide various resources and expertise and will contribute to the monitoring of compliance to the project goals.

The limited success of MWDA has led to a change in resource commitments from local and international sources. Yes, it is true that success attracts additional support and this has been true in the case of MWDA. For instance, once the initial grassroot efforts of the founding members were presented to individuals in Ottawa, in Ontario, Canada, there was an immediate interest from volunteers and scholars who organized fundraisers, collected and shipped materials for the community library and local schools, formed Maama Watali Foundation Canada, and even made self-sponsored trip to Luweero and Nyenga to provide hands-on help to MWDA. These efforts continue to this day and are continuously being made more robust through networking lead by these interested individuals. When local leaders saw the community library being initiated and volunteers from Maama Watali Foundation, Canada, working diligently with the local beneficiaries, they approached the organization, queried what was going on and then immediately included the activities on the community agenda of what they hoped to achieve by going forward. In addition, the members of the Rotary Club of Uganda became involved in the activities. Representatives of Buganda Kingdom separately committed to provide land (200 acres) so that the activities of MWDA could be expanded. North Carolina State University also committed to provide additional human and material support to ensure long-term sustainability and expansion of the activities of MWDA.

Conclusion

The discussion highlights that the increased participation of local women is contributing to a reorientation in socio-economic development policy focus in a rapidly changing Uganda. Clearly, once an organization is seen to be succeeding in its endeavours, then local politicians flock towards it and try to associate themselves with it. The study demonstrates that once focus is placed on empowerment of local women, there is not only a change in gender roles but also more crucially a change in the focus of development policy priorities and ultimately the allocation of financial and other resources.

Empowered women didn't only talk but started undertaking specific activities including library portion of the MWRIC, health promotion, credit for agriculture-related activities, soliciting funding for cooking stoves and history documentation. They began a transition from just 'talking' and have instead reverted to 'walking' towards their goals. Throughout the process, MWDA has been able to find leaders and champions. Women's burgeoning activities caught the attention of the local male-dominated leadership who were then influenced and wanted to be associated with the practical outcomes reinforcing the argument that success attracts support. Males were attracted to these activities in part because they could judge that they were successful and so participation could be considered an endorsement in performance. Males, who had previously ignored the women, are now listening more closely and turning to these outcomes as key information resources, exploring the possibility of allocating additional resources, and for policy prioritization and guidance. In addition, the women's activism has contributed to identification and development of leaders who are then in turn serving as role models within the community. The combined effect is that the goal of achieving full participatory democracy at the grassroot level becomes increasingly important and achievable. So once an institution can demonstrate success, then its priorities are taken more seriously by local decision-makers – once again reinforcing the adage that nothing breeds support like success.

References

Ahaibwe, G. and Mbowa, S. (2014). 'Youth Unemployment Challenge in Uganda and the Role of Employment Policies in Jobs Creation', 26 August 2014, Brookings Institution, http://www.brookings.edu/blogs/africa-in-focus/posts/2014/08/26-youth-unemployment-uganda-ahaibwe-mbowa

Basaza R., Kaija, D. and Ochola-Odongo, D. (2002). 'The Impact of HIV and AIDS on Children: Lights and Shadows in the 'Successful Case' of Uganda', Chapter 2 by Robert Basaza, Darlison Kaija and Dorothy Ochola-Odongo, June 2002, UNICEF Office of Research, http://www.unicef-irc.org/publications/pdf/aids_book/chapter2_ basaza.pdf

Business Week (2012). 'Women Hold 20% of World's Political Power, Report Says', 24 October 2012, http://www.businessweek.com/news/2012-10-24/women-hold-20-percent-of-worlds-political-power-report-says.

Bwambale, Taddeo (2013). 'For Uganda's Population, It's More Youth, More Problems', 26 February 2013, New Vision, http://www.newvision.co.ug/news/640143-for-uganda-s-population-it-s-more-youth-more-problems.html

GoU (2013). 'Budget Monitoring Report Third Quarter Financial Year 2012–2013 (Government of Uganda (GoU), Ministry of Finance, Planning and Economic Development, May 2013, www.finance.go.ug

OECD (2008). 'Gender and Sustainable Development: Maximising the Economic, Social and Environmental Role of Women', Organisation for Economic

Co-operation and Development (OECD), http://www.oecd.org/social/40881538.pdf

UBoS (2013). 'The National Labor Force and Child Activities Survey 2011/12: Child Labor Report', July 2013, Uganda Bureau of Statistics (UBoS) http://www.ubos.org/onlinefiles/uploads/ubos/pdf%20documents/NCLS%20Report%202011_12.pdf

UDHS (2011). Uganda Demographic Health Survey (UDHS).

UNICEF (2013). 'United Nations in Uganda Supports Efforts to Empower Grassroots Girls and Women in Uganda' UNICEF, Kampala, 8 March 2013 http://www.unicef.org/uganda/media_12331.html

WEforum (2012). 'Global Gender Gap Report' World Economic Forum (WEforum)'s Annual report, 2012; http://www.weforum.org/issues /global-gender-gap

World Population Review (2014). 'Uganda Population 2014' 19 October 2014. http://worldpopulationreview.com/countries/uganda- population/

WOUGNET (2014). 'WOUGNET Members Member Map' Women of Uganda Network (WOUGNET), November 2014, http://wougnet.org/members/member-map/

2

Grassroot Democracy to Women Empowerment

The Role of Village Assemblies in Kerala

JAYASREE PAUL

Abstract

Kerala has got worldwide attention for outstanding performance in human development and gender development indicators. But all these glorified achievements in these conventional indicators are masked by many discriminations and atrocities against women. The high conventional social indicators mask the real face of Kerala women, who are vulnerable to gender inequalities. The decentralized planning during the mid-1990s has given greater visibility to the gender issues for the first time in the history of Kerala. The decentralized planning conceived gram sabha or village assembly with a mission of ensuring people's participation in local governance as well as in decision-making and to facilitate empowerment of all weaker sections especially women in all dimensions. Although these novel strategies open up new avenues for uplifting women, their involvement as key agents to development is still neglected. A system rooted in gram sabha fails to bring up women in the limelight and is also unable to address their adverse conditions. In this context, it is essential to analyse the feasibility of gram sabhas in generating a favourable environment to focus on women. The present study is an attempt to assess the role of a women as decision-maker in gram sabha, identify those impediments in participation/decision-making and finally in women empowerment.

Keywords

gram sabha or village assembly, women empowerment, neighbourhood group (NHG), decentralized planning

The Context

The state of Kerala has been widely noted for outstanding achievements in human development and gender development indicators. The state enjoys a bouquet of bonuses like favourable sex ratio, high life expectancy, low fertility rate, low death rate and decreasing poverty ratio, thanks to notable achievements in female education. These achievements pushed her to the first rank among the Indian states in terms of Human Development Index and Gender Development Indicators (Government of Kerala 2005). But all these glorified achievements in terms of conventional indicators mask the Kerala women who are vulnerable to many sorts of gender inequalities. Her educational wisdom and access to health infrastructure and constitutionally mandated exposure to local body elections have not brought even slightest improvement in her representation in the mainstream politics. The paradox of Kerala women's abysmally low work participation rate (18.6%) concomitant with the high female literacy rate is much discussed. Women who exceed men in number have been pushed out from productive work, according to the census records, and her role in development is least acknowledged. The decentralized planning during the mid-1990s, has given greater visibility to the gender issues, first time, in the history of Kerala. The decentralized planning conceived village assembly or gram sabha (GS), with a mission of ensuring people's participation in local governance as well as in decision-making and to facilitate empowerment of all weaker sections, including women. Although these novel strategies open up new avenues for uplifting women, their involvement as key agents to development is still neglected. The present study is an enquiry into the role of GS as decision-maker to identify the impediments in participation/decision-making and finally in women empowerment. In short, the study probes into the problems, which arise in translating innovative ideas into concrete projects targeting women.

Statement of the Problem

Since the inception of Five Year Plans in the 1950s, radical measures have been implemented to raise women's access to resources and to empower, but in vain. Gender discrimination was glaringly visible in all streams of power structure. Dowry death, rape, wife-beating and domestic violence exist in all societies irrespective of caste, creed and region. Compared to other states of India, the lowest women work participation and the poorest political representation are other attributes of highly literate Kerala women. In this context, 73rd and 74th Constitutional Amendments, enthrusting upon decentralized planning brought sweeping changes by implementing three tier systems and reserving one-third of seats towards women in local bodies. The amendment elevated GS as the base for local governance. The state government of Kerala vigorously implemented these reforms in planning and gave it a popular name called People's Planning Programme (PPP) in 1996. PPP considered GS as an integral component of the local governance system and it ensured greater participation of women in the 9th Five Year Plan and preference to projects with gender issues.

Contrary to other states in India, the attendance in GS meetings in Kerala is dominated by women. The state government has given a special thrust to women empowerment by mandating at least 10 per cent of plan fund towards Women Component Plan (WCP). WCP is exclusively meant for women empowerment projects alone. The pity is that the participation of women in the plan preparation and decision-making was meager. Unfortunately, the strategic needs of women are not being addressed effectively and it distorts the noble aims of decentralized planning. The local governance rooted in GS fails to address their strategic needs. Indeed, the much glorified straight forward relation between literacy and women's autonomy is to be questioned. A grassroot level study is, therefore, required to assess her role in the decision-making and also identify the problems they face in decision-making. This micro-level study analyses the feasibility of GS in generating a favourable environment for women to speak out. The present study, conducted in the selected local bodies of Thrissur district, is an attempt to assess the participation of women in GS, identify those impediments in participation as well as in decision-making and finally in women empowerment.

Objectives

The study has the following objectives:

1. To analyse women participation and identify hurdles in her participation in the gram sabha's in Kerala.
2. To assess women empowerment
3. To examine the role of gram sabha in cultivating a spirit of empowerment among the women participants.

Hypothesis

1. H0: There is no association between NHG membership and organizational capacity.
2. H1: Organizational empowerment is closely associated with NHG membership.

Methodology

The study area was Thrissur district where panchayats have good records in implementing local planning effectively. Thrissur district bagged national and state awards for the best local body in the last successive years. A primary survey was conducted among adult women who were participants in gram sabha.

Sampling

There are 88 panchayats in Thrissur district which is divided in 16 blocks. In total, six panchayats were selected which constituted 7 per cent of the gram panchayats in the district. The women participants in the GS were the respondents of the survey. Two wards were selected at random from each panchayat and 50 women participants from two wards in a panchayat were randomly selected. Thus 300 respondents were selected for the survey.

Overview of Gram Sabha (GS) or Village Assembly[1]

The centralized planning during the 1950s was ineffective in constructing social and political networks due to the absence of local governing institutions. Neither GS nor even local body was given any priority in planning. The Community Development Programme as part of Five Year Plan was crippled by the poor local governance system. In this context, a committee headed by Balwantrai Mehta (1957) was appointed and he recommended three-tier Panchayati Raj system (PRI) with district panchayat at the top, community development block, at the middle and gram panchayat at the bottom. The three-tier system turned ineffective and many committees were appointed to improve the local governance. Finally, in 1993, the Parliament enacted 73rd and 74th Constitutional Amendments which brought drastic changes in three-tier system and mandated women reservation in local bodies. The amendment was a breakthrough for the section Article 243-A, which defines GS as a body consisting of persons registered in the electoral rolls relating to a village comprised within the area of local body at the village level. Accordingly, GS may exercise such powers and perform such functions at the village level as the legislature of a state may by law provide. GS is a deliberate body at the village level and basic unit of local self-government. It provides an ideal platform for people to present their needs and local problems. A typical GP has 10 to 25 wards.

Functions of GS are the following:

1. To identify the felt needs of the people and prioritize them
2. To give importance to functional devolution
3. To select beneficiaries and locations
4. To make suggestions to the problems identified
5. To examine annual statements of accounts and audit report
6. To review programmes of the work done
7. To suggest the locations of civic functions and to provide local public goods such as roads, waterways, street lights, etc.
8. To mobilize voluntary labour and contributions in kind and cash.

Decentralized Planning in Kerala[2]

In accordance with the 73rd and 74th amendments, Kerala Panchayat Raj Act (1994) and Kerala Municipality Act (1994) were passed. Elections to the local bodies were held in 1995 and the local bodies were constituted on 2 October 1995. Decentralization programme popularly known as People's Plan Campaign, (PPC) introduced in 1996, brought forth substantial changes in the role of local bodies in the decentralization process, planning and policy approaches.

Kerala Panchayat Raj Act 1994[3] empowers the GS to make decisions regarding the developmental issues in the locality. GS may be the first platform for our women to speak out at a public forum where, panchayat president, elected representatives and panchayat officials are present.[4] All the voters in a ward are the members of the GS. The GS is to begin with the minutes, the annual statement of receipts and expenditure, and the administration report of the preceding year. If in any circumstances, any decision of the GS could not be implemented, the president shall report the reason before the GS. The local bodies at village, block and district levels must give due consideration to the recommendations and suggestions of the GS. The attendance in GS is mandatory for availing beneficiary schemes announced by the local body. There would be three or four GSs at ward level in a financial year. Every voter can attend GS and each participant has every right to express one's needs and grievances in the GS. If the quorum of GS is less than 10 per cent, the local body has to convene a second GS. Prior to the GS meeting, the working group will be convened to discuss about the plan objectives and sector-wise allocations. The concrete decision related to plan objectives and sector-wise allocations must be evolved from GS. For this, the entire participants in the GS would be divided into a separate group based on different subjects such as road, women and children. Based on the recommendations of the group, the plan targets of local body will be formulated. The needs raised in GS will be discussed in development seminars. A printed development report will be prepared based on the GS of all wards. This report incorporates the plan and non-plan fund allocation to different sectors in a panchayat and other requirements pertaining to the area. Prior to the second GS, the working group would be convened to discuss about the plan proposal. The needs raised in GS will be discussed in development seminars.

The second GS is known as beneficiary GS in which the participants are divided into different groups who discuss that whom and in what proportion, the beneficiaries schemes of local body should be distributed. Finally they arrive at a consensus and the president or ward member reads out the list of beneficiaries for acceptance. The final GSs are meant to evaluate the programmes implemented and present audited statements.

Gram Sabha and Women Empowerment: Conceptual Framework

The concept of empowerment reflects how the vulnerable acquire 'power from within' out of collective intervention and develops inner ability to control resources to determine agendas and make decisions. Kabeer (1994) defined empowerment in terms of 'power from within' intending that the deprived group should cultivate an inner ability to control resources to determine agendas and make decisions. She defined empowerment as 'the expansion in people's ability to make strategic life choices' in a context where this ability was previously denied to them.

Many feminists defined empowerment as woman's individual self-reliance which exclusively depends on progress of individual without collective action. Individual empowerment generated out of education, skill development, access to capital and confidence may benefit herself but not the community as a whole.

Many definitions visualize that women get empowered when they play an active role in development process and participate only in the decision-making phase of political and economic institutions. Rowlands (1997) opposes this perception and she believes that this view of empowerment is consistent conventional definition (in terms of power over). It confines empowerment which only bring people who are outside the decision-making process into it. More than decision-making ability, to Rowlands, empowerment must include the process that enables them and develops self-esteem and critical thinking, supplemented by knowledge, new information and organization skill. Thus, empowerment is a multi-dimensional process of change and the beneficiaries are those who materialize change.

Planning becomes democratic, when those who were hitherto excluded take part in planning decisions. GS facilitates inputs from women for the local planning. Gram sabha is the right platform where women in the households also are involved in decision-making with regard to allocation of resources which would bring visible benefit to the women. GS is the first largest platform in their life for articulating their needs and aspirations.

The success of decentralized planning depends greatly on the proper functioning of GS which requires substantial participation of the people. Participation is a voluntary action of an individual. Effective participation is possible only if participants have any role in organizing the programme. This is possible in a situation where people themselves form an organization to satisfy their felt needs. Thus, beneficiaries and organizers are members of the same organization and they themselves plan and implement programmes, share duties and carry out evaluation, all is done by the members and for the members.

Result and Findings

Profile of Thrissur District

Thrissur, the geographical area of the present study, is considered as the cultural capital of Kerala. It has an area of 3,032 sq km. It has five taluks, 254 villages, one corporation, 16 block panchayats and 88 gram panchayats. It enjoys female literacy of 86.94 per cent and has sex ratio of 1,085 for 1,000 men (2001 Census).

In Kerala, generally, gram sabha is dominated by the backward caste because of their presumption that gram sabha is a platform for meeting the needs of backward caste or BPL families exclusively. Ninety-three per cent of women participants have schooling; 54.7 per cent of respondents are either casual workers or workers in national rural employment guarantee programme and 33.7 per cent are housewives.

Women Empowerment

Empowerment in the present study has been measured in terms of knowledge index, participatory index and organizational index of the respondents. The scoring indicators of knowledge index are understanding about purpose and functions of GS, awareness on women reservation bill and panchayat level plan programme. Participatory index is measured by the indicators such as physical and substantial participation with inclusion in decision-making. The indicators of organizational index consist of membership and participation in neighborhood group or any organization, discussion on the GS agendas within the organization and local organization capacity. Each index is calculated by assigning equal weights of one.

Index = $(x_1+x_2+....x_n)$ x100

?v

$x_1+x_2+....x_n$ = Sum of scores of indicators

?v = Sum of Weights

Using quartile estimation, the empowerment index is classified as follows:

Less than 25 per cent = very low empowerment

25–50 per cent = moderate empowerment

50–75 per cent = high empowerment

Above 75 per cent = very high empowerment

Table 1

Distribution of Empowerment Index

Index	*Knowledge Index*		*Participatory Index*		*Organizational Index*		*Empowerment Index*		*Empowerment Status*
	No. of Women	*%*	*No. of Women*	*%*	*No. of Women*	*%*	*No. of Women*	*%*	
< 25	3	1.00	0	0	39	13.0	6	2.0	Low
25–50	5	1.7	14	4.7	53	17.7	5	1.7	Moderate
50–75	112	37.3	181	60.3	175	58.3	207	69.0	High
75–100	180	60.0	105	35.0	33	11.0	82	27.3	Very High
Total	300	100	300	100	300	100	300	100	

Empowerment index is an average of scores of knowledge empowerment, participatory empowerment and organizational empowerment.

Empowerment Index = $(x_1+x_2+....x_n)x100$

?V

$x_1+x_2+....x_n$= Sum of knowledge, participatory and organizational scores

$?V_4$ = Sum of all weights

The empowerment is visible only in 27.3 per cent of women surveyed. Knowledge index is comparably in a better position, still a considerable number of them do not know the functions and responsibilities of GS. Poor knowledge and lack of organizational skill obstructs effective participation.

The index of organizational capacity is not at all impressive. Organizational empowerment is high in the panchayats where NHGs are active. Further, the hypothesis testing using Chi-square test was performed to find out whether there is any association between membership in NHG and organizational capacity.

Since P value is less than the calculated value, we can reject the null hypothesis and the result is highly significant. So it is proved that organizational empowerment is closely associated with membership in neighbourhood group (NHG) (Table 2)

Table 2

Result of Chi-square on Association between Organizational Index and Membership in Neighbourhood Group

P value value at 1 per cent level	.000
Calculated value	194.5
Degree of freedom	4
Inference	significant

Self-Help Groups and Gram Sabha

Self-help groups (SHGs) play a vital role in the empowerment of women. The major self-help group exclusively of women and for women is Kudumbasree. It is a state-sponsored poverty alleviation programme focusing primarily on micro-finance and micro-enterprise development. At the bottom of Kudumbasrere, there are Neighbourhood Groups (NHGs) comprising 10–20 women members. Meetings are convened on a weekly basis in the houses of NHG members. The participation of women in SHGs has greater influence in injecting organizing capacity of women for a common cause.

A greater proportion of women participants (80 per cent) are members of Kudumbasree. Among the member respondents, three-fourth of them regularly participate in Kudumbasree. There is weekly meeting in every Kudumbasree.

Any discussion in Ayalkootam prior to the GS meeting is beneficial for the effective participation in GS. This discussion can make the GS more participatory and more enlightening. Of the participants, 40.7 per cent agree that discussions were held in their respective NHG prior to the GS.

Problems of Gram Sabha

The distinguished feature of GS in Kerala is women domination in participation. GS, the base of grassroot democracy, suffers from the problems of malfunctioning which ultimately cripples down development process and later women empowerment programmes. The problems are analysed here.

Most of the participants do not have proper awareness about the purpose and powers of GS. A large proportion believes that GS is a body for distributing beneficiary schemes to the needy and for this the participation in GS is compulsory. A considerable proportion around 43.5 per cent believes that participation is required if and only if husband/sibling is absent.

According to Panchayati Raj Act 1994, at least 10 per cent of voters should participate in the GS and if the quorum is not satisfied, another GS is to be convened again. In order to avoid the inconvenience of second GS, the authorities just enter the names of voters to reach the 10 per cent level. This fudging of figures will definitely affect the decision-making powers of the local body and distort the objectives of decentralized planning.

The procedure of conducting GS is not as per the rules in Kerala Panchayati Raj Act 1994. Before the GS, the working group will be convened and would discuss the needs and priorities. The participants in the GS are supposed to divide into various groups and discuss on assigned subjects. After the discussion, each group has to make recommendations on plan proposal. At the end of the meeting, the final decision will be announced. In actual practice, process is in the reversing order. No group discussions were found in any panchayat surveyed. GS is just a platform where people get orientation about the current plan and programmes and submit beneficiary applications. The final decision about allocation of resources and distribution of beneficiary schemes are cooked in the local body office. Involvement in discussions widens her knowledge and the development process becomes more participatory.

Discussion at Kudumbasree prior to the GS meeting is beneficial for the participants of GS. This discussion can make the GS more participatory and more enlightening. Around 60 per cent participants do conduct discussion on what proposal has to be submitted before coming to GS.

The basic problem of GS in Kerala noted by all the scholars is that participation level of upper caste or high income families is very insignificant due to their strong conviction that GS is a platform meant for distributing benefits to the families of lower caste people or families below poverty line. This thwarts the participation level of women from upper castes and their knowledge level about PRIs is abysmally poor.

Conclusion

Gram Sabha gives greater opportunities to women for improving capabilities like participation in a public forum, decisions-making power with regard to resource utilization at ward level and above all greater opportunities for getting awareness about much acclaimed decentralized planning process at Panchyati Raj level. The overall empowerment stemming from active participation of the people in GS to a great extent depends upon the awareness of the people about its functions and powers. They hardly voice their own opinion regarding the selection of beneficiaries, location of implementing developmental projects, etc. The hindering factors identified in the study are lack of awareness about GS and its functions, lack of information about current and forthcoming projects, and poor organizational capacities.

Notes

1. Local self-government in rural area.
2. Participatory planning which paved the way for devolving all the powers, functions, planning and finance at lower levels.
3. Kerala Panchayati Raj Act 1994, Chapter II, Section (3) (1)
4. A task force of ward members, members of community-based organizations, officers and experts

References

Government of Kerala (2005). Human Development Report (1–2), State Planning Board, Thiruvananthapuram.

Kabeer, Naila (1994). 'Empowerment from Below: Learning from the Grassroots.' Kabeer, Naila. *Reversed Realities: Gender Hierarchies in Development Thought*, London: Verso, 223–263.

Kabeer, Naila (2001). Resources, Agency, Achievements: Reflections on the Measurement of Women's Empowerment, (in Discussing Women's Empowerment: Theory and Practice) SIDA Studies, No. 3, SIDA: Stockholm.

Kerala Panchyati Raj Act (1994). Government Press, Thiruvananthapuram.

Rowlands, Jo (1997). *Questioning Empowerment: Working with Women in Honduras*. Oxford: Oxfam.

3

Examining Manufacturing Jobs for Canadian Women in the Era of Global Capitalism

JUNE CORMAN, ANN DUFFY AND NORENE PUPO

Abstract

This paper examines the vulnerability of working women and men in the context of capitalist production practices by focusing on two plants in Welland, Ontario, Canada – John Deere and Henniges. This paper shows that management decisions regarding hiring policies and pay packages had significant consequences for women. It also explores the circumstances surrounding the closing of these plants and shows that these decisions had disastrous consequences for when women and men lose their jobs, they lose their livelihoods and must struggle to find other options to support their families. The analysis is based on interviews with workers at both the plants and publicly available information on ownership changes. The focus is on the consequences for working women and men of an economy system based on the wage-capital relationship that, by its internal logic, propels corporations to maximize profits through hiring strategies, remuneration packages and the location of plants. At both John Deere and the Henniges rubber plant, careful deliberations informed by competitive pressures related to, among other things, absence of tariffs and disadvantageous exchange rates, overran considerations of human costs as profits were prioritized.

Keywords

deindustrialization, women and manufacturing, plant closures, hiring practices, wage concessions

Introduction

Decisions made by globally based CEOs and their locally based managers can have disastrous consequences for workers, their families and their communities. This paper examines the vulnerability of working women and men in the context of capitalist production practices by focusing on two plants in Welland, Ontario, Canada: the John Deere factory and the Henniges rubber plant.[1] This paper examines management decisions regarding hiring policies and pay packages that had significant consequences for women. It also explored the circumstances surrounding the closing of these plants and showed that these decisions had disastrous consequences for when women and men lose their jobs, they lose their livelihoods and must struggle to find other options to support their families in a context where few were available.

The intention is not to glorify the heyday of manufacturing in Canada or the wage-capital relationship. Prior to the advances made by the union movement, the work was hard, often dirty and unsafe and supervisors had authority to rule idiosyncratically. People organized unions to ensure fair employment practices as well as reasonable rates of pay, benefits and pensions. Nor is the intent to glorify the patriarchic household structures that so often accompanied the male breadwinner model. The financial leverage, gained as breadwinner, structures inequities into marriage.

The aim rather is to focus on the consequences for working women and men of an economic system based on the wage-capital relationship that, by its internal logic, propels corporations to maximize profits through hiring strategies, remuneration packages and the location of plants. At both John Deere factory and the Henniges rubber plant, careful deliberations informed by competitive pressures related to, among other things, absence of tariffs and disadvantageous exchange rates, over ran considerations of human costs as profits were prioritized.

The livelihoods of working people across the globe are linked to each other by decisions made by the management personnel of multi-national corporations. In the context of policies of national and local governments, chief executive officers engage in routine decision-making to seek the highest rate of return that often results in buying factories, building factories, closing factories and relocating production. Given their mandate to be responsible to those who own the corporation, these decisions are made devoid of the positive or negative consequences for the people that will receive employment opportunities or lose jobs as factories close.

These decisions made as a response to the pressures of global capitalism, constrain the livelihoods of women, men and children in all corners of the world. Employment and consumption patterns of working people have increasingly become linked as free trade agreements permit companies to manufacture products at the source of cheap labour, and to sell these inexpensively produced goods almost anywhere. The abundance of people looking for work in countries such as Mexico, India, and China, and the absence of government legislation protecting workers means that corporations can squeeze workers to work long hours for low pay in unhealthy environments. As Prabhat Patnaik (2014) observed, owners of corporations benefit by dividing workers around the world when they shift employment away from some people and offer jobs to others. The culprit of both the absence of employment in some locations and poor working conditions elsewhere is an economic system, now global, that prioritizes profits over the well-being of people.

The working class in Canada, or more aptly put, those striving to be part of a working class in Canada, are vulnerable to job insecurity and job loss because most of the large manufacturing facilities in Canada are owned by multi-national corporations who can easily shift product to facilities in other countries or who have resources to build such facilities. Vulnerability is further increased by state negotiated agreements that waive off tariffs and instead prioritize binding free trade agreements. Throughout much of the 19th century and for interludes during the early 20th century, the Canadian Government used tariffs on manufactured goods to compel corporations to manufacture at least a portion of the goods sold in Canada. The Autopack is an example of an arrangement that required production of some automobile parts and automobiles to be produced in Canada. Canada now has entered into free trade agreements with many countries, such as Mexico, and with the consequence that our consumer markets are open to products produced elsewhere. The exploitative arrangements between capital and labour in these other parts of the world are not of concern to the Canadian government and are largely hidden from Canadian consumers, until televisions show images of those killed in fires or due to collapses of roofs and others who can barely support their family on low wages (Livesey, 1984).

Women in Manufacturing: Accessing Good Jobs

In Welland, Ontario, women's opportunities for jobs were always at the behest of powerful historical and international forces. In this globalized context, women experienced the brunt of corporate decision-making in full force as the jobs available were by and large determined by the hiring practices of private sector companies. Prior to any legislative requirements, they could discriminate in attempts to selectively choose the composition of their workforce. The post war boom in Canada and the advent of the 'car' era created demand for automotive products made from rubber and steel and companies responded by increasing their workforce. Companies, focusing on heavy manufacturing, already located in Welland capitalized on this demand and expanded their operations. These best-paid manufacturing jobs, such as Atlas Specialty Steels and John Deere were reserved for men. During the prosperous 1960s, women married to these well-paid factory workers, usually held jobs until marriage or until the birth of children, took time at home and some then returned to the labour force.

Women gained access to these 'good' jobs after the Human Rights Commission in 1979 forced all employers to discontinue discrimination against qualified women (Corman and Luxton, 2001). Women, who were finally hired by steel, automobile and other industrial manufacturing companies, were entitled to the same pay, benefits and pensions as men, given that they were covered by union negotiated agreements. These women, who were lucky enough to get these particular jobs, were able as men had been for previous decades to support their families, donate to charities, pay local, provincial and federal taxes and build communities in many ways.

Unfortunately, the timing of the Human Rights Ruling coincided with the decline in tariffs and also a downturn in demand for these products. Throughout the 1980s and 1990s, employment in some of these sectors, such as the steel industry in neighbouring Hamilton and the automobile industry in nearby St.

Catharines, slumped and those last hired – women – were those first to lose their jobs (Luxton and Corman, 2001).

While employers could not overtly refuse to hire qualified women after the 1979 decision by the Human Rights Commission, the work forces in heavy manufacturing in Welland, never the less, remained predominantly male. Atlas Specialty Steel never hired women in the plant and John Deere Welland Works only hired their first women on the job floor in 1987 and even at the maximum never exceeded 15 women out of a unionized workforce at the high of 600.

When John Deere posted a notice that they would accept applications from women in 1987, only four women joined the workforce.[2] This number is not surprising as many of the jobs in this plant required welding expertise. Other people though could work in the paint shop and do other forms of less skilled labour. One of the first women hired explained that she applied without any hopes of actually being hired. She had seen a notice that John Deere would hire women but she was pessimistic if her application would land her a job even though she had the qualifications: 'I started there in 1987, about twenty-two years ago. I had worked at Gencorp Rubber, now named Henniges. John Deere, back then, had a notice that they were going to start hiring women. So I put my name in. I was just playing around. I had worked at Gencorp for 12 years on piecework. I was the perfect candidate. I didn't think I would be hired; I didn't plan on quitting my job at Gencorp. It was like, boom, boom, boom and then I had to make a choice. I just felt like doing it. I gotta admit the difference pay made possible what I have today'. John Deere never looked seriously for women applicants and even by as late as 2002, only nine women were on the shop floor. Of the 15 women on the shop floor in 2008, one is in her 50s, 'At John Deere for 25 years, a lot of the girls were my age, in their late 30s and early 40s and one was probably 30'.

In efforts to make more profit and in the context of exchange rates between the Canadian and American dollar, John Deere began to insist on pay differential tiers for new hires. Senior people were grandfathered into tier-one. Those hired in 1998 achieved tier-two and those hired after 1999 would always earn the lowest in tier-three. Given that women were not hired in any numbers prior to the introduction of tiered wages, men were by and large the only people to benefit from a strategy to pay differentially based on seniority rather than lower pay for all. A woman explained: 'They have the old guys making between $27.00, $26.00 to $35.00, $40,00 depending on bonus; the young guys, or the medium, tier-two, from around $22.00 to $25.00; and us at $11.00 to $21.50 maximum all depending on the year in which you were hired'.

A woman described how pay differentials affected her: 'The guys that were hired prior to my group made double the money I did. When I got hired we were on a tier system where it took us six years to get up to full wage for our hiring group. And I'd never would match the money some of these baby boomer guys were making'. While a senior man described how he benefitted from the tiered wage system: 'Those who held jobs prior to the 1998 system were given a SHIP factor, any money you make, you multiply it by the SHIP factor. That would put us with high seniority, about 50 or 60 per cent higher than the others working beside us, sometimes higher'.

A man explained that under the continuous improvement pay plan introduced in 1999, himself, his son and his daughter all received different pay packages because each had been hired in different years, with his daughter being hired last. 'There were three in my family working there, I was at the top rate as if nothing (concessions) never happened. When new people come in such as my daughter, it would take six years to get to the top of her rate'. But she and others hired in her cohourt would never reach the rate achieved by either her father (on the most lucrative plan higher because of the SHIP factor) or her brother (hired in 1999 on the transition plan) doing the same work.

The junior people – women and men – hired after 1999 also were disadvantaged as they did not have seniority to bid on the jobs that had the most potential for bonus. For example, 'They were thirty-year guys. There were six of them in a CIPP Group, which is unheard of, they were the only group that had six guys and they were all thirty-year guys. They had that job so down to a "T" that they eliminated three guys. Now they're doing six-man work with three guys. Each guy was getting like $15,000–$20,000 every six months. Unheard of. My whole time there, I think I only made $2,000 extra in six months, (JDA3). As one of the members of a privileged three man team explained: 'I was probably the highest paid person in John Deere just for the simple reason that I was in a three-man team, and I understood CIPP. We started at five men but then we had to reduce to three. I showed them what we could actually make in dollars if everybody gives an honest effort. For three years we made unbelievable money. It was unheard of for a plant worker to make that kind of money.'

Having low seniority and therefore not having a choice on the work done by your team or the composition of the members of your team made people vulnerable to the disadvantage of being stuck in a big team. One explained, 'with the team incentive your team is only as good as your weakest link. If you are in a team that was 40 or 50 people you were beat. All you have to do is get one guy in a bad mood one day who says 'I'm not going to do anything', and everybody's earnings get hit'. In these circumstances, people with lower seniority could end up in jobs resulting in pay deductions due to low performance. For example, 'My first year under the tier system, I lost $5,000 off my pay cheque. I was losing $100 a week because once your team runs below the expected rate they docked it off your cheque if you don't have any reserve'.

The tiered system of unequal pay for the same work created tension at the plant and fostered dissension among workers. A woman explained how working next to a man who was doing the same work for twice the pay was degrading. 'It was very degrading, standing beside the same person doing the same job, earning anywhere like $10 less an hour. That really, really hurt me'.

She felt even more bitter when men drew the pay difference to attention. 'Shortly after I got hired, I was looking at my pay stub and some guy very sarcastically said, "Did ja want help taking this home?" I blew up at him. I know it was a joke, but it hurt. I just thought that was very cruel'. The sizeable pay differential led her to develop a dismissive attitude to work and to the company. '(The pay difference) felt like a stab in the back. From that point on, I just totally, 'that's it'. I am parked myself at John Deere and leaving when my husband retires'.

During the period that women were not hired by heavy manufacturing plants, other factories in Welland and throughout the province offered jobs to women in light manufacturing. The women in these plants received less pay than men in heavy manufacturing, especially prior to the implementation of the tiered pay but these jobs were a step up from service sector employment. The workforce at the Welland rubber plant was unionized, and consequently had guaranteed recall rights, regulated working conditions, earned twice the minimum wage, enjoyed benefit, and had a pension plan. Contrasting employment conditions with those less fortunate, and those more fortunate employees of General Motors, a rubber plant worker explained: 'You're gonna get more than the 10, 12, 15 dollars but we're not gonna make the thirty-two like GM guys. Never gonna happen.'

Historically, women workers predominated at the plant especially during the shortage of labour during the Second World War and thereafter until the 1980s. Gradually the workforce shifted to only half female by the closure in 2011. Competition for jobs in light manufacturing became scarce in direct proportion to the loss of high paying manufacturing jobs in heavy industry. Not only was the Welland rubber plant downsizing but also men who lost their jobs at Atlas Specialty Steels and other heavy industries competed alongside women for what had been women's work. Men then tended to hold union positions.

Initially, some jobs were done by men even when women formed the vast majority of the workforce. In the 1980s, men were more likely to work in the chemical mixing room, work on heavy presses and make bowling balls while women did joining work. As late as 2011, men still worked on the heavier presses and held the jobs in the mixing room. For example, as a woman explained: 'We have the mixing department and for the most part all the years it's been men. And it's kind of been like their domain. And it was a very dirty area, they had like long-term health affects because they were breathing in carbon, carbon blacks, and smoke. And it was heavy work so the women didn't want to go in there'. Eventually though some women did break into the mixing department.

When jobs were still formally segregated, an employee explained that 'there was an "A" Rate and a "B" Rate and the "A" rate paid maybe a dollar something, a couple of dollars more. "A" rate was what you call men's jobs'. Similarly, there were jobs exclusively done by women, such as finishing work. As a woman explained: 'You know, small parts, putting in inserts and guys would be working big presses, making hockey pucks'.

In 2011, by the closure of the plant, there were less formal restrictions on who did which job. 'Now it's kind of all combined. Like if you (a woman) bid on a job that used to be an "A", you could be to the front and get it'. Yet there were jobs that were still done more exclusively by men. For example, 'There are some jobs where it's mostly guys at the end of the plant where they mix the rubber. Not many women like that job. And there are probably physical demands, heavy and physical and dirty. It's mostly guys in mixing. Millwrights, actually no women. I never see any electrician women either. We had couple of supervisor women before but most of the supervisors as guys, in contrast, by 2011, there was much less segregation on the women's side of the plant as men work along with women in jobs that use to be women's preserve. For example, a woman explained: 'There is a mixture of women and men pretty well. In joining and finishing, they're a mixture. Finishing is mostly girls, guys and girls really.' She continued: 'We kind of mixed the jobs. Now it doesn't matter. She can do, he can do. One shift is guy on that job, next shift is woman on that job'.

Because women had formed the majority of the workforce at the rubber plant, and all its various owners maintained at least a 50 per cent female workforce, benefits that could be associated with seniority – pay, bidding for jobs, order of layoffs and recalls – were not structured along gender lines. In contrast to the situation at John Deere, where the recently hired women alongside junior men bore the brunt of wage concessions based on grandfathering senior workers into lucrative settlements and also the brunt of bonus systems that differentially privileged small or large teams with access to specific teams tied to seniority. Seniority, though, in neither case could protect these women and men from the most horrific management decision: to permanently close the plant. At both John Deere and the rubber plant, women and men on the labour side of the capital-labour had been expected by management to make a long-term commitment to return back to work day in, day out, year in, and year out. They were prepared to commit 30 to 40 years of their life to the company and in exchange hoped that the company would commit to job security. Neither the John Deere plant nor the rubber plant honoured this tacit commitment.

Women in Manufacturing: Permanently Losing their Jobs

By 2011, a confluence of global economic and political forces had motivated corporate powers, located outside Welland almost without exception, to systematically close the big manufacturing plants in the city. Those working in these plants had faced a number of devastating announcements concerning plant closures and layoffs, prompting some to describe the community as Canada's 'poster child' for deindustrialization. Not even its strategic location in terms of train and water transportation, its diversified manufacturing base, its skilled labour force, and its direct proximity to the US border could quell the closures. The decisions of corporate executives who responded to the relentless pursuit of greater profits by closing, downsizing and/or relocating Welland plants had created a perfect storm in the middle of the Niagara Peninsula – perfect in the sense of decimating the local economy and the local labour market (Duffy et al., 2013).

The John Deere announcement in 2008 was particularly momentous since it was the last large manufacturing plant still providing significant employment. Despite having 18 months previously entered into a three-year agreement with its labour force and having extricated important concessions such as tiered hiring, the US head office decided to move all manufacturing either to the United States or to new plants in Mexico. Workers, who uniformly believed the plant was producing a profit and was exemplary in terms of workplace safety, were devastated by this decision. They lost their jobs and prospects for their future. John Deere's announcement meant that 'the last big one' was closing too. These actions also triggered a cascade of business closures as warehouses, suppliers as well as local service industries (including retail outlets and restaurants) were forced to close. The women and men who lost their jobs with the closure of John Deere joined a long line of desperate people who were searching for the elusive job, which could provide a living wage and a retirement package (Duffy, Pupo and Corman, 2013).[2]

John Deere Company closed its farm machinery factory in Niagara in 2009, throwing 600 unionized employees, many welders, out of work. These workers made all-terrain vehicles and loaders and then painted them John Deere green. Lower wages in Mexico and protectionist sentiment by the then American President, led executives in the John Deere headquarters in the United States to reassign production to plants in Mexico and the United States. The women and men, who lost these jobs, entered a labour market that offered very little. Steel and auto plants were not hiring and most other jobs paid less, with few benefits or pension entitlement. Many of these women tried to restrain but even those who managed to certify as home care workers or social service workers ended up with less pay, less benefits and less pension entitlement.

The history of John Deere Welland Works, as outlined in its own publication, is a textbook example of management responding to profit-making opportunities in the context of state policies and wage differentials in various locals (John Deere: 1–30). Although the ownership of John Deere Welland Works did not have a complicated and checkered past as Henniges, as a multinational company with production facilities strategically located on almost all continents, the plant in Welland became subject to pressures to consolidate and to shift production to plants with the prospects of higher profit margins.

John Deere and Company, located in the United States, had acquired the Welland-based plant in 1912 in response to tariffs on American farm machinery entering Canada (welland.library.on.ca/e-services/local-history). Deere explained that high tariffs imposed by the Canadian government on manufacturing products, during this time period, created the financial incentive to produce equipment for the Canadian market in Canada. The Canadian market expanded exponentially after 1900 as homesteader's increased agricultural production in the western provinces.

The constraint to produce in Canada disappeared when the federal government in the early 1920s lowered the tariff: 'The Canadian import tariffs for agricultural equipment were so low that cost calculations indicated it was more economical to serve the Canadian market which was primarily for the Western Provinces, out of the Minneapolis branch' (John Deere: 5). The head office shifted production to American-based factories and mothballed the Canadian plant.

With the advent of the stock market crash in 1929 and the ensuing depression, the Canadian Government once again levied higher import tariffs on manufacturing products entering the country. According to Deere: 'In 1931, as a result of the introduction of major Canadian import tariffs on farm implements, and the desire to stay competitive in Canadian sales, the factory was recommissioned' (John Deere: 7). According to an ex-employee, at that time, Mr. Deere, speaking to the Welland workforce, promised to keep the plant open forever. Production of armaments for the Canadian military during World War

II and the post-war demand for equipment by farmers, now recovered from the decade of depression and drought, required additional workers for the plant in Welland.

In the 1950s, the tariff structure imposed by the federal government once again provided the financial incentive for management to shift production to the Welland Plant. The company explained: 'In 1958, Deere made the decision to begin manufacturing industrial equipment in Welland for the Canadian market. The heavy duty on industrial goods coming into Canada was the major reason for this decision' (John Deere: 9). In the context of these tariffs, production in Canada boomed during the 1960s though not for long. By 1968, the federal government eliminated the tariff on these types of industrial products and as a result: 'This meant it was no longer economical to maintain production of industrial products in Welland for just the Canadian market' (John Deere: 11). Production of farm equipment, though, continued.

In the absence of tariffs, fluctuations in the exchange rate between the American and Canadian dollar directly influenced the rate of return of producing product on either side of the border and as noted above in 1989, in the context of a high Canadian dollar, Deere had insisted on two-tier wage system at the Welland plant even in face of a strike. Widely fluctuating exchange rates continued to affect production decisions. In 2004, the Canadian dollar was only worth 65 cents American dollar while by 2008, the Canadian dollar reached a high of $106 per American dollar. In response to relative production costs, in 2007, John Deere continued to set up more factories in Asia and Mexico, and in 2008, they developed joint ventures in India and China.

Although management at the head office of John Deere in the United States did not issue an official explanation for the decision to close the Welland Plant announced in September 2008, the absence of tariffs combined with a high Canadian dollar provided financial incentive to shift production to underutilized capacity in the United States and to employ low wage workers in newly built facilities in Mexico. In September 2008, the company announced the closure of the Welland operation. Shortly after the closure, all the interior equipment was moved out, leaving only huge empty hulls.

The employees were thrown into a labour market, which contained no relevant jobs for their experience level. The people, who lost their jobs and hence their livelihoods when this plant closed, explained that quality, productivity and operating the plant in the black was never an issue. Rather, pressure to produce in the United States in the post-Obama era combined with low wage costs in Mexico fueled the decision taken in Moline, Illinois. Neither the employees nor their union was involved in dialogue regarding closing the plant and nor would the managers at the headquarters in Illinois negotiate with the union after the announcement to close the plant.

In contrast to John Deere, from the inception of the rubber plant in Welland, employees faced a different set of circumstances. While the John Deere plant in Welland remained owned by John Deere from 1912 to closure in 2009, the employees at the rubber plant experiences several different owners, often located outside Canada. The plant had already had four owners prior to 2001, when GDX Automotive, the largest supplier of vehicle sealing systems, purchased GenCorp and, in so doing, acquired the Welland rubber plant (welland.library.on.ca/e-services/local-history). GDX Automotive would be the last owner with an intention to make profit by producing rubber products for sale. After 2004, with the purchase by Cerberus Capital Management, a large privately owned investment company with holdings around the world, all subsequent owners were more intent on rationalizing productive capacity in consortium companies and then reselling the company (nytimes.com). But instead of focusing on the newly named, Henniges rubber plant in Welland, as the Union President, Joe Buote explained, Cerberus Capital Management, essentially 'walked away' and it was a 'long and frustrating time under Cerberus ownership' (Riopelle, 2007).

Through a series of purchases, including Metzeler North America and GDX Capital, Wynnchurch Capital located in Illinois, acquired the Welland rubber plant in 2007. For a short time, they operated all these assets, located in Canada, United States, Mexico, Germany, Czech Republic and China, under the name Henniges Automotive. Essentially Wynnchurch packaged two companies together that had similar production facilities and different customer lists. By purchasing much of the competition, production could be rationalized in fewer plants. The combination of Metzeler North America and GDX had created the No. 1 supplier of vehicle sealing systems in North America and the No. 2 supplier globally (welland.library.on.ca/e-services/local-history).

Wynnchurch as 'a private investment fund with experience with corporate carve-outs and restructuring' had a modus operandi to acquire companies, rationalize production and repackage for resale (wynnchurch.com). Within three years, by 30 November 2010, Wynnchurch sold the majority shares of Henniges Automotive to Littlejohn and Co with headquarters in Connecticut. Littlejohn had at that time a portfolio of $2.3 billion. According to company literature, founded in 1996 by Angus Littlejohn, the 'company makes majority or minority investments in companies with the intention of restructuring the assets and reselling the company often within three to five years' (littlejohnllc.com/manage.asp).

On 1 March 2011, working to further rationalize production of the consortium of Henniges rubber plants, Littlejohn and Co announced the closure of the Welland operation effective Fall, 2011. Down from a high of 1,100 employees, the remaining 300 women and men workers lost their jobs. A news release from the company said the facility 'was selected for closure because of the high relative cost of operation and its inability to remain competitive in today's market...The company will consolidate operations to existing facilities throughout North America including Canada, US and Mexico' (Johnson: 1). Once again, operating with the logic of an economic system based on profit, the decision-makers focused 'on creating value for investors' (littlejohnllc.com/manage.asp) in total disregard for the people who had devoted years of their lives to this plant and who were dependent on these jobs for their livelihoods.

With the closures of both the John Deere and the Henniges rubber plant, the workers felt betrayed by the companies especially because they had remained working at their respective plants through downturns while the company acted without any commitment to them or to the community of Welland. Both unions had accepted wage concession and had continued to produce quality product. Workers had hoped that such measures would safeguard their jobs. For some at both plants, a hurtful aspect of the closure was that neither company engaged the workforce or the community in discussions to save the plants. The final blow was that there was nothing they could do as individuals, as union members, as citizens and as voters (Pupo, Duffy and Corman, 2013).

Conclusion

With the enormity of the waves of plant closures in Welland, the entire community was transformed, shattering dreams for retirement, small business success and young workers' plans for a settled life near family and friends. High rates of unemployment increased, caseloads of community agencies had a ripple effect on local small suppliers, restaurants and stores. The idle industries and growing brown fields still call attention to those who profit from closure decisions and to a callous economic system fixed solely on the profit motive and stubbornly oblivious to the well-being of communities.

In both cases, the Welland plants was a small part of very large corporations, located outside Canada, with assets scattered throughout the world. With access to dispersed production facilities, executives could trim costs and increase revenue of the parent corporation by selling certain production facilities or by transferring production to lower cost facilities within the corporation. The welfare of the parent corporation took precedence over the welfare of the individual factories or particular employees or the communities hosting the production facilities. The decisions to abandon factories, lead directly to loss of jobs, loss of incomes and livelihoods, dislocated families and community disruption.

In the Canadian context, governments at the local and provincial level have little bargaining power to influence the agenda of multi-national corporations. The Federal Government, though, with control over monetary policy and trade agreements can directly set the investment climate to either encourage manufacturing in Canada or relinquish this responsibility in the interests of 'free trade.' By the 21st century, the Canadian Government provided few, if any, obligations on corporations to produce products in Canada for sale to the Canadian market. Without enforced encouragement, chief executive officers of multi-national corporations abandoned plants in Canada to locate in what they determined were more favourable investment climate.

From the vantage point of Welland's displaced women and men, nameless strangers – CEOs in grey suits – in distant boardrooms controlled their fate, ruined their livelihoods, and ransacked their community with little or no explanation for their actions. Workers who built equipment for John Deere and who made rubber automotive parts for Henniges saw themselves as responsible people who had reported to work on time, met their production quotas and quality checks, endured grueling working conditions day after day, year after year. Those factors that they controlled – quality of the production and the productivity and safety record at the plant – were not given as reasons related to closure decisions.

Working people and their unions have very little leverage to negotiate contracts or to negotiate to retain the company in operation or even to negotiate closure agreements when the owner also either operates similar-product plants in other locations has the capacity to build such plants. These negotiations are further complicated when the owners, such as venture capital companies, do not have a long-term stake in either the plant or for that matter the industry as a whole. Workers will never have leverage over closure decisions when maximizing profit constrains corporate executives to make decisions in the interests of the bottom line rather than in the interests of people.

People who lose their jobs due to plant closures and those who gain low paid, unsafe jobs are at the mercy of corporate decision-makers, who themselves, are constrained to maximize profits. By the 21st century almost all people are integrated into a global market economy. It is this system that requires analytical attention and organizational abilities.

Notes

1. The paper is part of an SSHRC-funded study of displaced workers and community change in Welland, Ontario, Canada (SSHRC-GRG #410-2009-2244). Unions at both sites provided lists of the first names and phone numbers of their members. This paper reports on interviews done between November 2009 to February 2010 with 50 John Deere workers and in 2010 with 40 Henniges workers. The Ethics Committees at both Brock University and York University approved the research protocols.
2. Interviews are coded by company such that JDA10, for example, indicates the person worked for John Deere, and was the 10th person interviewed by Ann Duffy. Similarly, HEN2 denotes that the person worked at the Henniges Rubber plant and was the second person interviewed by Norene Pupo.

References

Duffy, Ann; Pupo, Norene and Corman, June (2013). 'Public Sociology in the Context of Economic Restructuring', presented at the American Sociological Conference, New York.

Johnson, D. (2011). The Welland Tribune Website, Wellandtribune, CA, 2 March 2011, 1.

Littlejohn Website, littlejohnlle.com/manage.asp, 9 March 2012

Livesey, Bruce (2014). 'Where our Clothes Come From', Report in Business Magazine, 84–94.

Luxton, Meg and Corman, June (2001). *Getting By in Hard Times: Gendered Labor at Home and on the Job.* Canada: University of Toronto Press.

New York Times Website, nytimes.com Accessed on 15 March 2012.

Patnaik, Prabhat (2014). Public Address at the Society for Socialist Studies, Social Sciences and Humanities Congress, Brock University, St. Catharines, Ontario, Canada.

Pupo, Norene; Duffy, Ann and Corman. June (2013). 'Facing Plant Closure: Workers and their Unions in Times of Crisis', presented at American Sociology Conference, New York.

Riopelle, Maggie (2007). 'Changes at the Rubber Plant', *Welland Tribune*, wellandtribune.ca Accessed on 23 October 2007, 1.

Welland Library, Local History website http: //www.welland.library.on.ca/e-services/ local-history. Accessed on 5 March 2012.

Wynnchurch Capital Website, wynnchurch.com Accessed on 9 March 2012.

4

Public Employment Programmes in India and Inclusion

An Analysis

MANJU SINGH AND AGRIMA SINGH

Abstract

Gender equality and empowered women are catalysts for multiplying development efforts. Investment and planning of development efforts with perspective of gender inclusivity will yield high returns. Public employment programme in India is aimed at most vulnerable section of the society and align with the policy approach of inclusive growth. Public employment programme have long been considered as a main tool of development to target poor and vulnerable people including women. This paper seeks to examine the extent to which a public employment Programme – Mahatma Gandhi National Rural Employment Guarantee Act (MGNREGA) – considers gender specific social and economic concerns in its design to empower women in India. This is with the expectation that this will enable better understanding of gender dimension and also yield insights for policy design and implementation. This paper is based on a micro-study conducted in Rajasthan. Data was collected using interviews and focus group discussions. Key areas of data include gender analysis of public employment programme (MGNREGA) in India specifically in its design. Studies of such nature would be relevant for formulation of future policy design to address the issues underlying an increasing feminization of poverty and to yield the highest return of development.

Keywords

gender, inclusion, public employment programme, policy design

Introduction

It has been recognized that gender equality, empowerment of women, women's full enjoyment of all human rights and eradication of poverty are essential to economic and social development, including the achievement of all the Millennium Development Goals (OECD, 2010). Women's economic empowerment is a prerequisite for sustainable development and pro-poor growth. Gender equality and empowered women are catalysts for multiplying development efforts. Investments in gender equality yield the highest returns of all development investments (OECD, 2010). Attaining economic empowerment of women is a challenge and it cannot be achieved suddenly. Holistic approach and long-term commitment along with gender-specific perspectives in sound public policies are the prerequisites. Equal access at the design and execution level of policy and programming is essential. A nation's success in empowering women will depend on a response towards formulation of gender inclusive public policies specifically in its design and execution.

Research endorses that gender has an important role in relation to the impact of economic as well as social risks. The impacts of economic shocks at the community level are settled by, for example, gender distribution of labour markets and institutional norms which makes poor access and utilization of productive services by women. Assets of female-headed households are more vulnerable than those of men during crisis because of gender biases. Effect may more deepen in case sold assets are not replaced (Byrne and Baden, 1995). Imperatively social factors of vulnerability are equally significant as economic shocks and stresses for attaining sustainable livelihood and general well-being (CPRC, 2008). These risk factors reinforces through policy implementation and discriminatory practices rooted in institutions, community, household and individual from macro to the micro-level. Investment and planning of development efforts with perspective of gender inclusivity will yield high returns.

Public employment programme has long been considered as a main tool of development to target poor and vulnerable people including women. Public employment programme in India is aimed at most vulnerable section of the society and align with the policy approach of inclusive growth. It is realized that strong and focused efforts in public employment programmes are still lacking to ensure equal opportunities and access to all citizens without any bias of gender, caste, class, creed and disability. The gendered context of poverty and vulnerability has not adequately recognized in public policies (Holmes and Jones, 2009). It is vital that gender-sensitive measures are incorporated into policy, design and implementation. An exploration of policy and design of any public employment programme is imperative for the future policy implication to address question of gender equality.

The Study

The study focuses on a public employment programme – Mahatma Gandhi National Rural Employment Guarantee Act (MGNREGA) – that has been considered as an intervention in India to provide livelihood security to poor and vulnerable people. It examines the extent to which MGNREGA considers gender specific social and economic concerns in its design to support women in India. This is with the expectation that it will enable better understanding of gender dimension in public employment programme and also yield insights for the policy design and implementation.

The approach of the present study is based on secondary review of literature supplemented by a micro-study to have greater understanding of the work with real life personal interface in the field. The secondary review includes gathering and analysis of information of relevant work available in print and published on the web such as published reports, government documents, official reports, information in newspapers, magazines etc. A micro study in the state of Rajasthan in north-western part of India was carried out. This was conducted in two districts, Ajmer and Pratapgarh, during January-March 2012 and October-November 2013. Information was collected from key respondents through interviews which include officials of various cadre including District Collector, Block Development Officer, Junior Engineer and focus group discussions consisting eight–12 women working in MGNREGA on various sites.

The thrust area of the study includes review of general, gender inclusivity in the policy and design of MGNREGA and implications for future policy and programme design to address the issue underlying an increasing feminization of poverty in India.

Is MGNREGA Design Gender Inclusive?

This part of the paper focusses on the policy, design and implementation in MGNREGA particularly with reference to gender inclusion. This will review the extent of gender equality in the structure of MGNREGA and also how much it addresses gender question to contribute greater opportunities for women that simultaneously address unequal intra-household and community gender dynamics.

MGNREGA has already gone far ahead in including innovative design and monitoring system based on India's far ranging experience in managing rural livelihood. Many research studies have commented about the role of MGNREGA towards empowerment of women (Drèze and Oldiges, 2007; Drèze and Oldiges, 2009; ISST, 2006; Jandu, 2008). Rural women were hardly having livelihood opportunities prior to MGNREGA because of complex and varied reasons across India. Women were having very limited chance for agriculture and non-agriculture wage works besides care role for sick and elderly (Berman 2003; Chen, 1989). Consequently, they find themselves in vulnerable position with limited, seasonal and insecure earnings. In addition to vulnerability because of migration and involvement in construction, factory, mining and forestry work, women have to face hazards and the possibilities of injury. Many women conveyed that had they not worked on the NREGA worksites, they would have worked at home or would have remained unemployed (Khera and Nayak, 2009).

Although MGNREGA has been widely considered as powerful prospective to transform rural livelihoods through its rights-based approach to employment, this did not include transformation of gender relation as an intended goal. The design of the Act acknowledges women's role in the rural economy and women's experiences of poverty and vulnerability to some extent. There are some important clauses in the Act that make legal provisions relating specifically to women.

- One is, provision of the quota in the act targets to encourage women's participation in the workforce. This ensures that at least one-third of all workers registered under the scheme should be women [Schedule II (6)].
- Other is considering the women's care responsibilities, crèche facilities are to be provided when five or more children below the age of 6 are brought to the worksite [Schedule II (28)] to facilitate women's participation in the

programme. Women, especially single women, are given preference to work on worksites close to their residence if the worksite is 5km or more away (Ministry of Rural Development, 2008).

- Further, the Act states that equal wages to both men and women should be paid under the provisions of the Equal Remuneration Act, 1976 [Schedule II (34)].
- The guidelines suggest that while opening bank accounts for the workers, a considered choice between individual accounts and joint accounts need to be given by the bank. It suggests that different household members like husband and wife should be co-signatories in the case of joint accounts. Special care should be taken to avoid crediting family earnings to individual accounts held by the male head of the household which could affect economic powers of women. In the case of male-headed households, separate individual accounts for women members may be opened.
- Another aspect is regarding the supervisory workers at the worksite as mates that are designated for each work. Adequate representation of women among mates is ensured in its guidelines.
- One more aspect of gender sensitivity in the act is that women should be represented in local level committees, the social audit process as well as state and central level councils.

It is, thus, understood that MGNREGA by its policy and design helps women in expansion of employment opportunities. It facilitates livelihood opportunities at local level with ease, access to the work that is government and regular in nature, assuring predictable set working hours and less chance of exploitation. The work is socially acceptable and considered dignified and most importantly better paid than other works.

Inclusion in Work Opportunities

Women are getting opportunity of equal participation through quota in the design of implementation in MGNREGA. More than half of workers (53.3%) are women on the public work sites that are much higher than national work participation rate for rural women (24.8%, 2011–12)? At national level, women participation in MGNREGA is varied across states. At one extreme states like Kerala (92.62%), Pondicherry (83.95%), Tamil Nadu (74.68%) and Rajasthan (68.96%) have high participation, other extremes have low participation like Assam (24.8%), Jammu and Kashmir (19.8%), UP (18.76%) and Mizoram (22.71%). Variation in women's work participation may be explained in different ways. Factors that have encouraged women to work include work opportunities at the door step (Bhatty 2006; Khera and Nayak, 2009), a tradition of rural women working in the other's field (Narayanan, 2008), provision of equal wages (Khera and Nayak, 2009), innovative experiments in implementation like female mates system in Rajasthan (Khera, 2008), synergization of MGNREGA with Kutumbshree in Kerala (Vijaykumar and Thomas, 2008 cited in Pankaj A. and Tankha R., 2010). Regarding any formal provision of quota for single woman-headed HHs, although it is not assured in the act but women were satisfied over the preference given to single women in practice.

This informally reflects gender inclusion in the implementation of the programme. In almost all sites visited in the field during this study, most of the workers were females. Female-headed HH's participation in the works is encouraging ranging from 12–52 percentages (Institute of Applied Manpower Research, New Delhi, 2008). The nature of the programme supports mobilization of women towards paid from unpaid voluntary work. It is recognition and promotion of value for time and labour of women.

Apt Work Conditions

As the act stipulates that work be provided within 5 km of residence, women found it logistically easy with main task of household work. It was also reported that this issue is addressed with full concern. Most of the women are engaged in the work that is within 5 km distance and transportation cost is paid to them in case the site is far away (rarely). Women found it extremely easy to access work right near their own village with fix timings and set norms and rules. Moreover they felt no stigma attached to this work. Quality of work is pushed upward into the direction of decent work as MGNREGA workers claim the scheme has helped them avoid less dignified work. Another aspect of locally available work is that now women are able to cope with illness of family members and aged people well. Although, regarding flexibility in the timings of work in MGNREGA with specific requirements of women, it is not considered in any case. All has to follow the same time schedule. This practice limits wok participation of women specifically burdened with household responsibilities that requires lot of flexibilities.

Equity in Earnings

Other reason for gender acceptability under MGNREGA work is provision of statutory minimum wages. Even if sometime it is delayed MGNREGA has substantially helped jump in wages and the women's earning. Their own income stream is secured with this.

Sometimes women did not engage themselves in agricultural wages because of very low rates and they felt that it was not worth going out and to work for such a meagre amount. MGNREGA with the provision of equal wages enables women to access higher wages than earlier. The provision of equality of wages is bridging the wage differentiation and women are found highly satisfied. Parity of wages between man and women strengthening women's place at work assumes significance. Emergence of women workers as independent bread earner with their own income and control has significantly increased their level of empowerment like greater decision-making and spending power and exposure level. Paid employment opportunity outside the household, apart from other factors, increases the bargaining capacity of women by giving her better fall-back position (Agrawal, 1994). As suggested by Moser (1993), women's ability to earn outside the household increases their own perception of their contribution to their family.

Following this effect, women are able to avoid stress migration in search of work and sometime help postpone their migration. Private employers are under pressure to provide better working conditions. Positive effect on their bargaining power is also visible. On flip side, women are now overburdened due to participation in MGNREGA and there is no reduction in poverty of women. In some cases men in their group register their attendance and sit ideally somewhere in the village Panchayat that further increase women's work load. Another interested fact is that most of the women are not aware of the calculation method of wages but they assume that females receive less than males overall.

Equity in Choice of Work

One of the basic ways to think about MGNREGA from gender perspective is that how the created assets benefits women, the choice and design of work take women's interest into account. Existing design of MGNREGA largely focusses on building infrastructure at various sites as per the priorities listed in the Schedule 1 of the Act. It comprises water conservation, drought management, irrigation, land development, flood control and protection, rural connectivity to provide all weather access and knowledge resource centres. Women rarely raise voice in decision-making about the work sites. A blueprint approach reflects particularly in the choice of work in MGNREGA that lack the flexibilities to consider the ways in which gender concern can shape programme opportunities. There is total absence of flexibility and consideration regarding choice of work as per the skill and demand of women.

Recently government is showing some extent of flexibility and allowing dovetailing with some other schemes like MLA-LAD scheme.

There is no evidence of inclusion of social sector activities like education, healthcare, food processing and distribution, skill development and training related to farm and off farm sector where women can contribute well with ease and efficiency. Provision of social sector and other related activities blended with gender skill in the work choices of MGNREGA as shown in Figure 1 may expand service infrastructure in rural areas. This gender consideration and choice of work may provide employment for women as per women's ability and skills and reduce poverty on the one hand.

On the other hand, this will increase accessibility and availability of basic services in rural areas and facilitates opportunity for professional development of women as well. Employment activities in the area like care, education, health and hygiene, training in farm and off farm sectors, awareness generation, rural entrepreneurship, etc. may be included in the shelf of MGNREGA as per the local specific requirement. This approach will build the rural surroundings that certainly support in providing education, better health services, easy access to natural resources, higher productivity, reduce burden of care work and increase in awareness. Finally with reduced time poverty and mobility toward paid work it may improve quality of life of women.

Support in Women's Role in Family and Reproduction

Schedule II (28) of Act facilitates women's participation in the programme through providing crèche facilities when five or more children below the age of six years are brought to the worksite. The provision in design of MGNREGA is supporting women in family and reproduction roles to some extent. Women were found to be satisfied with the support provided in MGNREGA for child

Figure 1
Widenening Shelf of MGNREGA Activities

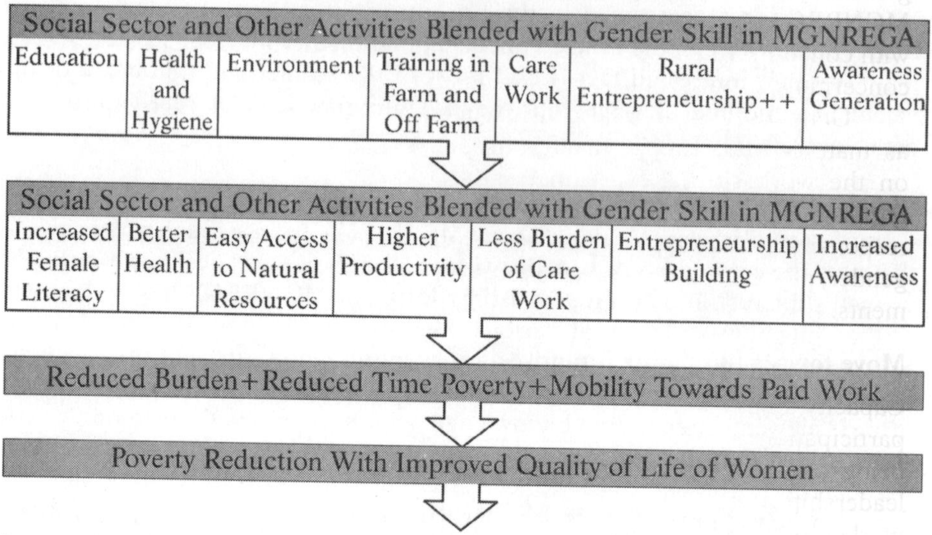

*e.g. energy conservation, solar energy, watershed management

+ Crop technology, seed management, pest management, plant and nutrition management, vermin compost, nursery, livestock care and management

++ e.g. marketing, computing, banking, leadership, food processing

care on the work sites (may not be fully in physical term). Responsibility of child care is assigned to one among them from their own group. This system helps both ways taking care of children and also of the women who need special consideration due to life cycle needs. She is paid wages as per the norms. Rotational system benefits all women requiring special help at work sites.

Group interaction pointed out some facts about gender sensitivity towards life cycle needs in MGNREGA. Thirty per cent quota of mates is reserved for person in special need like pregnant/old/sick. It was observed that women were not aware about any formal provisions regarding this dimension. But interestingly at the time of needs such as pregnancy, early motherhood and sickness, good care is taken by the group members among themselves. Thus, team spirit and group concept of MGNREGA facilitated all the women to face life cycle needs quite comfortably.

Effective gender inclusion beyond employment and income is possible with locale specific, gender sensitive strategies and modalities with or without guideline and provision in the act. Work allotment was done on the basis of specific needs of women/disabled/sick/old in some areas. Many activities that were considered as light work like watering tree under plantation programme and child care work was assigned in case of life cycle needs. Sometimes the group internally adjusted and helped their team mates in case of help.

Raising Women's Voice and Leadership

Mere physical representation in terms of quota may not always be effective, especially when it is unarticulated and unheard. MGNREGA is contributing in this direction in some sense. Women's assertion and active representation is now germinating through organization of women specific meetings among MGNREGA workers. This gives opportunity to share and resolve their problems with concern. MGNREGA is assisting poor women to have say in the decisions concerning resources that are influencing their work and life.

Gender sensitivity is also visible in terms of assignment of supervisory roles as 'mate' in MGNREGA. In a few instances females were assigned role of mates on the work sites. Female mates fully understand the gender concern and requirements at work sites. But in some work sites males were assigned the responsibility of mates for the whole group of female workers. Irrespective of gender, all women workers were found to be adjusting with each other's requirements.

Move towards Capacity Building of Women

Capacity building exercise of participants supports wider reach and active participation of any programme. There is no training and awareness programme being organized under MGNREGA although some time under dynamics of leadership, literacy programmes are conducted by PREARAK (field worker/motivator in literacy programme in a village). Adult literacy campaign to MGNREAGA workers provides training during lunch hour. Those who use thumb impression are the target group for literacy campaign. ANM (Auxiliary Nurse Midwife) at village level trains mates about primary healthcare and first-aid.

Some other awareness programmes exist, but not under aegis of MGNREGA. Awareness generation on child welfare, girl child, girl education, right to information, etc. were being organized under other government schemes or by some civil society organization.

Overall, there is a lack of investment in capacity building programme under MGNREGA. Women showed high inclination for rural-local-gender specific skill upgrading and awareness training that indirectly could help improve implementation of the programme like healthcare, livestock care, vermin compost, nursery, maintenance of solar equipment, food processing, basic computer and other rural farm and non-form technologies, etc.

Adding on Support

Another aspect of understanding gender concern in the programme was seen in terms of the support provided under MGNREGA in some areas. Women workers were quite contented on this aspect. They got all help and assistance at the time of registration and opening of accounts.

They accepted their limited level of information and exposure but were happy to share that ability to complete all formalities with assistance provided by officials and became quite independent in handling the issues. Gram sevaks (member of local self-government in village) also helped women in financial matters.

Related to the institutional connectivity of MGNREGA to other related programmes, women workers commented that considering their limitations to access opportunities, after joining MGNREGA, they got preference in other schemes, although, it is an unofficial and informal practice. They were easily able to access micro-credit from SHG, insurance for cattle and other schemes. Further it was reported that health insurance was not available for them.

MGNREAGA employment offers some relief and confidence in women particularly who are not getting any financial aids. Getting money advances from moneylenders were found to be easy as they are assured of getting money back now. MGNREGA is considered as a great help for widows. Regular earnings from MGNREGA have helped them to avoid hunger, migration and also made them cope with the sickness in the family very well.

Interaction with women workers reflects the insight as to how MGNREGA is helping women to take charge of their lives even as a spark with a small beginning. Their confidence and voice in family decision has risen after MGNREGA. They have started asserting with their own earnings after MGNREGA.

MGNREGA has made a significant contribution in improving the well-being of women (Khera and Nayak, 2009). The group also feels that violence against women has significantly reduced because of their involvement in MGNREGA and increased status. MGNREGA is helping women build ways towards happiness.

Approach of Performance Measurement

The Ministry of Rural Development (MoRD) has specially designed a separate website to provide up-to-date information on various aspects of MGNREGA at the state, district and panchayat levels and it provides extensive information on this huge programme. It has a significant role to make it more accountable and transparent in terms of access to information on its various aspects and working. Reports from MIS include year-wise financial reports, field visits and review reports, MIS presentations and audit reports. Financial reports cover wide information regarding employment, works, funds and account details extensively. Information related to employment aspect of MGNREGA includes data on employment status, pattern, progress report, period-wise employment, employment provided to disabled, work demand pattern, pattern of average wage, employment status of SC/ST, age-wise registered and employed person, total employment provided by various categories, etc. Further data on works, funds and account details is also provided in full extent.

Gender dimension is an important component of the design of analysis of any programme. Analysis of any outcome indicator needs gender as a primary category of analysis rather than a peripheral consideration. One of the key challenges seen in MGNREGA MIS is limited availability of gender segregated information and statistics. Gender segregated data on various dimension of MGNREGA, like employment demanded and offered, job card issued to households, average wage paid, wage expenditure, number of registered labour, households completed 100 days of employment, could be helpful for assessing the gender inclusivity. Similarly, data regarding account opened in bank/post office, details of members of joint account on the base of gender classification is also not indicated that may give useful insight regarding gender sensitivity. This can help predict gender related impact of MGNREGA access, unintended effects and identify potential mitigation approaches.

MGNREGA: Route to Transform Gender Dynamics

Literature seldom reflects gendered patterning in policy and programme design (Holmes and Jones, 2010). The ground work of the present study aims to examine the extent to which MGNREGA includes gender specific considerations in its design and to yield insights for policy design and implementation to transform gender dynamics. The following pointers may provide important impetus for successful implementation of MGNREGA that may address gender question aptly.

- Decades of international experience with social protection and with other poverty reduction programmes yield some general lessons to consider in formulating an implementation strategy (quoted by Kimsey from World Bank, 2004). Foremost is political committed leadership and effective programme strategy that requires significant institutional change in norms, rules, modalities and implementation.
- There is no successful blue print or design for appropriate gender inclusive programme. There is need to encourage a mindset that is willing to continuously learn, take calculated risks and closely monitor and evaluate results. Development and experimentation of alternative strategies and operational modalities with gender concern is the prescription for making the initiative gender inclusive.
- People-centric convergence with gender concern is need of the hour. Since convergence is a consultative output, capacity building of all stakeholders and community participation may facilitate appropriate gender concern in the programme.
- A complete shift from relief work approach to all-inclusive development approach is required for better management with gender concern. The work undertaken should change from taking up standalone works in typical relief work modes to inclusive development outlook. Planned and effective convergence for sustainable enhancement of productivity of earning of poor people specially women should become the vital focus of MGNREGA.
- Embracing two-pronged approach in MGNREGA has potential to ensure women's equal access by provision of easy and wider access to work for women on the one hand and on the other hand facilitate mobilization from unpaid work to paid work.
- Widening MGNREGA activities' shelf with social sector and related activities blended with gender skill in public works can attain multiple objectives simultaneously. This will reduce poverty, improve social service delivery in the area, provide employment opportunities for women and facilitate the professional development in the social service field for women.
- Gender segregated data of all measurement and outcome indicators with transparency can predict gender related impact of MGNREGA. This will help access unintended effects and identify potential mitigation approaches. Both qualitative and quantitative data presentation is essential to assess differential impacts of MGNREGA on men and women. This is crucial in order to inform policy evidence, improve programme design and reinforce accountability.

- An integrated MIS ought to serve needs of all stakeholders and role players. Building staff capacity w.r.t. gender orientation and sensitivity is essential for effective gender reach of the programme.
- A special effort is necessary to get women on board and make sure that they receive equal benefits. There is need of distinct strategies and activities to reach poor women. Perhaps the most simple (may not be easiest) is massive awareness generation using multiple channels of communication to ensure that women know their choices and rights for their betterment and equality.
- Information must be shared to all especially women regarding gender provisions to help reinforce all dimensions of successful execution. Not only formal MIS but open communication channels to reach all as Janata (People) Information System (JIS) is need of the hour. Locally adapted communication strategies like wall paintings in common place of village may be more reachable than computers.
- The appropriate mix of centralized management and decentralized implementation requires finely balanced trade-offs. Local women often have critical knowledge about the need and capacities. Balanced decentralization may foster greater programme flexibilities with gender dimension.
- Top officials should be prepared for open criticism and suggestion – a transparent open process will lead to long-term success. Sensitization of leaders (local as well national), executors, and technical staff for consultation and experimentation to adopt appropriate measure regarding gender interest can help achieve goal.
- Further the dissemination of what works and what does not, is useful to keep beneficiaries and implementers informed about results as well as encourage the public and politicians to remain supportive and encourage taking up programme.

Conclusion

Although MGNREGA did not include transformation of gender relation as an intended goal, the design of the Act acknowledges women's experiences of poverty and vulnerability to some extent. There are some important legal provisions reflecting gender concern but far more efforts are required for addressing gender question in policy and design. Beyond provision in design, all stakeholders must have a mindset that is willing to learn, take calculated risks and closely monitor and evaluate results. The success of gender inclusive design depends on a process of adaptation, readiness to learn from experimentation and courage to adopt new approaches. Development and experimentation of alternative strategies and operational modalities with gender concern is the prescription for making the initiative gender inclusive.

References

Agarwal, Bina (1994). *A Field of One's Own: Gender and Land Rights in South Asia*, Cambridge: Cambridge University Press.

Bhatty, Kiran (2006). 'Employment Guarantee and Child Rights', *Economic and Political Weekly*, 41(20): 1965–67.

Byrne, B. and Baden, S. (1995). Gender Emergencies and Humanitarian Assistance. BRIDGE Report No. 35, IDS, Sussex.

Breman, Jan (2003). *The Laboring Poor in India: Patterns of Exploitation, Subordination and Exclusion*. New Delhi: Oxford University Press.

Chen, Martha (1989). 'Women's Work in Indian Agriculture by Agro-Ecologic Zones: Meeting Needs of Landless and Land-Poor Women', *Economic and Political Weekly*, 28 October.

Drèze, Jean and Oldiges, Christian (2007). 'Commendable Act', *Frontline*, July, Volume 24, No. 14.

Dreze, Jean and Khera, Reetika (2009). 'The Battle for Employment Guarantee', *Frontline*, 26(01), 3–16 January.

Holmes, R. and Jones, N. (2009). *Putting the Social Back into Social Protection: A Framework for Understanding the Linkages between Economic and Social Risks for Poverty Reduction*. London: ODI Background Note.

Holmes, R. and Jones, N. (2011). 'Gender Inequality, Risk and Vulnerability in the Rural Economy: Refocusing the Public Work Agenda to take Account of Economic and Social Risk', ESA Working Paper No. 11–13. www.fao.org/economic/esa.

Institute of Applies Manpower Research (2008). All India Report on Evaluation of NREGA: A Survey of Twenty Districts, Programme Evaluation Office, Planning Commission.

Institute of Social Studies Trust (2006). *Women and the NREGA*. New Delhi: Institute of Social Studies Trust and International Labor Organization.

Jandu, Navjyoti (2008). 'Employment Guarantee and Women's Empowerment in Rural India', www.righttofoodindia.org

Khera, R. and Nayak, N. (2009). 'Women Workers and Perceptions of the National Rural Employment Guarantee Act in India', Paper at presented FAO-IFAD-ILO workshop, Rome.

Kimsey, M. included in Samson, Niekerk and Quene (2010). Designing and Implementing Social Transfer Programmes (Second edition). Economic Policy and Research Institute, South Africa.

Moser, Caroline (1993). *Gender Planning and Development: Theory, Practice and Training*. London: Routledge.

Narayanan, Sudha (2008). Employment Guarantee, Women's Work and Childcare, *Economic and Political Weekly*, 43(9): 10–13.

OECD DAC Network on Gender Equality, Gender Equality (2010). Women's Empowerment and the Paris Declaration on Aid Effectiveness Issues Brief 6 Paris

World Bank, FAO and IFAD (2009). Gender in Agriculture Sourcebook, The World Bank, Washington DC.

www.nrega.nic.in

www.ruralnic.in

5

Gender Wage Gap and Role of Fertility

A Cross-Country Analysis

NAMRATA SINGHA ROY AND ISHITA MUKHOPADHYAY

Abstract

This article critically confronted the discrepancies in wage participation relationship across gender, the role of education and skill formation in determining wages of male and female workers and the role of fertility in creating gender wage gap through its influence on female labour supply. With the data on 50 countries across world for two distinct periods 1995–96 and 2006–07, a Mincer wage equation was estimated. With relevant cross-countries heterogeneity, wages were like to increase with labour force participation and the impact of education on wage has shifted from primary to secondary education for male and from secondary to tertiary education for female. The impact of participation of women in determining wage remained significant over the decades and the importance of higher education got prioritized over time. Therefore the orthodox view that female were in disadvantageous position compared to male in labour market because of motherly duty is no longer applicable. The traditional pattern of high fertility rate and low female participation rate turned into positive association over the decades (1995–96 to 2011–12). The traditional 'U' relation is no longer appropriate to explain the fertility and female labour supply relation. It is now the rising part of the 'U' curve where majority of countries are operating. Moreover, the struggle to overcome the barriers created by fertility factors has started much earlier in developing countries than the developed countries. It is, therefore, the speaking of the working poor, where women had to keep uncared children to earn their means.

Keywords

wage differential, gender, fertility decision, female labour supply, education.

Introduction

A worldwide perspective in the field of labour market is that women are discriminated against salary even though both female and male do the same work. Two types of explanations have been attributed for these stylized facts: one is gender discrimination in the labour market, and the other is selection of men and women into different sectors and occupations, primarily in response to their different care responsibilities. That is, women are more likely to choose jobs that allow them to adjust working hours and to exit and enter the labour market more frequently and at a lower cost. The key reason for such type of job selection lies in the centrality of the mother's role in our society: the primary responsibility for child care lies with her. As women have compulsory child care duty, fertility or number of children plays a major role in female labour supply model. Fertility related variables account for the most important explained variation in several empirical model of female labour supply (Schultz, 1985). Children have been a focus in theoretical discussions of female labour supply, and in proposed explanations for why the behaviour and wages of women and men differ. The standard theory of labour market and fertility decisions, based on the work of Mincer (1975) and Becker (1975), explained the secular trends of fertility rates and female participation rates. According to that theory, the secular increase in female earning power raises the opportunity cost of the time allocated to child-bearing that in turn induces female to participate in the labour market and to have fewer children. As a result, the theory implies a negative association between female participation and fertility rates. But currently, a positive association is like to observe in most of developed and developing countries. Therefore, the orthodox view that females are in disadvantageous position compared to male in labour market because of motherly duty is no longer applicable. The present paper addresses the causal link from fertility to the participation of women in labour market and its impact on creating gender wage gap.

Literature Review

Several researchers have shown that gender gaps are affected by either gender specific factors including differences in the qualification of men and women and differences in the treatment of equally qualified women or wage inequality (Blue and Kahn, 1994; Katz and Murphy, 1992; Krueger and Summers, 1988). Along with them, Mincer (1975) provides a survey and expositions of the development of the earnings functions as an empirical tool for the analysis of the determinant of wage rates. The premier application was the study of the effects of investment in schooling and on-the-job training on the level, pattern and interpersonal distribution of life cycle earnings associated with the pioneering work on human capital by Becker (1975), and especially by Mincer (1975).

In largely separate streams of the literature on female labour supply, economists have argued that family responsibilities, and particularly children, will affect both the reservation and offered wage rates of women and that impacts on their labour supply will be mostly negative (Blau and Robins, 1988; Gronau, 1977; Hotz and Miller, 1988; Moffitt, 1984; Nakamura and Nakamura, 1992; Schultz, 1985, Lehrer and Nerlove, 1986). Several researchers have examined the effect of child care costs on the probability that married women with children will participate in the labour market (Connelly, 1992). They have estimated a structural Probit model of labour force participation showing evidence to support the prediction that increased child care costs lower the probability of participation. More recently a paper by Carrasco (2012) considers the estimation of the causal effect of fertility on female labour-force participation equations. The results indicate that exogeneity assumptions of children variables induce a downward bias in absolute value in the estimated negative effect of fertility on participation, although the failure to account for unobserved heterogeneity overstates this effect. Moreover, stronger effects of fertility are found when existing children are treated as predetermined but not strictly exogenous variables.

Any success in disentangling the causal mechanisms linking fertility and labour supply should lean to light on other substantive issues as well. For example, some theories of family behaviour also suggest that changes in wives' earnings affect marital stability (Becker et al., 1985). Given the wide and long standing interest in the connection between child-bearing and labour supply, hundreds of empirical studies report estimates of this relationship. The vast majority of these studies find a negative correlation between fertility and female labour supply.

Uncertainty regarding the causal interpretation of associations between fertility and labour supply arises in part from the fact that there are strong theoretical reasons to believe that fertility and labour supply is jointly determined (Schultz, 1985; Goldin, 1990). In fact, this endogeneity is reflected in the existing research agenda. On the one hand, papers on labour supply often treat child-status variables as regressors in hours of work equations, while on the other hand, economic demographers and others discuss regressions and models that are meant to characterize the impact of wages or measures of labour-force attachment on fertility. Since fertility variables cannot be both dependent and exogenous at the same time, it seems unlikely that either sort of regression has a causal interpretation.

In contrast with negative association between Total Fertility Rate (TFR) and Female Labour Force Participation Rate (FLFPR), numerous studies have consistently found reversed tendency from negative to positive in Western OECD countries (Brewster and Rindfuss, 2000; Ahn and Mira, 2002; Rindfuss et al., 2003; Engelhardt and Prskawetz, 2004; D'Addio and D'Ercole, 2005). Somewhat counter-intuitively countries with high rate of women's employment started displaying high fertility rates. The emergence of the positive correlation between women's labour force participation and fertility has usually been explained by the reduction in incompatibility between child-bearing and women's paid work, especially in countries with high female labour participation. The incompatibility was reduced through policies that support reconciliation of paid work and family, such as public child care for children below age 3, and also through policies supporting gender equality (Castles, 2003; Rindfuss et al., 2003; Brewster and Rindfuss, 2000; Luci-Greulich and Thévenon, 2013). Recently, Matysiak (2014) found that the cross-country correlation between the TFR and FLFPR R became positive also in former state-socialist countries of Central and Eastern Europe and attributed it to the emerging diversity of the region in policies supporting work-family reconciliation.

However, all these studies were based on period data, which, in the case of the period TFRs implies considerable year-to-year fluctuations and distortions due to changes in the timing of child-bearing. Analysis by Matysiak and Sobotka (2014) took a cohort perspective, using completed Cohort Fertility Rates (CFRs) and reconstructing Cohort Female Labour Force Participation

Rates (CFLFPs) at ages 25–39 years that provide consistent measures of labour force participation and fertility across the life cycle which are neither distorted by short-term fluctuations, nor by temporary effect due to fertility postponement. Their findings illustrate that the reversal in the cross-country correlation between the Cohort Female Labour Force Participation Rate and Cohort Fertility Rate indeed took place. In countries where the labour force participation of women born in the late 1940s was high the cohort, low the fertility. From cohorts born in the early 1950s, the cross-country correlation between CFLFPR and CFR started to be positive and for cohorts born in the late 1950s and in the first half of the 1960s, the correlation coefficient reached the maximum level.

Another study by Apps and Rees (2001) tried to investigate the underneath reasons for the existence of positive association between fertility rate and female labour supply in OECD countries. They accept the hypothesis that the reason for this lies in the combined effects of a country's tax system and system of child support, and they clarified this theoretically, using an extended version of the Galor and Weil (1996) model. The results suggested that countries with individual rather than joint taxation, and which support families through improved availability of alternatives to domestic child care, rather than through direct child payments, are likely to have both higher female labour supply and higher fertility.

Objective of the Study

Against this background, the study addresses the discrepancies in wage participation relationship across gender over decade and the role of education and skill formation in determining wages of male and female workers. At the same time, this paper focusses on the causal link running from fertility to the participation of women in the labour market and thereby its impact on creating gender wage gap.

Methodology

Wage rates or earning of an individual depends on a number of labour market factors as well as human capital factors like Labour Force Participation Rate, returns to education, experiences in the job market and so forth. Since this analysis is concentrated on employment which is visible, Labour Force Participation Rate (LFPR) has been taken as an important factor influencing labour market wage. Mainly ILO data base (LABORSTA) collected by labour force survey and World Development Indicators are used as data base for comparative analysis extent over 50 countries. By definition Labour Force Participation Rate for both male and female is basically the proportion of the population ages 15 and above who are economically active.

The data on average earnings, generally taken from establishment payrolls, which cover cash payments received from employers (before deduction of taxes and social security contributions payable by workers). The nominal value of country's currencies were converted into real values by using PPP Conversion factor at 2005–06 equivalent to make them comparable internationally (in terms of US $). Gross Enrollment Ratio Primary (GERP), Gross Enrollment Ratio,

Secondary (GERS), and Gross Enrollment Ratio Tertiary (GERT) and Expected Years of Schooling (EYS) are taken as explanatory variables which are assumed to influence a worker's productivity. EYS is a consolidated indicator showing an overall level of education.

Data has been taken for comparative analysis from two periods – one is 1995–96, the period of globalization and 2006–07 that is after a decade to see the impact of globalization on female labour supply over 50 countries; 2011–12 data has been taken for comparison purpose.

Model Specification

A Mincer wage equation (Mincer, 1975) where the dependent variable is the natural log of wage with human capital and labour market characteristics as the most important explanatory variables. A semi-log earning function is, therefore, estimated with Labour Force Participation Rate, Gross Enrollment Ratio Primary, Secondary, and Tertiary and Expected Years of Schooling as explanatory variables. The following structural wage equation is estimated:

lnW_i= á + âLPR_i +ãG?ER?_i+äEYS_i+u_i............(1)

W=Average Daily Real Wage (PPP adjusted at 2005–06 equivalent), LPR= Labour Force Participation Rate, GER= Gross Enrollment Ratio (primary, secondary, tertiary), EYS= Expected Years of Schooling.

Results

Gender Wage Determination

Table 1 represents the regression result where the dependent variable is average daily real wage and Labour Force Participation Rate, Gross Enrollment Ratio Primary, Secondary, and Tertiary and Expected Years of Schooling as explanatory variables.

Table 1

OLS Log Wage Human Capital Regression, Separately by Gender, 1995–96 and 2006–07

Explanatory variables	*1995–96*		*2006–07*	
	Male	*Female*	*Male*	*Female*
Labour Force Participation	0.79** (0.016)	1.21** (0.030)	0.55 (0.221)	1.59** (0.058)
Gross Enrollment Ratio, Primary	–0.12** (0.045)			
Gross Enrollment Ratio, Secondary		0.090*** (0.000)	0.331*** (0.000)	
Gross Enrollment Ratio, Tertiary				0.13*** (0.001)
Expected Years of Schooling	1.52*** (0.000)			
Adjusted R-squared	0.52	0.35	0.40	0.30
N	50	50	50	50

Note: 'p' values are in parenthesis. *Significant at 10 per cent level. **Significant at 5 per cent level, ***Significant at 1 per cent level.

Overall, it is found that with relevant cross-countries heterogeneity, wages are likely to increase with labour force participation and education and this holds true across countries. From Table 1, it is evident that impacts of labour force participation on wage for male has reduced. It has become insignificant in the year 2006 which indicate that increase in participation does not guarantee that wage will also increase. Participation in the labour market of male worker has increased over time, but wages are pegged at a minimum level. This is the situation of disguised employment where unlimited supplies of labourers are available to work at a lower wage. Gross Enrollment Ratio Primary (GERP) and Expected Years of Schooling (EYS) are statistically significant at 1 and 5 per cent level for male workforce in 1995 scenario but for the year 2006 secondary enrollment become statistically significant at 1 per cent level of significance, that suggest that higher level of education is required to get competitive salary in labour market. It contradicts the findings by Gronau (1977) that the 'long-run prospects for increased labour supply due to increases in education are, therefore, much more limited'.

For women, labour force participation rate has a consistent and significant impact to determine wage. For the year 1995, Gross Enrollment Ratio Secondary is significant at 5 per cent level of significance. But for 2006 Gross Enrollment Ratio Tertiary becomes significant at 1 per cent level for female workforce. The increase in participation of female labour forces are mainly induced by greater enrollment in tertiary education level. The impact of globalization is mainly confronted with the advancement of service sector which requires higher education and good skill formation. So the higher enrollment of women in tertiary sector ensures their enhanced opportunity to work in service sector. The lower adjusted R2 values for all estimation results are mainly attributed to data limitation.

From the above study it is evident that the impact of participation of women in determining wage remains significant over the decades and the importance of higher education got prioritized. Therefore, the orthodox view that the females are in disadvantageous position compared to male in labour market because of motherly duty is no longer applicable. The changing association between fertility rate and female labour supply is explained in following sections.

Fertility and Female Labour Force Participation: The Changing Trends

Figure 1 plots labour force participation of women against the total fertility rate over 50 countries. The traditional pattern of a high fertility rate and a low rate of female labour force participation is exhibited in 1995–96 that is during the era of globalization. After a decade, that strong inverse correlation stared to weaken and currently, positive association becomes evident.

The reversal in the correlation between fertility and women's labour force participation has important policy implications. It suggests that moderate fertility levels close to replacement are compatible with high involvement of women in the labour market if the institutional conditions in the country support work-family combination.

Figure 1

Trends in Total Fertility Rate and Female Labour Supply over the Years

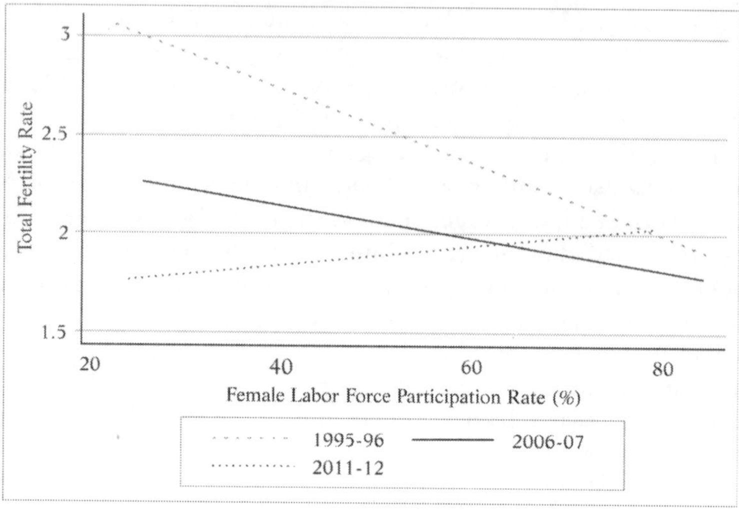

Fertility versus Female Participation: Experience from Developed and Developing Countries

Since fertility is no longer able to explain participation of women, then even high participation rates are coexisting with high fertility rate. Therefore, the traditional 'U' relation is no longer appropriate to explain the fertility rate and female labour force participation rate. It is now the rising part of the 'U' where majority of countries are working. To have a more intuitive understanding, Figure 2 established the fertility rate and female labour force participation rate relationship for developed and developing countries separately.

Figure 2

Trends in Total Fertility Rate and Female Labour Supply across Developed and Developing Countries over the Years

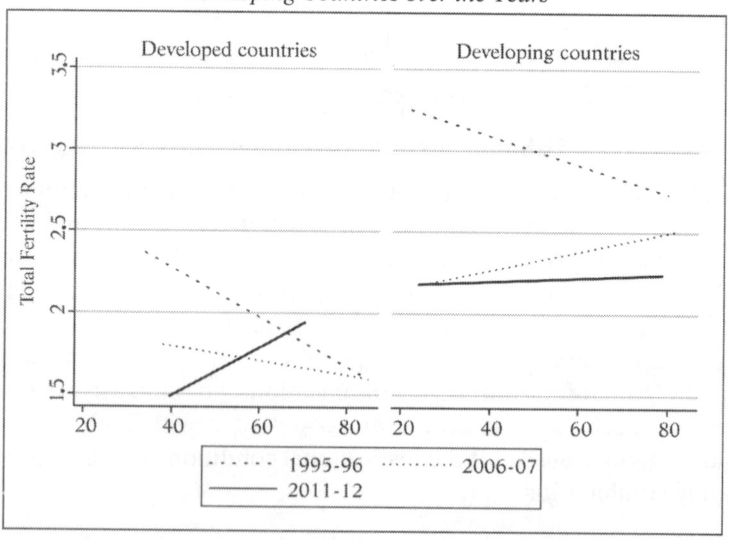

It is interesting to see that the positive association between fertility rate and female labour supply is a more recent phenomenon for developed countries. The negative association between female labour force participation and fertility rate was strong in 1995–96. After a decade, the association got weak and currently it is showing a high positive association. But remarkable is that for developing countries the trend towards positive association of fertility with female participation has started from 2006–07 onwards that is much earlier than the developed countries. So, the struggle to overcome barrier created by fertility induced factors has initiated at early stage than the developed countries. Therefore, both developed and developing countries are operating in rising part of 'U' curve. In developed countries with improved availability of formal alternative child care are likely to have high fertility with high participation of women. But what is happening to child care of developing countries? There are no formal child care facilities in most of the developing countries. For mothers of pre-school-age children, the decision to engage in paid employment typically implies the concomitant choice of a child care arrangement. The cost of child care can be an important factor influencing not only the decision about the type of child care arrangement to use, but also the decision to enter the labour market itself. Similarly, the wage that a mother can expect to earn in labour market activity can determine not only the decision to take paid work, but also the mode of care. Women in developing countries have to enter into the labour market, mainly informal jobs to earn the means. To do job for them is necessary rather sufficient for them for the survival of their family. They are the working poor. Is this, therefore, the speaking of the working poor, where women sacrifice child care and work to earn means? Policies are needed to take care of these issues.

Conclusion

This study focused on the role played by various factors that enhance productivity as well as participation of worker in the labour market. It is evident that overall with relevant cross-countries heterogeneity, wages are likely to increase with labour force participation and the impact of education on wage has shifted from primary to secondary education for male and from secondary to tertiary education for female. Thus, it is clear that globalization makes women more productive to stay in the labour market.

Changes in education have facilitated women's integration in the labour market. More educated women have traditionally exhibited higher participation rates than their less educated counterparts; so as education levels have increased around the world, more women have ventured into paid work. Similarly, changes in family formation have increased the labour market attachment for young women and women with small children. Increase in the age of marriage and decline in fertility are, thus, likely to have contributed to higher participation rates in most countries and regions. The impact of economic development and changes in education and family formation on female labour force participation varies across individuals, countries, and regions and ultimately depends on institutions, formal and informal, as well as on individual preferences.

Where changes in markets and institutions have aligned to strengthen incentives and erode constraints to participation, women have joined the labour force in large numbers. In contrast, where other constraints existed – particularly in informal institutions – or where market and institutional changes generated opposing forces, the impacts have been much more muted. Along with this result, the changing association between fertility rate and female labour supply exhibits that fertility is no longer deterrent for women participation in the labour market and, hence, not the sole reason for creating male female wage gap in labour market.

There are some unobserved factors that are operating in the labour market making lower wage of female labour a natural process. Since fertility is no longer able to sufficiently determine participation of women, then even high participation rates are coexisting with high fertility rate. Therefore, the traditional 'U' relation no longer exists between fertility rate and female labour force participation rate.

Analysing the trends between fertility rate and female participation rate for developed and developing countries separately revealed that the trend towards positive association between these two factors has started much earlier in developing countries than the developed one. Both developed and developing countries are currently operating in rising part of 'U' curve. In developed countries, with improved availability of formal alternative, child care is likely to have high fertility with high participation of women. But the child care facilities of developing countries are now questionable. Therefore, is this the trend of the working poor, where women sacrifice child care and work to earn the means? It is suggested that moderate fertility levels close to replacement are compatible with high involvement of women in the labour market if the institutional conditions in the country support work-family combination. Even absence of child care facilities cannot act as a deterrent in female labour force participation. Children are left uncared; their mothers are marginalized in the labour market. The question that therefore arises relates to the efficiency of the labour market, which needs to be addressed.

References

Ahn, N. and Mira, P. (2000). 'A Note on the Changing Relationship between Fertility and Female Employment Rates in Developed Countries', *Journal of Population Economics*, 667–682.

Apps, P. and Rees R. (2001). Fertility, Female Labor Supply and Public Policy, Discussion Paper No. 409, Bonn: IZA.

Becker, G., Elizabeth, L. and Robert, M. (1977). 'An Economic Analysis of Marital Instability', *Journal of Political Economy,* 1, 141–1, 188.

Becker, Gary S. (1975). 'Front Matter, Human Capital: A Theoretical and Empirical Analysis, With Special Reference To Education', in Becker, Gary S. *Human Capital: A Theoretical and Empirical Analysis*, with Special Reference to Education, New York: National Bureau of Economic Research, -22-0.

Becker, Gary S. (1974). 'A Theory of Marriage: Part II', *Journal of Political Economy,* S11–S26.

——-'A Theory of the Allocation of Time.' *The Economic Journal* (1965): 493–517.

Blau, D.M. and Robins, P.K. (1988). 'Child-Care Costs and Family Labor Supply', *Review of Economics and Statistics,* 74–81.

Blau, F.D. And Kahn, L.M. (1994). 'Rising Wage Inequality and the US Gender Gap', *The American Economic Review*, 23–28.

(1992). 'The Gender Earnings Gap: Learning From International Comparisons', *American Economic Review*, 533–438.

Brewster, K.L. and Rindfuss, R.R. (2000). 'Fertility and Women's Employment in Industralised Nations', *Annual Review of Sociology,* 271–296.

Carrasco, R. (2012). 'Binary Choice With Binary Endogenous Regressors in Panel Data', *Journal of Business and Economics Statistics,* 385–394.

Castles, F.G. (2003). 'The World Turned Upside Down: Below Replacement Fertility, Changing Preferences and Family-Friendly Public Policy in 21 OECD Countries', *Journal of European Social Policy*, 209–229.

Connelly, R. (1992). 'The Effect of Child Care Costs on Married Women's Labor Force Participation', *The Review of Economics and Statistics*, 83–90.

D'Addio, A.C. and d'Ercole M.M. (2005). Trends and Determinants of Fertility Rates in OECD Countries: The Role of Policies, Working Paper, No. 27, Paris: OECD.

Engelhardt, H. and Prskawetz, A. (2004). 'On the Changing Correlation between Fertility and Female Employment over Space and Time', *European Journal of Population*, 35–62.

Engelhardt, H., Kögel, T. and Prskawetz, A. (2004). 'Fertility and Women's Employment Reconsidered: A Macro-Level Time-Series Analysis for Developed Countries, 1960–2000', *Population Studies,* 109–120.

Galor, O. and Weil, D.N. (1996). 'The Gender Gap, Fertility and Growth', *American Economic Review*, 374–387.

Goldin, C. (1990). *Understanding the Gender Gap*, New York: Oxford University Press.

Gronau, R. (1977). 'Leisure, Home Production, and Work: The Theory of the Allocation of Time Revisited', *Journal of Political Economy*, 1,099–1,123.

Hotz, V.J. and Miller, R.A. (1988). 'An Empirical Analysis of Life Cycle Fertility and Female Labor Supply', *Econometrica*, 91–118.

Ketz, L. and Murphy, K. (1992). 'Changes in Relative Wages, 1963–1987: Supply and Demand Factors', *The Quarterly Journal of Economics*, 35–78.

Krueger, A.B. and Summers, L.H. (1988). 'Efficiency Wages and the Inter-Industry Wage Structure', *Econometrica*, 259–293.

Lehrer, E. and Nerlove, M. (1986). 'Female Labor Force Behavior and Fertility in the United States', *Annual Review of Sociology,* 181–204.

Luci-Greulich, A. and Thévenon, O. (2013). 'The Impact of Family Policy Packages on Fertility Trends in Developed Countries', *European Journal of Population*, 287–416.

Matysiak, A. and Sobotka, T. (2014). 'Did the Reversal in the Cross-Country Association between Women's Labor Force Participation and Fertility Really Take Place? A Cohort View'. Web: Http: //Epc2014.Princeton.Edu/Abstracts/140852. Budapest.

Matysiak, A. (2011a). Interdependencies between Fertility and Women's Labor Supply, Doredrecht: Springer.

Matysiak, A. (2011b). 'Fertility Developments in Central and Eastern Europe: The Role of Work-Family Tensions', *Demográfia*, 7–30.

Mincer, J. (1975). 'Education, Experience and the Distribution of Earnings and Employment: An Overview' in Juster, F. Thomas, *Education, Income, and Human Behavior,* New York: National Bureau of Economic Research, 71–94.

Mincer, J. (1962). 'On-the-Job Training: Costs, Returns and Some Implications', *Journal of Political Economy*, 50–79.

Moffitt, R. (1984). 'Profiles of Fertility, Labor Supply and Wages of Married Women: A Complete Life-Cycle Model', *Review of Economic Studies*, 263–278.

Nakamura, A. and Nakamura, M. (1992). 'The Econometrics of Female Labor Supply and Children', *Econometric Reviews*, 1–71.

Rindfuss, R.R., Guzzo, K. and Morgan, S.P. (2003). 'The Changing Institutional Context of Low Fertility', *Population Research and Policy Review*, 411–438.

Schultz, Paul T. (1985). 'Changing World Prices, Women's Wages, and the Fertility Transition', *Journal of Political Economy*, 1,126–1,154.

'Testing the Neoclassical Model of Family Labor Supply and Fertility', *Journal of Human Development,* (1990): 599–634.

6

Women in Engineering Labour Market in India

An Analysis

SEEMA SINGH

Abstract

Traditionally, the rate of women's participation in the engineering labour market in India is very low compared to other streams of education. However, from 1991–92, India experienced a major change not only in the macro-economic environment following the adoption of globalization and advent of Information and Communication Technology (ICT) but in the women's participation in engineering. The participation of women in engineering education has witnessed a threefold increase during the post-globalization period, reaching the figure of 27.9 per cent in 2010–11, which is more than the corresponding figures even for the developed countries, including USA (19 per cent) and Australia (11.5 per cent). In this backdrop, the paper discusses factors such as economic, educational, demographic and social which have led to such a significant increase in the women's participation. The findings derived at the end of the paper may also be used as reference for countries desirous of increasing women participation in their engineering labour markets.

Keywords

engineering labour market, market, discrimination, liberalization, gender.

Introduction

The perception of 'masculine' and 'feminine' traits, with the former being associated with assertiveness, leadership, physical strength, and dominance, and the latter with emotional, supportive, nurturing, and submissive characteristics, has been used to justify sex-differentiated roles (Parsons and Bales, 1955) not only in the family but for their workforce participation also as participation of female is more in 'Medical' education than in 'Engineering' education. The field of engineering has hitherto been considered mainly as a male bastion in India as in other parts of the globe. However, it has increased during post-globalization period and now, percentage of female students in the engineering education has become more than the corresponding figure for many developed countries. In this background, the paper discusses status of women in Engineering Labour

Market in India and factors both demand side and supply side which has led to such magnificent increase. The second section discusses the supply side aspect i.e. women in the engineering education in India. The third section portrays an international perspective. Factors such as economic, social, educational and demographic which have led to increase of women participation in engineering have been discussed in the fourth section. Last section concludes the discussion.

Women in the Engineering Education in India

The supply side analysis has been made in this section to understand status of women in the engineering labour market in India. As it is clear from Figure 1 that engineering has always remained least preferred stream of study for women. Percentage of women students in engineering was as meagre as 0.2 per cent in 1950–51 against the corresponding figures of 16.3 per cent in medicine and 7.1 per cent in science. In the successive years, the share of women in all disciplines of higher education and similarly, participation increased in engineering stream also and it rose in 1990–91 to 7.9 per cent in engineering, 33.2 per cent in medicine, and 32.9 per cent in science. However, in 1991–92, India experienced a major change in the macro-economic environment by adopting globalization and advent of Information and Communication Technology (ICT). During the post-globalization period, the participation of women in engineering education has witnessed a threefold increase, reaching the figure of 27.9 per cent in 2010–11.

Figure 1

Percentage of Women Students in Various Disciplines in India

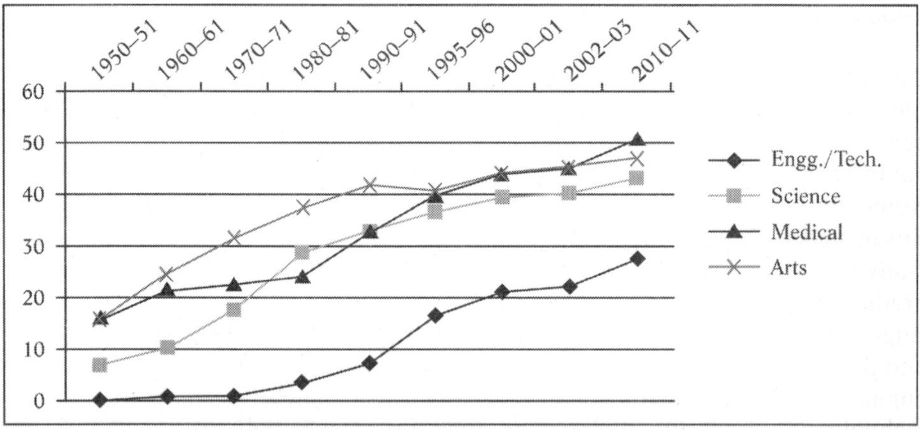

Source: For data upto 2002–03, Prabhuswamy and Raghvendra (2011). For data of 2010–11, UGC, Higher Education in India at a Glance. Data for 2010–11, UGC.

International Perspective of Women in Engineering Education

Throughout the world, women participation in engineering is low in comparison to other streams of education. According to Figure 2, it was just 11 per cent in China and 12 per cent in Japan. For Australia, it was 19 per cent. However, it came down to 11.8 per cent in 2010–11 (Kaspura, 2013). For USA and UK the corresponding data are 19 and 21 per cent, respectively.

Figure 2

Percentage of Graduate Women in Engineering, Manufacturing and Construction

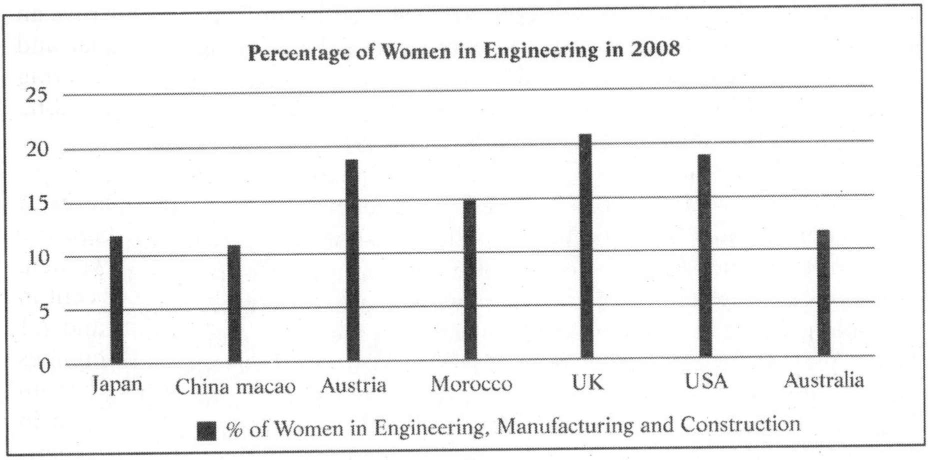

Source: Data for other countries except Australia is from UNESCO, 2010: Table 11-Tertiary Education/ISCED 5 and 6/Graduation by broad field of education/2008; 182–188.

Other socio-economic indicators of development for women may be very high in comparison of Indian indicators. However, these countries are having low participation of women in engineering. In fact in USA, women enrollment in engineering in last 10 years has decreased. In fact, the low participation of women students in engineering education has a historical and cultural background. Although engineers have very good prospect in the labour market, engineering programme and profession has a very nerdy image. According to University of California, Irvine sociologist Carroll Seron, 'Women don't stay in the profession because of the stereotypes'. Professor Seron, who is reporting on her research at Flinders University, says this makes engineering unusual compared to other once-segregated professions, like law and medicine, where women are at, or approaching parity. Professor Seron worked with colleagues Susan Silbey (MIT) Brian Rubineau (Cornell) and Erin Cech (Stanford) on a study of woman engineers' employment outcomes, including a study of under-graduates at MIT, the University of Massachusetts, plus the Olin College of Engineering (which aspires to gender parity) and women-only Smith College and their results don't tick any of the boxes that supposedly explain why women engineers give it away. It's not about ability, women with an interest in science, technology, engineering and math at university level can match men. Certainly the top 5 per cent of males outperform females on standardized tests, 'but you do not need to be in the top 5 per cent to be an engineer,' she says. Sometimes, women engineers who leave the profession go and work in other intellectually demanding STEM industries. And it's not about money. According to Seron, for STEM disciplines in general, 'the gender gap in earnings for women is significantly smaller, and essentially nil for younger cohorts in engineering.' It's not even because they are more likely than their peers in law and medicine to decide to have families instead. 'Women in engineering are no more, or less, concerned about this than their female counterparts across the university,' Seron says. The reason they leave is engineering culture. 'This is not a story of poor women who can't make it – they have options and they don't want to put up with male engineers who don't feel comfortable with women around them.' This starts, according to Seron, at university and continues in the workplace, with women feeling their competencies are undervalued by men. 'Professional role confidence is a significant predictor of persistence for men and women, but women enjoy significantly smaller endowments of expertise and especially career-fit confidence,' Seron says, 'Lots of engineering education is based on teams and male students stereotype women. These experiences persist in the workforce and women decide 'why bother?'.' The question as to why are men in engineering so much more uncomfortable with women than their peers in other professions like law and medicine where women are much more accepted needs elaboration. Seron says engineering education in the US began in the army (the original West Point curriculum trained engineers not technicians) and that may have something to do with it but she does not really know. But what she does say for certain is that the gender imbalance in engineering, 'is a wake-up call for work sites, they need to deal with the legacy issue of macho culture' (Matchett, 2011). But, in India the situation is changing fast.

Factors Leading to increase of Women in Engineering

It is clear from the foregoing analysis that women participation in engineering has increased manifold which is even more than many other developed countries. In this section, an effort has been made to figure out the factors, as economic, educational, and demographic and social, which have led to such an increase of women in engineering.

Economic Factors

Globalization and advent of Information and Communication Technology (ICT) has attracted many multinational and transnational companies to establish their base in India. Apart from other things, they are attracted for India's large scale English speaking engineering manpower at very reasonable salary (Singh, 2005). In addition to it, India's software is the largest foreign exchange earner for India which has led to large scale increase in demand for engineering manpower, especially, for women engineers as they are known for being better for table work. Even though there is no radical shift in the traditional 'patrifocal' ideology, an empirical survey of women in an engineering college demonstrates that the increase in women's participation is specific to computer-related fields in engineering, which is directly related to a vibrant market (Gupta, 2012). In the era of stiff competition, industries have realized the advantage of recruiting women engineers which is evident from the recent hiring trend as auto giants, Maruti and Yamaha, are hiring more women mechanical engineers for better productivity and aesthetic input in the design. Engineering firms declared their intent to accommodate work life balance of women engineers. Microsoft has a programme of re-employment of women engineers who have taken break from their regular career. Women First Council is a new chapter in HCL's 'employee first' philosophy. It is a council by the women, of the women, for the women, that provides an organized platform to address unique and special needs of the women. It gives 'women empowerment' a new meaning at HCL Technologies. The council gives its members ample opportunities to make a difference in their lives and those of their women colleagues. Wipro EcoEnergy has partnered with UN Women to Strengthen Women's Role in Business. Most of the firms are organizing seminars for their staff for gender sensitizing (Singh, 2013). Though companies are adopting affirmative policies to encourage women engineers but at the implementation level, how much flexibility will be given depends on the decision of the project manager and no one likes to compromise with the profit of the organization. Thus, no one likes to include the pregnant women engineer in his or her project team and so, even though she can work during her pregnancy, she stays without work, in the corporate terminology 'on the bench' and loses some perks which otherwise she could have earned. Many leave job and though there are programmes of re-employment, it is very difficult to continuously hone skill during the period of unemployment (Singh, 2014b). Women engineers have expressed lack of mentors for their retarded career growth (Wij et al., 2010).

Educational Factors

Engineering education has experienced exponential growth in last 20 years or so mainly through private initiative. Privatization of engineering education has provided a new hope to students who aspire for engineering education but are unable to make it to the elite institution, which are mostly government funded. The criteria for admission to private universities are less tough than the criteria for admission to public institutions. Along with general growth for engineering education opportunities, academia has provided other avenues to ensure higher participation of women in engineering education. Indira Gandhi Technological University (IGIT) located in Delhi, is exclusively catering to the engineering education of women. Further several women's engineering college have also emerged. Cummin College of Engineering for women in Pune, established in 1991, was first such college in the country. Now, there are 15 only women engineering college affiliated to the All India Council for Technical Education in Uttar Pradesh (AICTE) (Gupta, 2012). There are other ways also which have been adopted to ascertain participation of women in engineering. In Delhi Technological University (DTU) and PEC University of Technology, Chandigarh, there is reservation of one and two seats respectively for only girl child in all branches of engineering. There is 30 per cent reservation for women student in all engineering colleges of Maharashtra and 33 per cent reservation in Madhya Pradesh and Rajasthan. UGC, AICTE and DST have also several programmes for women scientists and engineers who are not in regular employment, to hone their R&D skills. However, very high gender inequality among the top rank was found in the study done by Rajasenan for the Engineering Entrance Examination in Kerala. The inequality quotients decrease if the analysis extends to incorporate all the candidates irrespective of their ranks. When the women are excluded from the top ranks, the opportunities for female students to get admitted into the best engineering colleges tend to reduce. This certainly will affect the employability of female engineering aspirants negatively. As per the ATMR (2008) the female employability problem is somehow circumvented with the increase in the number of seats in courses on ICT and ICT related subjects due to the emergence of the new career opportunities. These jobs are in tune with the female's choice and 'desirability' and therefore more females are exploiting this opportunity (Rajasenan, 2014).

Demographic Factors

During 1970s and later, family planning programme of India was enforced very strictly and progressively, it was accepted socially also and worked as peer pressure to accept smaller family norm of having two children. In such circumstances, irrespective of being son or daughter, families are taking good care of the education of their children. During 1990s, more private institutes/universities came up after modification in the governing laws of the University Grants Commission (UGC). Thus, the girls who were born after 1970 have an enhanced option to pursue engineering education rather than their older sisters.

Social Factors

The patrifocal family system continues to have significant consequences for the education of women even today. Educational decision in India is family decision as part of the 'patrifocal' culture. Educational decisions, in turn, are influenced by marital obligation of parents. Marriages are usually arranged by parents who consider it their sacred duty to fix a match for their daughters. The rule of hypergamy is followed, so that the grooms are better educated and older than the bride. The bride givers also have to dole out dowry (Gupta, 2012). The recent upsurge in women enrollment in engineering education justifies this rule. Parents invest in daughter's engineering education as it is easier for engineers to get suitable groom and dowry is also comparatively low for them. In fact, sometimes, they dictate terms at the time of marriage (Singh, 2014).

Conclusion

Enhanced employment opportunity for engineers after globalization and growth of ICT and ICT enabled services, have increased demand for women engineers. It is supported by large private initiative which has joined hands with the public funded institutes/universities in providing opportunities for engineering education. This suits to 'T' to the 'patrifocal' Indian social fabric in which marriages are usually arranged by parents, who consider it their sacred duty to fix a match for their daughters. The parents of bride also have to dole out dowry to the groom. In such circumstances, providing engineering education to daughter is good economics also because they have to give less dowry at the time of marriage. However, women engineers very often complain about lack of mentors as the reason for the retarded growth in their professional career. In such circumstances, role of association and societies like Women in Science and Engineering (WISE) and International Network of Women in Engineering and Science (INWES) has become very important in mentoring young women engineers in their professional career.

References

Gupta, Namrata (2012). 'Women Undergraduates in Engineering Education in India: A Study of Growing Participation', *Gender, Technology and Development,* Vol. 16(2): 153–176.

Kaspura, Andre (2013). 'The Engineers Australia Survey of Working Enviornment and Engineering Careers', Australia: Policy and Public Relations, Engineers Australia, web. 30 April.

Matchett, Stephen (2011). 'Giving the Hard Hat Away: Why Women Engineers Quit', http: //www.theaustralian.com.au/higher-education/giving-the-hard-hat-away-why-women-engineers-quit/story-e6frgcjx-1226142605381 Accessed on 15.9.2012.

Prabhuswamy, H.B.M. and Gundanty, Raghvendra (2011). 'Women in Engineering and Technical Education: A Statistical Analysis', *Golden Research Thought,* 01(06): 1–4.

Parsons, T. and Bales, R.F. (1955). *Family, Socialization and Interaction Process.* Glencoe: Free Press.

Rajasenan, D. (2014). 'Gender Bias and Caste Exclusion in Engineering Admission: Inferences from the Engineering Entrance Examination in Kerala', *Higher Education for Future,* Sage Publication, http: //hef.sagepub.com/content/1/1/11 retrieved on 12.4.2014

Singh, Seema (2005). 'MNCs Effect on Employment of Engineers', *The Indian Journal of Technical Education,* Vol. 28(2): 38–44.

Singh, Seema (2013). 'Best Practices of Indian Academia and Industry to Retain Women Engineers' in the seminar on Women and Higher Education: Challenges and Prospects, organized by University Women's Association of Delhi in Collaboration with Women's Studies and Development Centre, DU at the ILLL, DU, New Delhi on 22 February.

Singh, Seema (2014). 'Self-restrain or Discrimination: Participation of Women Engineers in India', Fourth International Conference on Industrial Engineering and Operations Management (IEOM) at Bali, Indonesia, 7–9 January.

Singh, Seema and Lee, Fenton Susan (2014). 'Women Engineers: A Comparative Study between India and Australia', *International Journal of Advancements in Research and Technology,* Vol 3 (7): 108–122.

UGC (2012). 'Higher Education in India at a Glance', University Grants Commission Publication, New Delhi, UGC web April 30.

UNESCO (2010). 'Global Education Digest: Comparing Education statistics Across the World', UNESCO Institute for Statistics, Canada.

Wij Sangeeta, Rao, Nalanjana and Sohail, Prerna (2010). 'Women in Science and Engineering in India', at the time of launch of Women in Science and Engineering (WISE) India at 17 September.

7

Women Entrepreneurs' Access to Finance in Small and Medium Enterprises

A Conceptual Framework

CLARET P.E. MENDONCA AND A. H. SEQUEIRA

Abstract

Literature on women entrepreneurs is predominantly evidenced on the poor, less educated women in micro-enterprises. These make up 98 per cent of the women-owned enterprises. The potential women entrepreneurs, who are a growing group of well-educated, urban-based women who can start ventures that go beyond self-employment and make a positive contribution to the economy is under researched. However, there are several challenges that these women face in starting and sustaining enterprises. Literature evidences the problem of availability of, and access, to finance as the most critical element to the start-up and consequent performance of any enterprise. Other studies support the notion that women entrepreneurs are disadvantaged by their gender. The lack of sex disaggregated data from the suppliers of credit masks this reality. Thus, a need arises that there is a clear case for more detailed research on sources of funding available to women in small and medium enterprises, the cost of finance, the terms of finance, and in particular, the experience of seeking external finance. The paper attempts to examine the phenomenon of Indian Women Entrepreneurship in Small and Medium Enterprises and their access to finance. A qualitative research methodology was adopted to capture women's perceptions of the experience of raising finance for their businesses at start-up and the further growth phase. In this process, the authors attempted to give voice to their experiences as intrinsically interesting in the context of their situation, and not just in comparison with the assumed 'norms' of male entrepreneurial activity.

Keywords

women entrepreneurs, small and medium enterprises, access to finance, start-up.

Introduction

According to the Millennium Development Goals Report (2014), India has the largest share of the global poor in 2010, i.e. 32.9 per cent earning less than $1.25 per day. Added to this, unemployment and poverty remain as the burning issues of the nation. On the other hand, India is a country with about 63 per cent population currently in the working age group of 15 to 45 years, which is a factor in its favour. No country, however, can guarantee employment to all its citizens. One of the alternatives could be seen as self-employment or entrepreneurship. Studies, however, show the evidence that the nascent entrepreneurship prevalence rates to be the highest in the 25–34 age group. Studies also point out that about 5–6 per cent of this age group have access to some kind of skills (EDI, 2014) which need to channelized into productive employment. This being the scenario, the position of women is still vulnerable in terms of status and employment.

Status of Women

In India, women constitute half of the population, but only 35 per cent of them are a part of the labour force and a mere 13 per cent are entrepreneurs. The female literacy rate is much lower than that of males – 62 per cent versus 85 per cent (Census of India, 2011). Such a scenario affects the number of women entering into higher education. Similarly, the representation of women on the corporate boards is also less. Moreover, according to UNDP (2013) report, India ranks 132/186 in gender inequality and Women's Entrepreneurship Development Index, 2013, has ranked India as 16 out of the 17 countries.

Women-owned MSMEs are around 3.01 million, which represent 10 per cent of all MSMEs. Their contribution is 3.09 per cent of industrial output and the employment generation is 8 million. They are mostly characterized as of smaller size, home based, limited access to finance, lower profits, limited access to markets and limited business skills and, therefore, have limited opportunity for growth (Kolb, 2013). Approximately, 90 per cent of their enterprises are in the informal sector. The current situation in the developing countries like India evidences that women are pushed into entrepreneurship, because they do not have any other employment opportunities (IFC World Bank Group, 2014). Personal demographics of men and women entrepreneurs are similar, but, business and industry choices, financing strategies, growth patterns, and governance structures are dissimilar (Greene et al., 2003).

Women entrepreneurship is an economic issue, not a gender-equity issue (Mitchell, 2011). The significance of women entrepreneurship to the economy can be fully understood from the World Bank Engendering Development Report, 2013, which reports that women reinvest up to 90 per cent of their income in the education, health and nutrition of their family and community creating greater development impact. They create new jobs for themselves and other women, bring innovative products and services to the market, and by virtue of being different, provide different solutions to management, organization and business problems (Strong, 2009). The women's markets represent an opportunity bigger than China and India combined. The credit gap for women SMEs in developing countries is estimated to be between $260–$320 billion, creating great opportunities for commercial banks to provide innovative services for women in their entrepreneurial ventures (IFC World Bank, 2014).

There is, perhaps, no greater initiative a country can take to accelerate its pace of entrepreneurial activity than to encourage more of its women to participate (Reynolds et al., 2001). The role of women in building the small business economy and driving economic growth in countries around the world is increasingly being recognized (Kelly et al., 2010). Against this background, the paper seeks to capture women's perceptions on their access to finance for their businesses.

The Problem Statement: The most recent Global Entrepreneurship Monitor report drawing on annual national assessments of entrepreneurial activity, shows that women's participation in entrepreneurship varies greatly according to country (Kelly et al., 2010). India lags behind other Asian countries in promoting entrepreneurship. Around 80 per cent of adults in India are non-entrepreneurs (India-GEM, 2013). A study by Gallup World Poll of 20 economic entities in Asia revealed that, India ranked in the bottom quartile on several important indicators of a well-functioning entrepreneurial ecosystem. The same study states that India is abundant in entrepreneurial talent. Most Indians are optimistic and persistent, but few are willing to take risks due to inefficient institutional support, lack of access to start-up finance, no training and mentorship, and lack of judicial infrastructure to enable trusting relationships.

Availability of, and access to, finance is a critical element to start and consequent performance of the business. Locating, accessing and managing finance is a critical and most challenging task for most entrepreneurs (Allen et al., 2008). The 4th All India census of MSMEs indicated that only 5 per cent of the enterprises in the sector had access to formal finance, while over 92.8 per cent were self-financed. RBI data shows that the share of SSIs in the gross bank credit from scheduled commercial banks is decreasing (In 1990–91, 15.42%; In 2006–2007, 6.34%). The availability of start-up funds is still worse. Lack of access can be seen as a focal point which has an impact on other dimensions of quality of life which are inter-connected and also on social, economic and political empowerment together with overall well-being (UNECE and WBI, 2009).

Studies on women entrepreneurs in developing countries have focused mostly on the poor, less educated women in micro-enterprises in rural areas (Huq, 2000). Few studies have focused specifically on the financing of women-owned/led businesses in 'hi-tech' and potentially high-growth sectors (Blake and Hanson, 2005). Lending to women owned micro, small and medium enterprises as a distinct segment is still unexplored when compared to lending to MSMEs in India. Due to lack of segmental focus and, perhaps, due to higher perception of risk, formal financial institutions have made little efforts to better understand this segment. There is a lack of awareness among bankers of the potential business opportunity presented by this segment. Access to capital is crucial to start-up and growing companies. Undercapitalized companies have lower sales, lower profits and generate fewer jobs.

Literature Review

The literature is organized in themes and sub-themes to get a good glimpse of the work done in the field of women entrepreneurship – women entrepreneurs in SMEs – their gender perspective and entrepreneurs' personal attributes further analysed as physical and psychological attributes; their motivation and their founding strategies. Another theme would be women entrepreneurs' context – family capital, social capital, general and gender-specific constraints; government policies and programmes. Finally, the framework proposes a practical, creative solution to build a vibrant entrepreneurial ecosystem for women entrepreneurs.

Women Entrepreneurs in SMEs: A woman entrepreneur is one who has started a business alone or with other women, or is someone who is a principal in a family business or partnership, or is someone who is shareholder and manager in a publicly held company (OECD, 1997). A high potential woman entrepreneur, who is the subject of this study is defined as 'innovative, market expanding, and export oriented'.

Gender Perspective: India ranks 114 among the 149 nations in Gender Gap Index; economic participation-134/149; health and survival-141/149; political empowerment-15/149 (WEF, 2014). Gender inequality is an issue and has been rightly included in the agenda of Millennium Development Goals, 2014. Increasing women's economic opportunities and entrepreneurship can boost gender equality, positively contribute to per capita income growth, and reduce poverty (Sen and Mukherjee, 2013). Gender-gap in entrepreneurial activity varies across countries and yet, it is an unrecognized source of economic growth (GEM, 2012). Gender effects choice of sector and preference for particular business finance (Constantinidis et al., 2006). Entrepreneurship interactions and discursive practices appear gender neutral, or gender blind, which renders masculinity invisible and becomes universal parameters (Bruni et al., 2005). There is a need to address gender blindness, gender bias, androcentric and gender polarization which have dominated research (Neergaard et al., 2005). 'Heroic Entrepreneurial Narrative' is a product of social, economic and historical factors with an embedded assumption that leadership involved in establishing and running an enterprise is naturally male (Hamilton, 2004). Organization theory defends a 'gender-neutral' position (Gherardi, 2003). Studies on gender/entrepreneurship and gender/finance, assumes comparative equivalence and underplays and underrepresents the experience of femaleness. Women are represented as blemished men who must be assisted to become honorary men, to succeed in the existing paradigm of entrepreneurship (Marlow, 2002).

Entrepreneurial experiences have also been the focus of researchers. Research tends to define women entrepreneurs experiences in relation to those of men. Entrepreneurship (both research and practice) has been a man's domain (Bird and Brush, 2002). Women's experiences of starting and growing businesses are overlooked, or compared to those of men in a way that excludes, subordinates or marginalizes them, even if unintentionally (Martin and Collinson, 2002). Gender is a major factor that affects start-ups too (Chu, 2000).

Women Entrepreneurs' Personal and Psychological Attributes: Indian woman manages one of the most complex organizations – the household – with its multi-dimensional and interplay between the sexes, different age groups and different stakeholders. Women have mastered the art of negotiations, reconciliation, qualities of patience, understanding and emotional intelligence (Kollan and Parikh, 2006). In India 32 per cent of early-stage entrepreneurs (25–34 age group) are women (India-GEM, 2013). Indian entrepreneurs have abundant entrepreneurial talent (i.e. business thinking, optimism, and persistence), but lack willingness to take risk (Gallup Survey, 2012). Goals, motives, female identity and personal characteristics affects growth orientation. High growth entrepreneurs are ambitious, high risk takers, have high energy levels, view self, their families and ventures differently. Obstacles are viewed as opportunities (Arasti et al., 2012). Women have low societal perceptions of opportunities, low capability perception, greater fear of failure, low motivation and do not know entrepreneurs. In developing economies, more people are with intentions than taking steps to start an enterprise (GEM Women's Report, 2012).

Research has also looked at the demographics and personal attributes of entrepreneurs. Successful women entrepreneurs are young and experienced. Their corporate exposure helps in identifying and starting the businesses (Pinelli, 2011). Women do not follow traditional career models (Knorr, 2011) Women entrepreneurs are highly educated, in their forties, less entrepreneurial in experience (Hunter and Leone, 2010). Women have communal qualities (expressiveness, relatedness, kindness, supportiveness, timidity). Stereotyping becomes prescriptive. Entrepreneurs are perceived to have masculine characteristics (Gupta, Turban, Wasti and Sikdar, 2009). There is a relationship between women's perception of their roles and the type of business started. The major in college impacts the type of business started. Perceptions are important, they impact entrepreneurial intentions and business success (Hunter, De Casperis and Paul, 2009). Women entrepreneurs make things happen, challenge the status quo, are adroit, goal oriented, socially driven, confident, big dreamers, consensus builders, perfectionists and energetic (2008 International Council for Small Business World Conference on India). Socialization makes women perceive opportunities differently (DeTienne and Chandler, 2007). People engage in entrepreneurship, if they believe they have the skills. Women believe they lack specific and general human capital skills (cf. OECD, 2004). Women's leadership, their visions and business models differ from men. They change with developing and leading business (Fenwick, 2002). Characteristics of women in low-income groups significantly differ from women in medium/high income groups. Their development differs from males because of career interruptions (Kantor, 2001). Women's management style demonstrates relational skills, mothering is carried over to business, mutual empowerment, and team work (Buttner, 2001). Perceived self-efficacy is positively related to intention of starting own business. Personal factors, learning experiences and contextual background have impact on one's self efficacy (Chen et al., 1998).

Entrepreneurial cognitions-individuals' perception of their ability (level of expected performance) and their self-efficacy (that is, the level of confidence in their own skills) are important to be successful (Bandura, 1982). There is a significant relationship between entrepreneurial cognitions and leadership (Langowitz and Minniti, 2007). There are no specific personality types – Contingency theory supports this (Chu, 2000). Entrepreneurial opportunities are legitimized through individual's perceptions of their knowledge and skills (Busenitz et al., 2000). Entrepreneurial event and experience changes a person. It changes perceptions, attitudes about risk, level of personal and business confidence and belief in one's self (Stevenson, 1990). Career stages reflect and interact with the individual life stages and events (Bowen and Hisrich, 1986). Woman entrepreneur's education is mostly in social sciences; experience predominantly in services and retail; and is unable to get start-up capital or loans (Hisrich and Brush, 1986).

Women Entrepreneurs' Motives to Start an Enterprise: Need to achieve; job satisfaction; economic payoffs; independence (Shwartz, 1976), glass ceiling; flexibility to handle family responsibility; personal challenge (Scott, 1986), traditional socialization (Brush and Hisrich, 1991), entrepreneurship perceived as positive; perception of competence (OECD, 2004), opportunities perceived in the environment; entrepreneurial intentions; opportunity/necessity motivation (GEM, 2012), status (Manolova, Brush and Edelmana, 2008), and family situation and context (Brush, 1990) are some of the motives to start an enterprise.

Women Entrepreneurs' Founding Strategies: Convert hobbies to businesses; rely on personal skills; difficult times employ short-term strategies to survive (Perez and Bui, 2010), mixed-sex founding team benefits women entrepreneurs in male dominated contexts (Godwin and Stevens, 2006), mitigate work-family conflict through role elimination, role reduction and role sharing (Shelton, 2006), bootstrapping or contingency financing plans (Brush, et al., 2006), interlocking directorates in family firms (Chua, Steier and Chrisman, 2006) are some of the founding strategies of women entrepreneurs.

Contextual Factors

All entrepreneurship is contextually embedded in the social, cultural and political institutions which influence the values, norms, motives and behaviours of individuals (Minniti, 2009). The Gallup Study of 2012 has found India lagging behind other Asian countries in promoting entrepreneurship. Entrepreneurial talent is abundant, but contextual factors are unfavourable.

Family Support

Quintos, Senior. Vice-President of Dell, said, 'Successful women entrepreneurs have a supporting spouse and family' (Simhan, 2013). Family support is vital to start/grow business (Vossenberg, 2013). There is strong relationship between business and family (Jennings and Brush, 2013). Factors affecting women entrepreneurship are motherhood, spousal self-employment, state initiatives, childcare and maternity (Klyver et al., 2012). Offspring of entrepreneurs have access to key entrepreneurial resources. The socialization contributes to strong entrepreneurial mindset (Bar Nir et al., 2011). Family friendly policies have a positive effect on women's self-employment (OECD, 2004). Children of successful entrepreneurs are more likely to choose to become entrepreneurs. (Delmar et al., 2000b). Parents provide the child with vicarious experience – to judge their capabilities in relation to others. (Chen et al., 1998). Status of parents affects the start-up and the subsequent performance (Aldrich et al., 1997).

Social Capital

Social capital and networks are important determinants for recognition and exploration of entrepreneurial opportunities (Stenholm et al., 2011). Network diversity – women mostly married, friends, family are less likely to have membership in entrepreneurs' associations (Hunter and Leone, 2010). Women use formal and informal networks in search for capital (Gatewood et al., 2008). Theory of Social Capital is reaffirmed. Relationships with entrepreneurs, bankers, accountants, consultants, family and friends is a source of valuable information, advice and access to resources. External finance is key to business survival and growth. Social contacts with decision-makers (financial institutions and banks) will improve chances of receiving funds (Manalova et al., 2005, 2006). Social roles/place may exclude them from social networks creating information asymmetries (Welter et al, 2006). Entrepreneur's social network structure explains creation and success of a venture (OECD, 2004). Women develop self-concept linked to their interactive relational connections (Fenwick, 2002). Social Network theory explains how status is attained or how social capital can be used to achieve personal goals (Adler and Kwon, 2002). Relational theory is a useful frame of reference to know how women entrepreneurs build relationships. Mothering role is carried over to workplace. Women lead in a participative and democratic manner. They train subordinates (Buttner, 2001). Entrepreneurial networks show quantity and quality of the links between a firm and the external environment (Carter et al., 2001). Networks inform about loan deals available and help access private resources (Uzzi, 1999). Strong personal networks are good for family related tasks and not for business (Lin, 1999). Social networks are structures (describe how individuals are connected) and processes (describe interactions) (Larson and Starr, 1993). Women's networks are similar to men's in terms of activity and density. Women have more men in their networks but men have few women in their networks (Aldrich, 1989). Weak tie networks are as important as strong tie networks (Aldrich and Zimmer, 1986b).

Women Entrepreneurs Gender Specific Constraints Regarding Access to Finance

In developing economies, 35 per cent of small firms report that access to finance is a major obstacle to their operations. It is constrained by market failures and cultural phenomena. Low competition among banks diminishes the access of firms to finance. This effect is stronger if financial development is less advanced, if the share of government banks is higher, and if, credit information is less available or is of low quality. Information problems lead to credit rationing and exclusion from financial markets even in equilibrium. Credit markets have serious principal agent problems, adverse selection and moral hazard. The non-price barriers such as product design features, red tape, no financial institutions near-by, poor regulations, and documentation of requirements may be discriminating against potential customers (GDFI, 2014). Women mostly do not need high capital outlay to commence business. They rely on personal savings and family to finance their businesses. The guarantees needed for external financing may be beyond scope of their personal assets and credit track record. There is no statistical significance between women entrepreneurs starting in male dominated sector and access to financing (Kyalo et al., 2013). Lack of finance accounts for twice the proportion of business discontinuance among women entrepreneurs compared to men in US and Israel. Hence, it is a universal problem (GEM Women's Report, 2012). There is scarce research on women and equity capital. Women are left out of wealth creation process by both equity suppliers and seekers (Knorr, 2011). Availability of adequate, timely and affordable credit is a big issue for the MSME sector and women entrepreneurs in particular (Prime Minister's Task Force Report, 2010). Access to finance is seen as part of the 'financial inclusion approach' and a new perspective for analysing the inequality within the financial sector. Access to finance is broadly defined as access to products (e.g. deposits and loans) and services (e.g. insurance and equity products) at a reasonable cost. Women's access to bank loans is made difficult because of legal issues concerning property rights. Women's businesses seem to be concentrated mostly in the service sector where usually the output is hard to quantify in the absence of physical assets and this becomes a barrier in accessing finance. Women allocate a significant amount of time in unpaid work makes it difficult to obtain the same performance as men who spend less time for unpaid work. The demand-side barriers – male signature for opening an account and for credit; Borrowers Property Rights – access to collateral; women lack access to networks; less financial literacy; domestic responsibilities; limits on women mobility, the supply-side barriers – financial institutions lack technical know–how to design products that suit the needs of women clients; the strong link between legal framework for secured transactions and secured registry; government and financial sector policies-unintended effects; small number of women in the board (UNECE and WBI, 2009). Access is needed for contingency planning, credit and wealth creation. A lower access to finance in the case of women leads to the idea of gender hierarchy where women hold an inferior position (Rajan, 2008). The financial institutions have intentionally limited their exposure for reasons – these businesses carry high risk; high cost of delivery and limited access to immovable collateral (MSME Census, 2007). Women business owners are less likely to apply for all forms of external capital. The findings do not support if the primary reason is fear of being turned down (Orser et al., 2006). Difficult to raise finances at the early stages because of low equity base and lack of cash flow to sustain debt finance. Financial institutions, being risk averse, also usually do not finance such ventures. There is a need to create a window for start-up funds (Report of the Committee on Technology Innovation and Venture Capital, 2006, Planning Commission). The aspirations and the expectations of women entrepreneurs on the demand side and the perceptions held by bank lending officers of women entrepreneurs and female type businesses on the supply side both affect the finance lending decisions (Carter et al., 2005). Availability of finance is a critical element to the startup and consequent performance of any enterprise. Women entrepreneurs are disadvantaged by their gender (Marlow and Patton, 2005). A general lack of unsecured lending appears to dissuade many people from setting up their own businesses in a culture characterized by risk aversion and fear of failure (O'Reilly and Hart, 2003). The concept of the 'discouraged borrower' where a creditworthy individual who does not apply for finance because they believe they will be rejected (Kon and Storey, 2003). Female founders are more risk averse and less likely to expect debt financing. The hypothesis that the effects will be mediated/tempered by non-financial resources were not supported (Carter, 2002). Women like men begin and run small businesses which don't interest bankers. Only one discrimination found against women was higher demand for collaterals. Most discrimination was due to communication problems arising from intercultural bias, as bankers (men) tend to consider female entrepreneurs as women first. The other reason is the lack of financial competencies (Orhan, 2001). The major banks tend to offer only traditional products, primarily secured loans and overdrafts: 'with a few exceptional cases banks have not moved beyond secured lending' (The Ulster Society of Chartered Accountants, 2001). Financial needs and financing options available to SMEs change throughout the firm's life cycle. Access to debt finance is affected by the positive association between the debt ratio and asset structure (Burger and Udell, 1998). There exists significant differences in loan officers' response to female and male applicants. Different and tougher criteria are used to evaluate performance potential of women entrepreneurs. She has to be better than the equal. There is a need for education to loan officers to sensitize them to the gender stereotyping (Fay and Williams, 1991). Male loan officers compared to female loan officers perceived a larger gap between the attributes of successful entrepreneurs and the attributes of women (Buttner and Rosen, 1988). Access to start-up finance is the top most financial issue. In all sectors, women use substantially less start-capital then men. Women encounter, more than men, credibility problems when dealing with bankers. This problem impacts the performance, survival and growth of women-run businesses (Schwartz, 1976). Regulators concern more with general financial data for inflation control, financial stability and less about a gender approach. Financial institutions are usually organizing their data around accounts rather than customers. Demand-side data are provided by individuals and households surveys. Their comparability might be hampered by the different measurements that are employed. Collection of data is time consuming and costly (UNECE and WBI, 2009). Small businesses are held back by tough local conditions some of them are unable to raise huge collaterals demanded by banks. They are too big for microfinance institutions but too small for conventional banks (Kimathi, 2009). Institutional aspects of entrepreneurship affect women differently (Baughn, Chua and Neupert, 2006).

Government Policies and Programmes: Entrepreneurship policies across the globe do not regard self-employment as entrepreneurship. Rather, entrepreneurship has some element of innovation and growth potential. In India, the informal sector accounts for about 89 per cent of the gross value added and almost 98 per cent of employment in MSMEs, of which over 64 per cent units fall in the self-employment category. Hence, the policies and programmes should also be supportive of the informal sector.

There is too much emphasis on poverty alleviation for the bottom tier and not enough for the women in the middle who could have the biggest impact (Aidis, 2014). MSME policy focuses on existing enterprises or a group of enterprises (clusters), and its target client is the firm. We need a separate Act to encourage the potential entrepreneurs. Policy-makers should insist on data from which needs of women can be understood and the progress seen. There is a plethora of policies such as – Micro, Small and Medium Enterprise Policy; Manufacturing Policy; Competition Policy; Industrial Policy; Science and Technology Policy; National Design Policy; etc., that have direct and indirect implications for entrepreneurship. The efforts are fragmented and have no strategy content. The present status of entrepreneurship education in India is poor and lacks strategic direction. Technology Business Incubators (TBI) have emerged as the major source of innovation across the globe. India has only 115 TBIs. A number of registrations like TAN, PAN, VAT, EPF, ESI, Central Excise have to be obtained. These formalities are time consuming and tiring. Property registration takes a long time and stamp duty and transfer charges differ from state to state. A number of clearances have to be obtained from Central and state governments like, NOCs from Pollution Control Board, land use permits, power, water and sewerage connections, etc. (EDII, 2014). In terms of ease of starting a business, India ranks 179; dealing with construction permits 182; getting electricity 111; registering property 92; getting credit 28; protecting investors 34; paying taxes 158; trading across borders 132; enforcing contracts 186; resolving insolvency 121, among 189 economies (World Bank Group: Doing Business, 2014). MSMED Act, 2006; SARFAESI Act, 2002; The Regulation of Factor Bill, 2011; RBI Policies regarding MSME Finance, Institutions such as Credit Bureau; Collateral Registry; The SME Stock Exchange; ISARC (India SME Asset Reconstruction Co. Ltd.) have limited impact on Small Industries. Existing programmes of the Indian Government for SMEs – NMCP, MSECDP, CLCSS for Technology Upgradation; CGS, ISO 9000/ISO 14001 Certification Reimbursement; MSME MDA, participation in the international exhibitions and fairs; financial assistance for using Global Standards GSI in Bar Coding; Purchase and Price Preference Policy have not percolated to the needy small enterprises. Women are not a monolithic category; rather, policies and programmes for them should begin with a diagnosis of their personal characteristics and motives aimed at strengthening pull motives that comprise a base for more viable and innovative entrepreneurial activity (Sarri and Trihopoulou, 2005).

Creating an Entrepreneurial Eco-System for Women Entrepreneurs

Socio-cultural environment in India is favourable towards entrepreneurship (41% of adults see good opportunities to start a business) (India-GEM, 2013). The need of the hour, therefore, is to augment the supply of well-groomed opportunity and innovation driven women small and medium entrepreneurs. It will help redress the twin problems viz. unemployment and poverty. Across the world, business processes have undergone a sea change in the post liberalization era. It is, therefore, important to create a friendly entrepreneurial eco-system for both sexes.

Protecting creditor rights; regulating business conduct; setting standards for disclosure and transparency; promoting credit information – sharing systems and collateral registries; educating and protecting consumers; Competition policy to reward better performers; policies to expand account penetration; innovations in technology – such as mobile payments, mobile banking, and borrower identification using biometric data; innovative financial products, such as index-based insurance; improvements in lending to micro and small firms can be achieved by leveraging existing relationships; financial education has a measurable impact if it reaches people during teachable moments; leveraging social networks; delivery mode matters, too. Simple rule-of-thumb training is more effective (GFDR, 2014). Customized offerings with deep understanding of the market; build a brand and develop tailored products; customize policies, processes, and systems to align to their needs; promote friendly environment; deliver non-financial services, and enabling environment; co-create a risk capital fund; equal rights to property; simplify collateral requirement; women-focused policies; online customer care support; and DFIs to be activated (MSME Finance, IFC Report, 2014).

It is also important that creating an environment where starting own business becomes a natural career choice. Coordinated resources, training through creative types of financing besides availability of bank finance also assumes significance. Small business owners are consulted and educators from kindergarten to higher levels made to understand entrepreneurship. Various levels of government need to be aligned and coordinated (Greene, 2013). Financing innovation; introducing more growth-oriented training and technical assistance; providing more market access assistance; increasing access to the internet; improving business environment; highlighting cultural acceptance (http: //www.unctadxi.org/Sections/DITE/) also become critical.

Framework

Entrepreneurial finance; government policy; government entrepreneurship programmes; entrepreneurial education; R&D transfer; commercial and legal infrastructure; entry regulation; physical infrastructure and cultural and social norms (Kolb, 2013; GEM Report, 2012; OECD, 2004) are important conditions for access to finance. Gender-sensitive value chain analysis to integrate women into the value chain, create capacity building enterprises, associations and policies; training tools; public policy to stimulate and support women entrepreneurs (http: //www.ilo.org/wed, 2012) also become important conditions.

To enable access to capital, market developing policies – improve country's contractual and information frameworks; market enabling policies – regulatory frameworks for leasing and factoring; market harnessing policies-prevent imprudent lending; increasing the supply of equity aggregators, VC funds, and local banks to support SME sector (Bouri et al., 2011) assume significance.

Three Main Pillars of Enabling Environment

Legal and regulatory framework; government support; and financial infrastructure support (MSME Census, Ministry of MSME, Annual Report 2009–2010) are the pillars of enabling environment. For a level playing ground, access to the same Entrepreneur's Toolkit – secure property rights, rule of law, and economic freedom is needed. Entrepreneurs in health, education, and community formation need the same level playing field and freedom that enabled entrepreneurs in technology (Strong and Mackay, 2009). Commercial bank partnerships with MFIs to increase access for women; mainstreaming gender in formal financial institutions; specialized women's banks; integrated credit registries; mentoring, training in non-traditional businesses; increase financial literacy and awareness; having more female voices at the decision-making table; sex disaggregated data are important. At national level – improve legislative framework and monitor the impact of their policies by collecting sex-disaggregated data; provide incentives and support for the financial institutions to increase the number of women among the customers.

At the international community – Promote training for financial institutions; increase the awareness of the women's needs in terms of financial products; underline the potential benefits for the financial institutions; collect sex-disaggregated data in their field for international exchange. UNCTAD should integrate gender dimension in all areas of work and ensure its programmes are well designed from the gender perspective, increasing women's access to finance and economic opportunities (UNECE and WBI, 2009). Enterprise development; supply chain and marketing practices; expand business relationships with women-owned enterprises; support gender-sensitive solutions to credit; ask business partners and peers to respect the company's commitment to advancing equality and inclusion; respect the dignity of women in all activities; ensure that company products, services and facilities are not used for human trafficking or sexual exploitation (Mills, 2013). They propose a gender aware framework comprising five Ms. The framework is rooted in the premise that entrepreneurship is socially embedded and draws from institutional theory. It extends three Ms – market, money and management, described as the building blocks of business viability. It adds 'motherhood', representing the household/family context, proposing this has a large impact on women in the entrepreneurial process. The fifth "M" is the meso (intermediate structures and institutions) and macro (expectations of society and cultural norms) environment (Brush, de Bruin and Welter; 2009; Davidsson, 2003; Bates et al., 2007). Heavily regulated countries have fewer new firms (Capelleras et al., 2008). Females will be pulled into self-employment by the Vision for Women Entrepreneurship and normative support for entrepreneurship (Baughn et al., 2006). Women are heterogeneous. They differ in education, work experience, age, social class, ethnicity, religion and country of residence. Effective policy has to take into account what it means to be a woman and her idiosyncratic experiences. Existing women entrepreneurs can give important insights and their voices need to be heard. Developing women's mastery and vicarious experience will bring change on supply side. Educate society on value of women entrepreneurship. Entrepreneurship capital spans political, legal, cultural and business values and is shaped by a diverse set of policy instruments, including education, training and taxes (cf, OECD, 2004). Formal regulatory institutions can create entrepreneurial opportunities, influence the extent to which female entrepreneurship can develop and affect the types of enterprises in which women engage (Welter et al., 2003). *Training* – participatory and incremental through female instructors; *Credit* – flexible finance that meets the developmental needs of the enterprise and loan guarantees; *Counselling* – individual based, on problems specific to business and hiring female consultants (SCORE model); *Mentoring* – MELLOW model; *Information sharing/network formation* – One stop shops, trade fairs, Internet, taking issues up to national and global level; *Incubators* – Incubatorelmpresedonna, Italy and ACE net Model; *Market assistance* – improving market access and transparency, standardizing market operations and reducing corruption; *Advocacy* – through ILO, UNIDO, OECD, UNIFEM, ESCAP, governments and NGOs (Kantor, 2001).

Informalize Formal Financial Sector

Financial institutions can learn a lot from informal financiers – small and short term loans; savings facilities are readily available; collateral arrangements are imaginative; and rapid disbursements with less paperwork (Hilhorst and Oppenoorth, 1992; Bouman, 1989). In US, corporations have to spend 5 per cent of their procurement budget with women owned businesses. Businesses with potential for growth need more handholding to develop their infrastructure (Stengel, 2014). Nurture skills and behaviours that facilitate growth, specifically in financial management area (Carter and Allen, 1997). Local support is crucial (Sullivan et al., 1997). Gender-based training programmes empower women to manage their lives within the constraints of the new economy (Servon, 1996). Positive attitude towards women business owners from business and political leaders (Burr and Strickland, 1992). Entrepreneurship Education + 21st century skills + Educational Institutions + Multi-Stakeholder Partnerships = Effective Governance; Economic success; Delighted constituency (Cisco, Intel and Microsoft, 2009) was also highlighted in research. Experiential learning is core to developing entrepreneurial knowledge, skills and attitudes. The core experience needs to be built around authentic adult relationships and role models; hands-on experience; and exposure to real economic risks. High expectations and belief in a young person's ability to succeed ('efficacy') are critical to success. Programmes need to be deeply embedded in, and connected to, the communities in which they operate. They also have to be very clear about the targeted outcomes and to tailor programming to the targeted outcome. It is important to be very modest about expectations for sustainable enterprise development in young adults. To promote women's entrepreneurship network building and providing access to start-up resources, schools and educational programmes also have a valuable role to play (Integral Assets Consulting, Inc., 2006). Against this background, this paper proposes a conceptual framework for women and their access to finance. The framework is given below.

Proposed Conceptual Framework

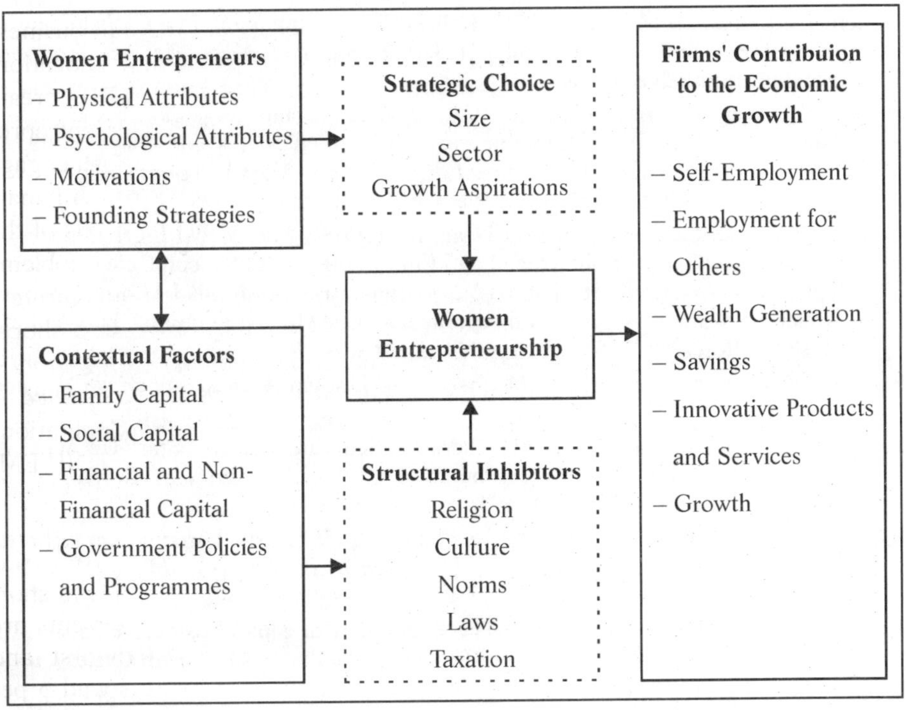

Conclusion

No economy can afford to squander any resource, particularly a resource as valuable as the energy and talents of half its population. However, even in the industrialized world, no country offers women the same degree of opportunity as men. And in developing nations, there are often substantial barriers that keep women from earning a living (EY, 2014).

Women-owned enterprises – whether small, medium or large – are an important economic source for growth. In developed countries, women are creating businesses at a greater rate than men and are equally contributing to the GNP of their economies as they invest their profits in education, their family and their community. If given the opportunity through innovative solutions to overcome financial and non-financial barriers, woman can thrive and be a profitable segment for financial institutions. Traditional measures of economic development and business performance often do not capture the true transformational benefits of women businesses. Connecting with women owned businesses is not CSR or levelling the playing ground. It is a business imperative (Lawton, 2010) which goes a long way to provide women's access to finance thus leading to economic development in the developing context.

References

Aldrich, H.; Elam, A.B. and Reese, P.R. (1997). Entrepreneurship in a Global Context, in S. Birley and I.C. MacMillan (eds.) *Strong Tie, Weak Tie and Strangers*, London: Routledge, 1–25.

Aldrich, H., Reese, P. and Dubini, P. (1989). 'Women on the Verge of a Breakthrough: Networking between Entrepreneurs in the United States and Italy', *Entrepreneurship and Regional Development*, 1, 339–356. Aldrich, H. and Zimmer, C., Entrepreneurship through Social Networks (1986).

Allen, I., Elam, A., Langowitz, N. and Dean, M. (2008). The Global Entrepreneurship Monitor 2007 Report on Women and Entrepreneurship, Babson College: Babson Park, MA. Arasti, Z. et al. (2012), A Qualitative Study on Individual Factors Affecting Iranian Women Entrepreneurs' Growth Orientation, International Business Research, ISSN 1913–9004 (Print).

Bandura, A. (1982). 'Self-Efficacy Mechanism in Human Agency', *American Psychologist*, 37: 122–147.

Barnir, A. and McLaughlin, E. (2011). 'Parental Self-Employment, Start-Up Activities and Funding: Exploring Intergenerational Effects', *Journal of Developmental Entrepreneurship*, Vol. 16 (3): 371.

Baughn, C. et al. (2006). The Normative Context for Women's Participation in Entrepreneurship: A Multicountry Study, *Entrepreneurship Theory and Practice*, Vol. 30 (5): 687–708.

Berger, A.N. and Udell, G.F. (1998). The Economics of Small Business Finance: The Roles of Private Equity and Debt Markets in the Financial Growth Cycle, *Journal of Banking and Finance*, 22, 613–673.

Bird, B. and Brush, C. (2002). A Gendered Perspective on Organizational Creation, *Entrepreneurship: Theory and Practice*, 26(3): 41–65.

Blake, M. and Hanson, S. (2005). 'Rethinking Innovation: Context and Gender, Environment and Planning', 37, 681–701.

Bowen, D.D. and Hisrich, R.D. (1986). 'Female Entrepreneurship: A Career Development Perspective', *Academy of Management Review,* 11: 393–407.

Brush, C.G.: Carter, N.M.: Gatewood, E.J.: Greene, P.G. and Hart, M.M. (2006). *Growth-Oriented Women Entrepreneurs and their Businesses*. Upper Saddle River, New Jersey: Financial Tinco Prentice Hall.

Brush, C.G. and Hisrich, R.D. (1991). 'Antecedent Influences on Women-Owned Businesses', *Journal of Management Psychology,* 6(2): 9–16.

Brush, C.G. et al. (2006). 'The Use of Bootstrapping by Women Entrepreneurs in Positioning for Growth', *Venture Capital,* Vol. 8(1): 15–31.

Busenitz, L.W.: Gomez, C. and Spencer, J.W. (2000). 'Country Institutional Profiles: Unlocking Entrepreneurial Phenomena', *Academy of Management Journal*, 43(5): 994–1003.

Buttner, H. (2001). 'Examining Female Entrepreneurs' Management Style: An Application of a Relational Frame', *Journal of Business Ethics*, 29(3): 253–269.

Buttner, H. and Rosen, B. (1988). 'Bank Loan Officers' Perceptions of the Characteristics of Men, Women and Successful Entrepreneurs', *Journal of Business Venturing*, 3, 249–258.

Carter, N.M. (2002). 'The Role of Risk Orientation on Financing Expectations in New Venture Creation: Does Sex Matter?' *Frontiers of Entrepreneurship Research*, 170–181.

Carter, S. et al. (2006). 'Gender, Entrepreneurship and Business Finance: Investigating the Relationship between Banks and Entrepreneurs in the UK', in *Growth Oriented Women Entrepreneur and their Businesses: A Global Research Perspective*. Cheltenham, UK: Edward Elgar Publishing. 373–391.

Chen, C.C., Gene Greene, P. and Crick, A. (1998). 'Does Entrepreneurial Self-efficacy Distinguish Entrepreneurs from Managers?' *Journal of Business Venturing*, 13(4): 295–316.

Chu, P. (2000). *Journal of Enterprising Culture*, Vol. 8(1): 67–84.

Chua, J., Steier, L. and Chrisman, J. (2006). 'How Family Firms Solve Intra-family Agency Problems using Interlocking Directorates: A Comment', *Entrepreneurship Theory and Practice*, 30(6): 777–783.

Constantinidis, C., Cornet, A. and Asandei, S. (2006). 'Financing of Women-Owned Ventures: The Impact of Gender and Other Owner- and Firm-Related Variables', Venture Capital, Vol. 8(2): 133–157.

Delmar, F. and Davidsson, P. (2000). 'Where do they Come From? Prevalence and Characteristics of Nascent Entrepreneurs'. *Entrepreneurship and Regional Development*, 12: 1–23.

DeTienne, D.R. and Chandler, G.N. (2007). 'The Role of Gender in Opportunity Identification', *Entrepreneurship Theory and Practice*, Vol. 31(3): 365–386.

Fay, M. and Williams, L. (1993). 'Gender bias and the Availability of Business Loans', *Journal of Business Venturing*, Vol. 8, 363–376.

Fenwick, T. (2002). Lady Inc.: Women learning, negotiating subjectivity in entrepreneurial discourses. International Journal of Lifelong Education, 21(2): 162–177

Gherardi, S. (2003). 'Feminist Theory and Organizational Theory: A Dialogue on New Bases', in *The Oxford Handbook of Organizational Theory: Meta-Theoretical Perspectives*, Oxford: Oxford Press. 210–36.

Godwin, L.N.; Stevens, C.E. and Brenner, N.L. (2006). 'Forced to Play by the Rules? Theorizing How Mixed-sex Founding Teams Benefit Women Entrepreneurs in Male-dominated Contexts', *Entrepreneurship Theory and Practice*, 20: 623–42.

Green, C.J., Kirkpatrick, C.H. and Murinde, V. (2006). 'Finance for Small Enterprise Growth and Poverty Reduction in Developing Countries', *Journal of International Development*, 18: 1017–1030 (13).

Gupta, V.K. et al. (2009). The Role of Gender Stereotypes in Perceptions of Entrepreneurs and Intentions to Become an Entrepreneur, *Entrepreneurship Theory and Practice*, 1042–2587, Baylor University.

Hamilton, E.E. (2004). 'Whose Story is it Anyway? Narrative Accounts of the Role of Women in Founding and Establishing Family Businesses', Entrepreneurship and Enterprise Development Working Paper Series.

Hilhorst, T. and Oppenoorth, H. (1992). Financing Women's Enterprise: Beyond Barriers and Bias. Amsterdam, Netherlands: Royal Tropical Institute.

Hisrich, R.D. and Brush, C. (1986). *The Woman Entrepreneur: Starting, Financing, and Managing a Successful New Business*. Lexington, MA: Lexington Books, Inc., http: //eir.dell.com/wp-content/uploads/2013/ 06/Gender_GEDI_Executive_Report-FINAL-FINAL-5_31.pdf

http: //msme.gov.in/MSME-Annual-Report-2011-12-English.pdf

http: //www.esa.doc.gov/sites/default/files/reports/documents/women-owned -businesses.pdf

http: //www.gemconsortium.org.Global Entrepreneurship Monitor,(2012)

http: //www.goldmansachs.com/citizenship/10000women/index.html (2013) http: //www.worldbank.org/

Kantor, P. (2001). Promoting Women's Entrepreneurship Development based on Good. Practice Programmes: Some Experiences from North to the South. Geneva: ILO/SEED.

Kelley, D.J. et al. (2010). Women's Report, Global Entrepreneurship Monitor.

Kimathi, J. (2009). Going it Alone, Msafiri, November 2009–January 2010, Edition 69. (Working paper).

Klyver, K. et al. (2012). More Gender Equality, Less Women's Self-employment: A Multi-Country Investigation. *Global Women's Entrepreneurship Research: Diverse Settings, Questions and Approaches,* Karen Hughes and Jennifer Jennings (eds), Edward Elgar, 171–188.

Knorr, H. (2011). 'From Top Management to Entrepreneurship: Women's Next Move?' *International Journal of Manpower*, Vol. 32(1): 99–116q.

Kollan, B. and Parikh, I.J. (2005). A Reflection of the Indian Women in Entrepreneurial World. WP No. 2005–08–07. IIMA.

Kon, Y. and Storey, D.J. (2003). 'A Theory of Discouraged Borrowers'. *Small Business Economics*, 21(1), 37–49.

Kyalo, T. et al. (2013). 'Access to Finance-Hindrance to Women Start-up of Enterprises in Male Dominated Sectors in Kenya', *Prime Journal of Social Sciences*, Vol. 2(5): 315–319.

Langowitz, N. and Minniti, M. (2007), 'The Entrepreneurial Propensity of Women', *Entrepreneurship: Theory and Practice*, Vol. 31(3): 341–64.

Larson, A. and Starr, J.A. (1993). A Network Model of Organization Formation, *Entrepreneurship: Theory and Practice*, 17(2): 5–15.

Lawton, Sue. (2010). 'Connecting With Women Entrepreneurs: Equality or Business Imperative?' *International Journal of Gender and Entrepreneurship*. Vol. 2(), 291–294.

Lin, N. (1999a). 'Building a Network Theory of Social Capital', *Connections*, 22(1): 28–51.

Lin, N. (1999). 'Social Networks and Status Attainment'. *Annual Review of Sociology*, 25: 467–487.

Manolova, Tatiana S., Brush, Candida G. and Edelman, Linda F. (2008). 'What do Women Entrepreneurs Want?' *Strategic Change Journal*, Vol. 17(3–4), 69–82.

Marlow, S. and Patton, D. (2005). All Credit to Men? Entrepreneurship, Finance and Gender, *Entrepreneurship: Theory and Practice*, Vol. 29(6), 717–736.

Martin, P.Y. and Collinson, D. (2002). Over the Pond and Across the Water: Developing the Field of Gendered Organizations, Gender, Work and Organization, 9(3), 244–265.

Mitchell, Lesa (2009). Overcoming the Gender Gap: Women Entrepreneurs as Economic Drivers. Kauffman Online Foundation (www.kauffman.org).

Minniti, M. (2009). 'Gender Issues in Entrepreneurship'. *Foundations and Trends in Entrepreneurship*, Vol. 5(7–8), 497–621.

Neergaard, H., Shaw, E. and Carter, S. (2005). 'The Impact of Gender, Social Capital and Networks on Business Ownership: A Research Agenda', *International Journal of Entrepreneurial Behaviour and Research*, 11(5), 338–357.

O'Reilly, M. and Hart, M. (2002). The Household Entrepreneurship Survey: Northern Ireland (Northern Ireland: InvestNI).

Orhan, M (2001). 'Women Business Owners in France: The Issue of Financing Discrimination', *Journal of Small Business Management,* Vol. 39 (1): 95–102.

Orser et al. (2006). *Entrepreneurship: Theory and Practice*, Vol. 30(5): 643–665.

Pinelli, M.T. (2011). http: //www.ey.com/Publication/vwLUAssets/Nature-or-nurture/$FILE/Nature-or-nurture.pdf

Reynolds, P.D. (1997). New and Small Firms in Expanding Markets. *Small Business Economics*, Vol. 9 (5), 79–84.

Sarri, K. and Trihopoulou, A. (2005). 'Female Entrepreneurs' Personal Characteristics and Motivation: A Review of the Greek Situation', *Women in Management Review*, 20(1): 24–36.

Schwartz, E. (1976). 'Entrepreneurship: A New Female Frontier', *Journal of Contemporary Business*, 5(1), 47–76. Scott, C. (1986). Why more women are becoming entrepreneurs. Journal of Small Business Management, Vol. 24(1), 37–44.

Sen, G. and Mukherjee, A. (2013). No Empowerment without Rights, No Rights without Politics: Gender-Equality, MDGs and the post 2015 Development Agenda, Working Paper Series.

Smith-Hunter, Andrea E. and Leone, Joshua, (2010). Evidence on the Characteristics of Women Entrepreneur in Brazil: An Empirical Analysis. *International Journal of Management and Marketing Research*, Vol. 3(1): 85–102.

Stenholm, P.; Heinonen, J.; Kovalainen, A. and Pukkinen, T. (2011). Global Entrepreneurship Monitor-Finnish 2010 Report. Publication of Turku School of Economics, Finland,

Stevenson, L. (1990). 'Some Methodological Problems Associated with Researching Women Entrepreneurs', *Journal of Business Ethics*, Vol. 9, April-May, 439–446.

Tonoyan, V., Budig, M. and Strohmeyer, R. (2010). Financing for Growth Northern Ireland. The Ulster Society of Chartered Accountants.

Uzzi, B. (1999). 'Embeddedness in the Making of Financial Capital: How Social Relations and Networks Benefit Firms Seeking Financing', *American Sociological Review*, Vol. 64, 481–505.

Vossenberg, S. (2013). Women Entrepreneurship Promotion in Developing Countries: What Explains the Gender Gap in Entrepreneurship and How to Close It? Maastricht Business School, Working Paper No. 2013/08

Welter, F. and Smallbone, D. (2003). 'Entrepreneurship and Enterprise Strategies in Transition Economies: An Institutional Perspective', in Kirby, D. and Watson, A. (eds.) *Small Firms and Economic Development in Developed and Transition Economies: A Reader*. Aldershot: Ashgate, 95–114.

Welter, F.; Smallbone, D. and Isakova, N. (eds.). (2006). *Enterprising Women in Transition Economies*, Aldershot, UK: Ashgate.

8

Another World

Gendered Work and Existence

MITOO DAS

Abstract

This paper attempts to depict the journey of a woman entrepreneur (a beauty salon owner) from the North-East of India (Imphal, Manipur) to Delhi and the life she has built after overcoming many odds. Following the qualitative method/technique of life history with the help of interviews and conversations used effectively in anthropology, concerns revolving around social, cultural and political issues like identity, gender, family, religion, education, migration, space, etc. are looked into.

This paper is proposed as an endeavour in the form of a preliminary investigation for a future attempt to investigate and research migrant women entrepreneurs from the North-East and based in the capital city of India, Delhi. This narrative of Rebecca can provide an outlet to comprehend various issues like the trials and tribulations that women face, particularly not being a local of the place where one decides to set up one's own business; the need to open up businesses in an alien space; information about concerns like legal identity to procure loans, gendered employment, etc. can give a better picture of the entire situation. Organizational problems which act as hindrances in the establishment and survival of migrant women entrepreneurs from the North-East was also attempted. Finally an effort is made to analyse the findings academically and to comment on the present scenario and propose means for viable, secure and women friendly schemes, particularly for migrant women.

Keywords

narrative, life history, women, migrants, entrepreneurs, north-east India, identity, prejudices, inefficient policies, measures.

Introduction

People all over the world have always shifted from one place to another for the purposes of education, work, leisure, travel, adventure or something more permanent, like creating a new location for the purpose of livelihood. This happens at a regular pace and with each new transformation in economic, cultural and social scenarios, such shifts are increasing in diverse ways. Hence, it is no surprise that in the contemporary world, women, like men, traverse to places outside their native realm on their own, and if circumstances permit, establishes a life for themselves in the new realm. Even when this is not a new phenomenon, such movement of women needs to be visited to understand the sociological, political and cultural implications that are associated with it in the present scenario. The contemporary causes connected with migration of women are also important to locate in view of changing roles and identities women seek today.

Discourses on migration, gender and work together can create a vast gamut of knowledge which can play an effective role in any academic and policy-making setting. It is interesting to note that the meaning of migration as associated with economy has changed vastly with migrations been understood variously due to the influence of globalization. Migration is not just a physical and social transaction, but very much 'an instrument of cultural diffusion and social integration' (Bannerjee and Raju, 2009). Migration which results from the wish to attain a better livelihood opportunity can among myriad jobs also facilitate the entering into the informal sector and investing oneself in the service industry as an entrepreneur. And these migrants, interestingly in creating a new space for themselves in the form of work, also carry with them and over time build affective 'values and behavioral systems of communities, forming a culture of migration' (Thapan et al., 2013). Women migrants are observed to be significant role players in 'carrying their indigenous traits to the new settlement'. This as Bal (2003) views it, perform as adjusting devices for a migrant in the accommodating society. However, this entire process of moving into a new, alien space and establishing a life worthwhile is not without complex hardships and ordeals. This is more so for in the case of women, as the existing patriarchal system prevalent in India, does not take lightly to women trying to build a life of their own, both monetarily and socially.

The Journey

This paper is a narrative of a woman entrepreneur who hails from Imphal, Manipur, which is situated in the north-eastern part of India. Her name is Rebecca Remmei and she runs a beauty salon named, Remmei in north Delhi, India. Her small business falls under the informal sector, more specifically in the service industry. Using the popular method of life history and unstructured interview utilized by anthropologists regularly to collect verifiable data. An attempt is made to understand the following in terms of migrant women entrepreneurs to a metropolitan city:

1. To present that there is an influx of women migrants from the North-East to metropolises in order to create a financially independent space (as entrepreneurs) for themselves.
2. To investigate the hurdles that are faced from the moment of the shift which continue throughout ones' working life.
3. To examine the gender related reasons behind the problems faced.
4. To examine the reasons behind entrepreneurship which exhibit gendered businesses.

5. To examine the mental and physical trauma that one goes through due to the ongoing struggle to survive in a competitive world dominated by men who are not socially supportive of women entrepreneurs.
6. To highlight the shortcomings of government managed schemes for women entrepreneurs, especially for migrant women and analyse if there is scope of amending or creating schemes at policy levels.
7. To analyse the findings and to comment on the present scenario and propose means and measures for viable, secure and women friendly schemes, particularly for migrant women.

This study is as a preliminary investigation for a future attempt on investigating and researching migrant women entrepreneurs from the North-East and based in the capital city of India, Delhi. This narrative of Rebecca can provide an outlet to comprehend various issues like the trials and tribulations that women face, particularly not being a local of the place where one decides to set up one's own business; the need to open up businesses in an alien space; information about concerns revolving around social, cultural and political issues like identity, gender, family, religion, education, location, etc. information about skill-based employees who assist them in their work; the acquisition of such employees, their security, etc. can also give a better picture of the entire situation. The absence of a legal/official identity of the host space to start an entrepreneurship also makes it difficult to start a business in terms of procuring sponsorship, investment and loans. For this, they have to be dependent on either some already officially settled family member, relative, friend or any other helpful acquaintance. This does create an uneasy and limiting situation for them. If this problem is resolved, their social identity as a woman, and that too a migrant, makes them doubly disadvantaged and act as deterrents because investors, do not trust or are eager to assist women to start any business. Hence, the different stages faced by such women to create spaces of their own, is relevant in studying and analysing the schema of layers that constructs women within patriarchy, location, and gendered employment.

There are other technical and organizational problems which act as hindrances in the establishment and survival of migrant women entrepreneurs from the North-East. We will, as the paper unfolds, describe all concerns taking into the case of Rebecca Remmei as our point of reference. However, before addressing the life history of Ms. Remmei, an attempt is made first to comprehend a little about what the informal sector is in which she and many women like her are associated with.

The Informal Sector: An Overview

Informal sector has been defined and understood diversely. Despite many research studies inquiring and trying to come to a definite meaning, it has somewhat remained ambiguous (Perera, 1994; Mitullah and Wachira, 1997; Bivens and Gammage, 2004; Nwaka, 2005). It was the International Labour Organization (ILO) in 1972 which brought to the international world a definition in its Kenya Mission Report. It defined informal sector as a 'way of doing things characterized by ease of entry and exit; reliance on indigenous resources; family ownership; small scale operations; labour intensive and adaptive technology; skills acquired outside of the formal sector; and unregulated and competitive markets.' (ILO, 1972). Since then, there were many definitions outlining the term informal sector. With change in time and situations, ILO introduced another definition much later, which states that, informal sector comprises a 'range of economic units in urban areas which are largely owned and operated by single individuals with little capital and labour and which produces and distributes goods and services with a view to generating income and employment to the persons concerned' (ILO, 1997). Newer definitions have been coming in time and again, however India as a country has not had a definitive description expressing what informal sector means in India. Academics and policy-makers in India have certainly discussed it enormously while researching the sociological and economic connections of the informal sector. However there was never a concrete definition of it. Many organizations too in India, like the National Sample Survey Organization (NSSO) and Directorate General of Employment and Training (DGET) have come up with definitions but these have been designed keeping in view their own specific interests (Naik, 2009). Naik who has worked as a consultant with the National Commission for Enterprises in the Unorganized Sector (NCEUS), which falls under the Ministry of Small Scale Industries, states that 'keeping in view of a uniform definition of informal/unorganized sector in India, the NCEUS set-up a Task Force to review the existing definitions and formulated harmonized definitions of informal/unorganized sector employment and informal/unorganized employment' (2009). By reviewing the Indian condition, the following definition has been proposed: 'The informal sector consists of all unincorporated private enterprises owned by individuals or households engaged in the sale and production of goods and services operated on a proprietary or partnership basis and with less than 10 total workers'. This definition was proposed based on data collected by NSSO between 1999–2000 and 2004–2005. Naik points out that this definition too is not flawless as it does not categorize enterprises, which he feels is problematic as for example, agricultural activities exhibit characteristics of an enterprise and hence needs to be accommodated (2009).

This paper without entering into a debate on the afore mentioned issue, places Remmei's profession and similar entrepreneurships as fitting to this classification provided by NCEUS.[1]

This paper particularly aims to delineate the concerns of migrant women entrepreneurs from the North-East India in the beauty service industry. Having placed the beauty salon enterprise as under the informal sector, a detailed narrative about Rebecca Remmei as an entrepreneur is then provided. The life history method utilized for this purpose is a significant method in anthropology. This method provides vital information about the respondent's entire life experiences. This is used to critically view and understand occurrences from the perspective of a larger society and culture. Instances about Rebecca gathered from her journey of becoming and practicing the life of an entrepreneur, can tell what provisions she has been offered as a member of society and a nation.

The Entrepreneur

The Entrepreneur, Rebecca Remmei, was born in 1976 and spent her childhood and early teenage years with her parents and siblings in Imphal, Manipur. She belongs to a sub-tribe of the Naga tribe called Rongmei, one of the major tribes found in Manipur. Her brother was the first among her siblings to move out of his state due to a government posting in Delhi. Other than her elder brother, she has three sisters, all younger than her. Her father is a retired government school teacher and her mother runs the house and has never been in any formal employment. They are practicing Protestant Christians.

When Rebecca reached her 10th standard, her brother noticed that she did not have an effective education in her home town. To make her foundation stronger, he decided to shift her to Delhi as after living there for a few years he realized it provided greater facilities and opportunities in every aspect of life. She was admitted to the Apex Public School to do her 11th and 12th in Burari, Delhi. This was in 1992. She stayed in the school's hostel during this period. Once her schooling was completed she got admitted to Indraprastha College for Women in the University of Delhi to do her under-graduation. She took up Political Science as her main subject of study. After becoming a graduate she joined the Department of Political Science in the University of Delhi through correspondence (distance mode) and simultaneously joined the Blossom Kocchar's College of Art and Design in Nehru Place, New Delhi, to achieve a formal training in beautification for both hair and body.

She mentions that from a young age she was always interested in putting make-up and styling herself up, including her sisters, relatives and friends. When she started her Masters in Delhi due to her free time, she reasoned with herself that a formal training in a knack she possessed would only help her in some form or the other. She did not at that time think that she would utilize her learning in the form of her future career. By the time she concluded her Masters, she also attained her Diploma in Beauty and Make-up from Blossom Kocchar's Institute. On its completion, she landed up as a trainer through the institute's placement scheme, with celebrity make-up artist Sylvester Rodgers, popularly known as Sylvie at her salon in Delhi. After a short stint with her, she joined a salon named Zako in Greater Kailash, Delhi, where she worked for three years. She earned a good package too. She worked for Sylvie and Zako between the years 2000 and 2004. It was here that while teaching young novices, through hands-on training, her skills got better and more effective. She got offers from people who were acquaintances of the owner to partner with them or to work for them. As she was not serious about taking this up as a career she refused all such offers at that point of time. However, she realized her worth in her work, and acknowledging the fact that people thought she was capable to provide professional service convincingly, she contemplated on starting her own beauty salon, a business which she could call her own. She always felt in her heart that a government job was boring and not her cup of tea. She finally took the risk and decided to give it a try. She knew she was good at her work, the problem lied in creating, building, accumulating and getting the permission and legal space to start her work. Gradually after consulting her family, she decided to set up her own beauty salon and become a woman entrepreneur in Delhi itself rather than going back home and starting at a safer, easier known space. This was because Delhi, as a mega city, a metropolis also offered greater achievement opportunities than her own home town.

In this, her family supported and encouraged her. In fact in the beginning, her parents and her brother provided her the money she needed to invest in her business, ranging from procuring a space on rent, buying equipments, setting up the salon to getting a licence for it, etc. This they had to do as she was unable to take a loan from any bank. This was because banks do not consider a migrant without a valid identity of the host space to be eligible for loan. She opened her salon through the category of sole proprietor as opening her salon through the available government schemes did not work for her, being a migrant woman from the North-East.[2] Looking back, she says the fact that she got into something she loves doing, and transforming it into her work, her career, is something she never regrets about. She is with something she loves doing and hence there is never a dull moment. It is also exciting to see her business grow and flourish. In all this her family has always without fail been empathetic. But there were relatives and neighbours who did attempt, though not successfully, to discourage her and her family from starting this business. They said that being a single woman, in a different city, starting a business on her own, that too, a salon, it would turn to be a bad decision in the long run. Running of a salon is deemed to be a lowly job for many. However, she did not let such advices deter her and she believed in herself and her potential and went ahead with her plan. Being religious she also believed that God will see her through thick and thin.

She finally opened her salon, Remmei (her family surname) in the year 2005 in a locality called Outrem Lines in North Delhi she took the place on rent. Though she had spent her training and trainer days in South Delhi, she opted for North Delhi as most of her clients here were students living in North Delhi who informed her that there was a lack of good beauty salons in that area. She ran Remmei in Outrem Lines for four years and shifted to a nearby space called GTB Nagar, which is mostly a commercial area. Her new address is strategically located with the metro station just a step away. At present she is doing well in her venture with an employee base of five girls.

Though this account sounds simplistic, it is not actually so. Rebecca from the start has faced immense difficulties and issues in the setting up of her beauty salon and establishing herself as a successful woman entrepreneur. There have been innumerable incidents and blockages in her journey as a professional business woman. The fact that she is a woman, a migrant from the North-East has mostly worked against her.

In everyday life she observes and notices that women and men from the North-East are looked at differently. The lives they live, the physical appearance that they possess, the language that they speak, the food that they eat, are not easily accepted by host societies from 'mainstream' India. Due to this Rebecca has had to face immense problems. People are not friendly and their own religiosity and social upbringing linked with patriarchy, make them look down upon her and people like her. This effects adversely as the host society closes them out, views them degradingly, considers them to be of 'loose character' and 'easily available'. As the locals are not able to accept people from the North-East as one of their own, they certainly try not to assist them, professionally or otherwise to become one of their own.

From the time she decided to start her business and went looking for a space to start her enterprise, she has only faced obstacles. In view of the fact that she is not a local from Delhi and without any valid identity or large amount of money to assist her at that time, she had to resort to dubious means to get her enterprise started. Her first agenda was to set up a working space. For this she met a property dealer with her brother through whom she procured a space on rent. The owner was a Punjabi local. In this her brother always acted as her representative as the men were not ready to talk to her. As her business got running, with clients visiting her and her work flourishing, the landlord started demanding more money and harassing her mentally endlessly. Many arguments ensued and many a times she had to take help of her men cousins to confront her landlord. The women of the house also abused her verbally commenting lowly on her looks (ethnicity) and on her status of a working woman. As if this was not enough, the MCD (Municipal Corporation of Delhi) harassed her for money on and off threatening to close her business if they did not receive the money on time, pointing out that she was running her business in a residential area.

After four years of immense mental trauma, she decided to request her property dealer to provide a solution. She met him with her elder brother and both of them apprised him of the situation. As her brother knew him from before, they were able to convince him to offer a better solution. Luckily for Rebecca, the property dealer who had a commercial space to rent in GTB Nagar, offered to give it to her on rent. This solved many issues for her from then on. She agrees that her business has been doing well after the shift. There was never a problem with accumulating clients, but here she is free from the everyday ordeal which definitely affects her work positively.

Other than this, in both her old work space and the new one, designing the space according to her needs was also tormenting. From procuring of raw material and goods to building the infrastructure to instructing the carpenters and other workers, she was distressed to figure out that no one listened to her seriously. Eventually to get things done her way she had to take help from her brother-in-law who handled these issues comfortably by virtue of being a 'man'.

As far as her employees are concerned, information collected from her and also from them revealed the following realities. She has five employees as of now. However, this ranges from four to six but not lesser or more than the mentioned numbers to assist her in running her salon. These girls are mainly from her own state Manipur but hailing from different towns and cities including Imphal. They have shifted to Delhi to look for a better opportunity in terms of livelihood as most of them come from families who are not affluent. They had heard about her from family, friends and acquaintances.

Rebecca's first step after taking in new girls is to train them vigourously through hands-on sessions and teaching them earnestly the nitty gritties of make-up and other beauty treatments ranging from hair treatments to body treatments. During this period the girls are called interns. She keeps them for a contract (which actually is not formal however does acts as a deterrent) period of one year or two years depending on their work performance. During this period she keeps them at her house with her, and almost lives like a family where they also share the kitchen.

The reason for care beyond a professional relationship is because of the religious obligations that Rebecca feels due to her being a Christian. She looks after their needs and helps them out when they are new in the city. By doing this she feels she is performing her duties as a true Christian.

She pays a salary from ₹ 7,000 to 15,000 depending on the category of the workers. Though a few of them have stayed back with her many leave once they have been trained in search of better jobs elsewhere. Even though at a personal level she does provide support monetarily and otherwise, due to the lack of job security and social security in her business, they prefer to leave.

In her parlour all women employees as mentioned earlier are from her own home state. This is because she feels comfortable to communicate and adjust with them in a better way than she would have, if she had employees from other places. There is also the sense of gratitude which many of them show due to the virtue of belonging to the same native land and being protected by her.

As far as her society back home is concerned, she believes among protestant Christians, a woman who works is not looked down upon but lauded. There are others mostly from the rural areas, where women who venture to make a livelihood on their own are ridiculed. However some form of patriarchy does exist in the home front where finally women after going back handle the household chores too. She has seen this in her own home too. Her brothers too are protective towards her and are always offering their assistance to her.

This profession, where she hails from is considered to be a woman centric profession and most salons she is aware of are run by women. In Delhi though there are men running salons, women certainly out number them in this profession with beauty salons being seen in every nook and corner of Delhi run by women. Most of them are housewives with supportive families trying to earn an extra buck for their homes.

Now that she lives in the metropolis with a comfortable life she lives in fear of everything coming to an end abruptly. Though as a migrant, she has brought along with her, her own cultural identity which she sustains by associating with people based in Delhi from her tribe. she still knows that living the life without the security the government through its schemes can provide.

She, however, insists that one should always follow one's dreams and should do what one is passionate about. Other things fall into place with time. She is optimistic and faces all kinds of hurdles positively.

This narrative which is an account of one woman nonetheless opens up avenues for debates and deliberations. Anthropologically this portrayal allows us to look into women, particularly women who migrate to opportunistic spaces and decide to chalk out livelihood prospects for themselves. Such portrayals let us view critically how spaces, identities, movement, religion, cultures, patriarchy and of course gendered roles are practiced and comprehended in society.

Women entrepreneurship which falls in the informal sector has been designed to allow women, among many things, to create a niche for themselves and at the same time to facilitate financial assistance to one's family and community. But this design is not without its shortcomings.

Interpretation

Rebecca who is a migrant woman from the North-East India represents women who have come to the urban space of Delhi, for better education and a better life. However, the host community has been extremely insolent and uncouth in their conduct in terms of facilitating an easier and hassle-free existence in their midst. It exhibits how a migrant woman has to face difficulties while setting up her business.

It is common knowledge that as citizens of India, everyone has the constitutional right to settle and work anywhere in the country. However, the existing policies fail to provide this fundamental right enshrined in our Constitution. Every citizen in India also has the right to lead a dignified and satisfactory life and it is the duty of the government and also academics and researchers, to keep working towards ways by which members residing in society can lead an equal, valued and just life, socially, economically and politically.

India is a diverse nation and although policy-makers and researchers try their best to frame schemes and strategies to benefit all, certain inherent flaws remain. Sometimes, if not in the scheme itself, then definitely in its delivery as between the scheme and the proposed profiteer there is a long chain of corruption, exploitation, castetism and racist attitudes which makes the process a complicated one. Hence, the schemes of the Indian government though catchy on the forefront, when it comes to the actual implementation of these, they are far from being effective. Some schemes just remain on paper or they are modified/stopped before it reaches the beneficiary.

In the absence of an identity proof of the host space, a migrant's original identity is generally not accepted for professional purposes, loan procurement etc. It is known that an identity card containing one's home town address should be effective enough anywhere in India, however at the practice level of dissemination of policies, these are used as hindrances. It is rather distressing that even after 50 years of independence there is no successful attempt by the government to provide a universal identity card to our citizens (which can be valid anywhere in India to obtain benefits of government services and schemes). Hence no wonder the migrant entrepreneur in their initial phase are faced with hurdles which starts from procuring a valid identity (card) for themselves in the destination place. This hurdle continues for the migrant woman entrepreneur even while procuring a space for business, in the behaviour of people whom the woman migrant entrepreneur has to deal while starting a business clubbed with comments on ethnicity and character, especially when one is from the north-eastern part of India. All these things have made the survival of self-employed migrant entrepreneur women tough.

These instances depict sociological conditions prevalent in society which even while talking of women's equality, attempts to see to it that there are actually no changes in women's lives. This is done to resist the alarm that is felt when the comfort of one's normative patriarchal life is threatened. Women who tend to survive on their own are usually looked at with suspicion. The structural presence of society creates structural discrimination. Structural discrimination refers to rules, norms, generally accepted approaches and behaviours in institutions and other social structures that constitute obstacles for subordinate groups to the equal rights and opportunities possessed by dominant groups (Mohapatra, 2012). Women in the informal sector are by virtue of the fact of being women are treated as inferiors. And women who are migrants, of a different religion, caste, and ethnicity are more vulnerable to structural discrimination apart from gendered discrimination.

Structural discrimination takes us to the idea of social risk. Following Roshini Narendran's (2012) modified concept of Slovic (1999, 2004) and Finucane et al. (2000)[3] social risk, Narendran states that social risk are incurred due to mobility constrains, male hegemony, perceived discomfort, social stigma and institutional void. Taking Rebecca again as an example, it is clearly observed that with mobility comes constrains, with hosts not accepting the migrant's presence. Male hegemony is seen from how men behave in various contexts (see above) to confirm their superior identity while dealing with women entrepreneurs. The abuses of the land lord at Rebecca's success or the carpenters not relenting to her orders of designing her salon in a particular way are just a couple among many more examples which comment on the men's need to remain superior to women.

Perceived discomfort is another risk that women entrepreneurs face, i.e. dealing with unpleasant situations. Rebecca had issues buying her equipment and other raw material from male-run markets as their behaviour was usually sleazy to say the least. She was always accompanied by her cousins or brother-in-law in such situations.

Social stigma is another issue which women entrepreneurs have to deal with. Though in Rebecca's case this was not seen, there were instances where people from her neighbourhood did tell her parents to not run a business alone as she is a woman and that too unmarried. Also in terms of religious beliefs, staunch Hindus may not visit Rebecca's parlour thinking their religiosity would be compromised.

Besides these issues, if entrepreneurship is placed alone, it is certainly a male-dominated industry. As much as it is an economic industry it is equally a cultural one. It is commonly found that a huge number of women entrepreneurs in India take up businesses which are attributed as easily manageable and ones which do not alter much of their femininity. Hence, women are generally seen working in the areas of cloth making, handicrafts, food products, beautification, etc. These emphasize work which evidently show an extension of their domestic competence in which they are apt. There is nothing wrong in taking the same to the market and making an earning out of it, however it hardly helps in the overhauling of the existing perceptions of femininity and masculinity and what is created and stays is a gendered occupation. Thus, we find men to be involved in entrepreneurship which validates their identities of the patriarchs of Indian society. As Bruni et al. (2004: 407) puts it, 'entrepreneurial action is an archetype of social action and, as the institutionalization of values and symbols, it can be related to gender for a cross-reading of how gender and entrepreneurship are culturally produced and reproduced in social practices.' The behaviour exhibited in gendered services is enacted as situated practices in symbolic spaces of the public, private, gender, entrepreneurship, etc. And men certainly would not like to be present in the smaller enterprises known for being women centric, in fear of their identity as men being questioned.

In fact the presence of men in the beauty industry or men running such industries as cited in Rebecca's account are not men who are heterosexual. Such ventures are not generally considered to be masculine enough for men. In spaces where the image of masculinity runs sharply, a man needs to carefully consider starting a beauty salon if he wishes to project a heterosexual, unambiguous, 'he-man' image (Ahl, 2006). 'Though men do work in the service industry, their participation still remains lesser than women due to societal constrains'. (Swinney et al., 2006).

Further issues which entrepreneurs, particularly women face, are managing their employees. With no proper and efficient norms introduced by the government to assist the lives of such employers in the informal sector, many have no option but to look for different jobs all the time. It also hampers the progress of the present employer. In Rebecca's case, besides the salary and the personal social support that she provides, she is unable to protect their lives through social security (health provisions, pension, fixed income etc.).

Finally this paper, before placing some recommendations and suggestions for facilitating migrant women entrepreneurs (and workers) in an equitable way, looks at the problem of being a migrant from the North-East in a mega city. A report published in *The Times of India* on 24 January 2014 (timesofindia.indiatimes.com/city/delhi/81-of-northeast-women-harassed-in-Delhi-Survey/articleshow/29270244.cms), based on a survey conducted by Jamia Millia Islamia, mentions that 'sixty per cent of women, who have migrated from northeast India to the four metros: Delhi, Mumbai, Kolkata and Bangalore – have reported harassment and unfair discrimination on a daily basis. While 23 per cent of respondents said they have been harassed by landlords, 42 per cent said they faced verbal abuse. A total of 26 per cent reported heckling and molestation'. This survey pointed out that migrant women face deprivation, hardship, racial discrimination and abuse which are extremely pronounced among women from the North-East.[4] The North-East for many in the mainland is an idea. Majority of the people are ill-informed about the people of the North-East. Acharya in the review of a book published in 2012 on migration from the North-East says, 'The region was and is still treated as a frontier province inhabited by exotic people alien to the mainland culture and civilization lacking linkages and integration with the heartland. Many find it difficult to locate the provinces and the people as part of "India" ' (http: //www.newasiabooks.org/review/northeast-migrants-delhi).

Many people including women come from the North-East due to many pull and push factors. One of the major push factors is the rampant insurgency, violence and unrest that makes the people from these areas to view a metropolis like Delhi, as a safe haven with multiple choices, be it in education, job opportunities, business ventures, etc. This can be seen as the pull factors also, as due to globalization the possibilities of survival have increased manifold, attracting people from the fringes and small towns. In fact, in Manipur itself, government-run schools are showing huge amount of decline in their delivery. It has been noted that about classes worth 100 days in a year are not conducted. This is due to the socio-political situation of the region which will lead to adverse consequences in the future (Chandra, 2010: http: //www.countercurrents.org/

chandra 081210.htm). This is observed in the case of Rebecca too, where due to suffering from a bad education system, her family decided to shift her to a better school in Delhi.

However, such influxes also bring to notice the kind of interests generated when ethnic minorities are placed in modern Indian cities like Delhi, along with the question of identity and citizenship in contemporary India. The 'main-landers' view this movement for survival as an encroachment of their space from the borders.

The ethnic identity, language, religion, etc. act as deterrents and the mainlanders resort to racial discrimination to assert their spaces and own identity as superior and hence in possession of authority. Words like 'chinky', 'sexy' are usually thrown at women (men too) perceiving them as women with low morals, as they understand it. It is found that due to the absence of strict patriarchal norms on the North-East women in their own societies where women's views and opinions are valued, these at the migrated space works against them, where men think of them to be loose which makes them vulnerable to sexual and mental abuse. This is part of what Chandra calls as 'social profiling'.

Beauty salons, like that of Rebecca's, run by people of the North-East are seen as places available for illegal sexual activities. It is, indeed difficult to run a business due to such preconceived scenarios.

It is never easy for a migrant woman from the North-East to set up a business. The issues mentioned above to explain the behaviour towards migrant women from the North-East says amply about the ordeals migrant women entre-preneurs had to face. With the government interventions not having enough strength, migrant women resort to safer means like taking protection of their men while dealing with professional situations or in their day-to-day dealings. Moreover, women who are migrant workers also do not find any solace in terms of safety and security. Not only are their jobs ill protected, they have to face harassment, (racial, sexual and mental) due to their physical and social distinc-tiveness. Their vulnerability to such assaults remains unchecked.

The Way Forward

This paper with more investigations of similar kinds in the future proposes to put together a few suggestions which may further be revisited and revised. Though the Government of India has, under the Ministry of Micro Small and Medium Enterprises, Department of Women and Child Development Programme, etc. presented various schemes for women, yet there are many loop holes which need to be worked on.

In the light of poor, irrelevant and ineffective government policies, to start a business in any part of the country outside their own state for migrant women is a concern that needs to be dealt with seriously and meticulously. The creation of newer or amended schemes and policies may give respite and hope to, many eager to enter such ventures. The role of civil society bodies, NGOs, corporate houses practicing CSR (Corporate Social Responsibility) in the realization of newer and progressive policy implementation can also be of immense signifi-cance if they act as unbiased consultants and mediators in the progress of migrant women entrepreneurs.

In view of this the following suggestions are placed here:

- Any entrepreneur requires a continuous flow of funds not only for setting up of his/her business, but also for successful operation as well as regular upgradation/modernization of his/her unit. Although the government (both at the central and state level) has been undertaking several steps to cater to this, yet due to their weak credit-worthiness and weak economic base of women migrants, it becomes difficult to obtain financial assistance from the commercial banks and financial institutions. The process of obtaining loans for migrant women should be made more flexible without collaterals.
- Government income generating activities should be integrated with other problems of the small entrepreneurs like the problem of raw material, skilled manpower, marketing, and utilization of capacity.
- In addition to the special schemes for women entrepreneurs, various government schemes for MSMEs should provide certain special incentives and concessions for migrant women entrepreneurs. The government should give relaxations to migrant women to facilitate their participation.
- Entrepreneurship Development Programmes to cater to the needs of potential women entrepreneurs should have special components for migrant women.
- By and large government policies are more idealistic than practical. Even though they are designed keeping every human in mind, the access of migrants to these government welfare schemes is non-existent. Ration cards, health insurance and pension schemes are luxuries they can only dream of. In view of this for any state its social security schemes and social services should be extended to the migrant and particularly to women migrant entrepreneurs and workers, who are not part of any scheme. The social services like water, electricity, LPG connection, etc and social security schemes like old age pensions, health insurance, death and disability pension should be treated as fundamental entitlements for migrants who are denied this in absence of valid identity. It is also recommended that these schemes need to be more sensitive towards the migrant entrant.
- The government should strictly usher in universality of identity. Any address of one's residence or place of work should be treated as an address representing one's nation. This and only this can give them a universal identity. The government needs to make strict mention in their policies about the validity of such identities in black and white, so that one is not abused while trying to procure a scheme in a different state than one's own.
- We are concerned here about four elements i.e. migrant, women, North-East and entrepreneur. Intervention from government is vital in all these four. The government has different Ministries looking after them with different policies and schemes. Here a convergence of the schemes in all these Ministries is strongly recommended.
- Notwithstanding the government's attempt to bring migrants under existing government schemes it is high time that the government should form specific health and social welfare schemes for protection of migrants.

- The government also needs to sensitize the implementers in all levels and sections about the diverse nature of the procurer, more so if one is a migrant, a woman and from the fringes. Such officials/implementers should be orientated and trained to address people of different gender, ethnicities, identities, religions, spaces as simply citizens and provide equal attention. On not doing so, strict action in terms of suspension from job, temporary stopping of increment, obstruction of promotion, etc. should be taken. At the same time officials facilitating and helping migrants and women to set up their enterprises should be awarded meritoriously.
- Along with sensitizing administrators and office personnel, the government should also put up community orientation programmes and visits to schools to convince them and create awareness about different cultures, structures, ways of life and teach them to respect and value them. Introducing information of the fringes, the North-East in this context, in the form of textbooks can help young minds from an early age to understand them similarly and appreciate their presence as they do their own. This can help in the acceptance of migrant women and others in the host space by the locals more thoughtfully.
- NGOs, private sector, civil societies can assist the government in better and effective ways. This they have been doing for years in their own way. Volunteers can inquire and look into the existing situations of the migrant entrepreneurs, find out how they manage and provide a concrete report to the government to actually make their situations better.
- Finally, there is a dire need to conduct a survey of the migrant population living in various metro cities across the country. The survey data will help design the policies and schemes more effectively and efficiently.

Conclusion

To conclude, the success stories like that of Rebecca, a migrant woman entrepreneur, are not because the government and the society had helped her achieve it. It is because of their grit and acumen that they have come so far. Sadly to reach this far in life these women did not get the support of the implementers, the banks, and the society at large. It is time that the claim that India makes about unity in diversity is actually practiced and acknowledges their own space to be also the space of their own neighbours from the frontiers of India. This can happen only when we learn to respect and treat fellow migrants, especially women from a different ethnicity, culture and religion as one's own. Thus this effort in creating a conducive environment will change their 'another world' to their 'own world'.

Notes

1. An enterprise is classified as proprietary if an individual is its sole owner and as partnership. It excludes all corporate entities, registered co-operatives, trusts and other legal entities. Going by this NCEUS proposition, Remmei's venture falls under this category.
2. The sole proprietorship is the simplest business form under which one can operate a business. The sole proprietorship is not a legal entity. It simply refers to a person who

owns the business and is personally responsible for its debts. A sole proprietorship can operate under the name of its owner or it can do business under a fictitious name, such as Nancy's Nail Salon. The fictitious name is simply a trade name – it does not create a legal entity separate from the sole proprietor owner.

3. Slovic and Finucane et al explained that an affect heuristic guides a person's perception of risk. Studies of risk perception examine the judgments people make when they are asked to characterize and evaluate hazardous activities and technologies. Narendran for her paper utilized the perception of risk as the fear of being socially penalized by society, which falls under *social risk*.
4. Duncan McDuie-Ra. 2012. Northeast Migrants in Delhi: Race, Refuge and Retail. Amsterdam: Amsterdam University Press.

References

Ahl, H. (2006). 'Why Research on Women Entrepreneurs Needs New Directions?', *Entrepreneurship: Theory and Practice*, 30(5): 595–621.

Bal, G. (2003). 'Transnational Migrants: Punjabi Women in Canada' in Paramjit S. Judge et al. (eds.), *Development, Gender and Diaspora: Context of Globalisation*, Jaipur: Rawat Publications.

Bannerjee, A. and Saraswati Raju (2009). 'Gendered Mobility: Women Migrants and Work in Urban India', *Economic and Political Weekly*, XLIV, 28: 115–23.

Bivens, J.L. and Gammage, S. (2004). 'Will better Workers lead to better Jobs in the Developing Work?', in Avirgan Tony, Bivens Josh L. and Gammage Sarah (eds.) *Good Jobs, Bad Jobs, No Jobs: Labour Markets and Informal Work in Egypt, El Salvador, India, Russia and South Africa*, Washington DC: Economic Policy Institute.

Bruni, A., Gherardi, S. and Poggio, B. (2004). 'Doing Gender, Doing Entrepreneurship: An Ethnographic Account of Intertwined Practices', *Gender, Work and Organisation*, Special Edition: Beyond Boundaries, Vol. 11(4), 406–429.

Finucane, M.L., Alhakami, A., Slovic, P. and Johnson, S.M. (2000). 'The Affect Heuristic in Judgments of Risks and Benefits', *Journal of Behavioral Decision-making*, Vol. 13, 1–17.

International Labour Office (1972). 'Employability in the Global Economy: How Training Matters', *World Employment Report*, Geneva, Available at http: //www.ilo.org

International Labour Office (1997). 'Employment, Incomes and Equality: A Strategy for Increasing Productive Employment in Kenya', *World Employment Report*, Geneva, Available at http: //www.freepatentsonline.com/article/Journal- International-Business-Economics/208535028.html

Mitullah, W.V. and I.N. Wachira (1997). 'Informal Labour in the Construction Industry in Kenya: A Case Study of Nairobi', Available at http: //www.ilo.org/wcmsp5/groups/public/@ed_emp/@emp_policy/@invest/documents/publication/wcms_asist_8175.pdf

Mohapatra, K.K. (2012). 'Women Workers in Informal Sector in India: Understanding the Occupational Vulnerability', *International Journal of Humanities and Social Science*, Vol. 2, No. 21.

Naik, A.K. (2009). Informal Sector and Informal Workers in India, Paper presented at IARIW-SAIM Conference on 'Measuring the Informal Economy in Developing Countries', Nepal: Kathmandu.

Narendran, R. (2011). 'Are the Female Entrepreneurs of Beauty Salons in India, Victims of Bad Publicity?' *International Journal of Diversity in Organisations*, Communities and Nations, Vol. 11(1): 47–56.

Nwaka, G.I. (2005). 'The Urban Informal Sector in Nigeria: Towards Economic Development, Environmental Health and Social Harmony', *Global Urban Development Magazine*, 1(1): 1–11.

Perera, R. (1994). Accommodating Informal Sector Enterprises in the Urban Built-Environment: Introduction. Human Settlements Development Programme, School of Environment, Resources and Development. Bangkok: Asian Institute of Technology, 1–14.

Thapan, M.; Singh, A. and Sreekumar, N. (2014). 'Women's Mobility and Migration Muslim Women Migrants in Jamia Nagar, Delhi', *Economic and Political Weekly*, XLIX, 23: 96–104.

Slovic, P. (1999). 'Trust, Emotion, Sex, Politics and Science: Surveying the Risk-Assessment Battlefield', *Risk Analysis*, Vol. 19(4): 689–701.

Slovic, P.; Finucane, M.L.; Peters, E. and MacGregor, D.G. (2004). 'Risk as Analysis and Risk as Feelings: Some Thoughts about Affect, Reason, Risk and Rationality', *Risk Analysis*, Vol. 24(2): 311–322.

Swinney, J.L.; Runyan, R.C. and Huddleston, P. (2006). 'Differences in Reported Firm Performance by Gender: Does Industry Matter?', *Journal of Development Entrepreneurship*, 11(2): 99–115.

9

Impact of Capacity Building Programmes on Women Entrepreneurs

A Study in Odisha

ARPITA KUMARI MISHRA AND SITA VANKA

Abstract

Capacity building programmes act as powerful tools to overcome the problems faced by women entrepreneurs. They are also the means to make the women's lives better not only in short term but also create space for long-term interaction and building a bond seeking change in women's status (Deborah Eade, 2005). Focusing on this aspect of women and development, the present paper is based on the field data and investigates how capacity building programme affects entrepreneurial performance of women entrepreneurs of Odisha, a state in eastern India. An attempt is also made to understand those factors which constrain or support the effective association in managing the enterprise. Primary data was collected from 106 women entrepreneurs who have been exposed to the programme and had started their enterprises. The results reveal that various socio-economic and demographic characteristics have significant impact on involvement of women entrepreneurs in their enterprise management. The study revealed that entrepreneurial development is a function of the person in interaction with the environment.

Keywords

capacity building, entrepreneurship, women, India.

Introduction

'Capacity Building' refers to an action to create, reform or support activities that facilitate sharing of experiences, knowledge and strategies and such sharing of actions demand and create networks. The capacity building efforts facilitate conscious rise and serve as a site for interaction among women, thereby connecting women across spatial boundaries of home and the village. It is an alternative approach to appraising the success of development interventions. Challenges to women entrepreneurs cover a wide spectrum, including level of education; inter-role conflicts emanating from greater parenting responsibilities, a dearth of financial assistance and socio-cultural constraints (Ghosh and

Cheruvalath, 2007). Although men and women experience personal problems, women recorded more difficulties. This is especially true with regard to a lack of self-confidence and not being taken seriously by providers of funds when applying for funds (Bridge, O'Neill and Cromie, 2003). It is widely acknowledged that women have access to fewer resources than men. In this scenario, F. Stephen and Ammu Josephes has pointed out that such barriers include the harsh economic realities of women's lives, male resistance, women's lack of access to literacy, numeracy and other functional skills. Thus, the challenge in this century is to work towards the economic, social and political development, with many questions emerging about women's development in entrepreneurial contexts.

Capacity building is very important for women entrepreneurs. The issue of capacity is critical and the scale of need is enormous, but appreciation of the problem is low: the link between needs and supply is weak; there is a lack of realistic funding; there is need for support for change; training institutions are isolated – communications are poor; development of teaching materials is inefficient and alternative ways of capacity building are not adequately recognized. (Lafontaine, 2000). Appropriate intervention for capacity building can be devised only if some initial insight has been gained into the general opportunities and constraints that woman entrepreneurs typically face.

Global Scenario

In recent years, the concept of capacity development has received unprecedented attention as a critical goal of international development policy. Though often vaguely defined, the term 'capacity development' has been widely used and accepted by many developments professionals as a way to describe some of the critical roadblocks to reaching the Millennium Development Goals and stimulating sustainable growth in the developing world. 'Capacity Building' is included in the programmes of most international organizations that work in development – the World Bank (World Bank), The United Nations (UN) and non-governmental organizations (NGOs) like Oxfam International. In the UNDP's 2008–2013 'strategic plan for development', capacity building is the 'organization's core contribution to development.' The UNDP promotes a capacity building approach to development in the 166 countries it is active in. Capacity building provides a wide range of different and innovative approaches that enables individuals, organizations, institutions and societies to perform well in what they intend to achieve. Capacity building as a development paradigm is found in almost all countries in Africa, Bangladesh, Germany, Zimbabwe, Uganda, Kenya, Tanzania, Ghana, Indonesia, India, Vietnam, etc.

Indian Scenario

Promotion of small and medium-sized entrepreneurs has been a conscious policy of the government at both the central and state levels in India. Support for small and medium-sized entrepreneurs in India have been fine-tuned over time and have been proactive – anticipating challenges and threats. In the six decades since Independence, it has moved from protection to promotion and, lately, to facilitation and advocacy. Prior to the Economic Reforms of 1991, the focus of small and medium-sized entrepreneurs development policies was mainly on protection (reservation of items for exclusive production by SSIs, for example) and concessional incentives (such as tax rebates and subsidies). With liberalization and the opening up of the markets in 1991, this focus shifted to strengthening the competitive edge and capacity building through facilitation and infrastructure. Major emphasis was placed on quality certification, technology upgrading, and market exposure. In India, with the popularity of liberal discourse on gender, 1990s saw a marked depoliticization of capacity building efforts, influenced by the popularization of gender neutral and gender ameliorative training by bilateral aid agencies, the Indian government and some NGOs. Gender neutral training of women aimed at strengthening skills of women in areas defined by gender-based division of labour, with a view to increasing productivity and income of poor households. For example, training of women on technical aspects of silkworm rearing and dairying, particularly in the area for which they are responsible as per the existing gender-based division of labour. Gender ameliorative training, on the other hand, aims at strengthening capacities of women for improving their day-to-day condition, but not their long-term position vis-à-vis men. Conventional entrepreneurship training of women is an example of gender ameliorative training. Such training programmes aim at teaching women the techno-managerial aspects of managing microenterprises and thereby improving their condition within families and in the markets. In India, there are several such providers, including governmental, non-governmental, and international organizations providing support for the capacity building of women entrepreneurs. For example, SEWA, the Association of Women Entrepreneurs of Karnataka (AWAKE), FICCI [Federation of Indian Chambers of Commerce and Industry] Ladies Organization (FLO), Myrada, Mahila Samakhya, RUSEC in Tamil Nadu, TREAD (Trade Related Entrepreneurship Assistance and Development) envisaged in 9th Five Year Plan in which capacity building is one of the component for self-employed ventures by women.

Odisha Scenario

The Government of India has enacted the Micro, Small and Medium Enterprises Development Act, 2006 with a view to providing a comprehensive legal framework to address the needs of both the manufacturing and the service sector MSMEs, particularly to enable the MSMEs of the country to face the emerging challenges in globalized and competitive market. The Government of Odisha has also notified Industrial Policy Resolution-2007 (IPR-2007) which provides for specific fiscal as well as non-fiscal interventions to develop the Micro, Small and Medium Enterprises of the State. Despite abundant natural resources and human resources, the growth of MSMEs in Odisha is not at par with the national and international standards. The new wave of industrialization being witnessed in Odisha today, especially in the metal, power, cement, petro-chemical, IT, tourism sector and the current growth in the services sector provide enormous opportunity for the growth of Micro, Small and Medium Enterprises in the State. To overcome the hurdles, in the development of MSMEs in the state, the Government of Odisha has declared a policy known as Odisha MSME Development Policy-2009. The policy intended to maximize growth of existing MSMEs, to reduce sickness of MSMEs, to provide opportunities as well as promote local entrepreneurial talent, to maximize avenues for employment generation, etc. Under this policy, women entrepreneurs are also encouraged when women entrepreneurs setting up new MSE shall be entitled to additional two years fiscal incentives relating to VAT under IPR-07 subject to being otherwise eligible for the said incentive and also subject to the overall absolute limits prescribed for the said incentive under IPR-07.

In addition to the government, the NGO sector in Odisha gained momentum in the early 1980s for its socio-economic programmes, especially in developing and promoting people's organizations and community centred activities. Establishment of Grain Bank, Seed Bank, Community Fund and formation of committees such as Village Health Committees, Joint Forest Management Committees, etc. to protect the interest of the communities were among the activities that were undertaken. NGOs have played a significant role in addressing issues of women's empowerment in the state through savings in the form of kind and cash which began in mid-1980s involving women members of the households by forming 'Mahila Mandals'. This was initiated for collective learning and to act as vehicle for fostering collective bargaining by some of the leading NGOs like CYSD (Centre for Youth and Social Development), Gram Vikas, and Fellowship during early 1990s. While the entry of NABARD in Odisha was in mid-1990s did encourage the bankers and NGOs. Since 2000. Centre for development Research and training (CENDERET), major donors like UNDP United Nations Development Programme), DFID (Department of International Development), EU (European Union), WFP (World Food Programme) and INGOs (International Non-Government Organization) like CARE, IGSSS (Indo German Social Service Society), Action-Aid, etc. have taken interest in development of women. Against this background, the issue has gained significance which demands attention of scholars and studies in this direction.

Review of Literature

This study is centred on the issue of women entrepreneurship and the changes that occurred through capacity building process. Capacity is the ability of individual, organization and societies to perform functions, solve problems and set and achieve goals. Capacity building builds on and harnesses rather than replaces indigenous capacity. It is, thus, based on learning and the acquisition of skills and resources among individual and organization (Vallejo, 2006).

A majority of research points to the fact that capacity building has a significant impact to entail the sustainable creation, utilization and retention of that capacity, in order to reduce poverty, enhance self-reliance and improve people's lives (Vallejo, 2006; Watkin and Kevin, 1995; Revivo-Steiner, 2006). These studies were empirical in nature and aimed at different geographies and sectors.

Literature evidenced that capacity building programme occurred primarily at the organizational level. The major thrust that capacity building provides to organizations is to develop skills and resources so that they can achieve their objectives and serve their stakeholders more effectively. The capacity building activities include improved governance (accountability systems and leadership), administration (human resource, financial management, and legal matters), planning (positioning, strategy development, innovation, project management-including project initiation, development and implementation), improving access to funding and income (marketing, fundraising, procurement and income generation) and more effective delivery of services(sector specific skills, partnership and collaboration, advocacy and policy change) (McKinsey, 2001; Parker, 1993; Lafontaine, 2000).

Stuides also highlighted the impact of capacity building on women entrepreneurs and quite a few case studies are found in this direction (Deborah Eade, 2007; DAC Network on Governance, 2006; Sakiko Fukuda-parr, Carios lopes and Khalid Malik, 2002; Radhakrishnan, 2008). Literature raised different issues, some of which are common to all, others were comparisons and contrasts. In particular, in terms of what can be learnt from them relates to an understanding of capacity and capacity building. How to go about building, developing and mobilizing capacities; how evaluation is done in capacity development programmes and processes, etc. There are several components of capacity building which help women entrepreneurs to establish and run enterprises successfully. Some of them are to build self-confidence; provide guidance to women entrepreneurs to start and manage the enterprise; promote women entrepreneurs' opportunities and capacity to effectively participate in the economy, including low-income women and women in small and remote villages; provide examples on how the private sector can encourage and build the capacity of women entrepreneurs; expand their access to extension service credit, education, information and training and influence the process of knowledge creation; to invest in building the productive capacity of women entrepreneurs through networks, training which can pull women out of poverty, increase efficiency and empower them to engage in local, national and international markets; and help women improve their marketing activities in order to strengthen the export competitiveness of products and services of their small and micro enterprises. Capacity building does not begin and end with NGOs, or with donors nor with 'civil society'. Rather, capacity building involves the whole network of relationships in society: within, between, and among households, neighbourhood, grassroots or community-based organization, union, training institutions, research bodies, government ministries, the private sector, NGOs and donor agencies – whether official or non-governmental – with creating new relationships of mutuality and reciprocity within a given society and beyond and promote the setting up of funds for women-owned businesses, to improve their capacity to take advantage of global and regional trade agreements.

Studies also reviewed the concept of capacity building, advocacy for capacity building, equated capacity building with training and described the approaches to capacity building. It was interesting to note that capacity building from a strategic, statewide perspective is complex (Loza, 2004). There are many dimensions to capacity building, which are further complicated by the variations of geography. Donors themselves contribute to this complexity, creating a patchwork of funding and approaches based on their particular interests, geographies and philosophies.

Literature has also pointed out that analysis of capacity and capacity building approached are carried out through three different levels of analysis

(UNDP, 1994) – the individual (human skill), the organizational and the institutional. The recognition of the relation between these three dimensions or levels is fundamental in the emerging paradigm for capacity building among the international donor community.

Capacity building indicators acquire operational value when they refer to concrete development objectives and the actors towards which capacity building project are directed (Eade, 2007). In abstraction, indicators lose analytic utility; thus, to build indicators it is essential to address two central questions: (i) capacity for what? (ii) capacity for whom? Indicators of capacity of a statistical agency, for example, will be different from indicators of organizational capacity of public bureaucracies.

Studies also emphasized the relevance of gender equality to capacity building. The feminist framework used for capacity building of women entrepreneurs was focused in studies (Rathakrishnan, 2008; Kiran Mirchandani, 1999). Feminist capacity development provides an opportunity to open up the frameworks and policies of capacity building and development to gender issues. The authors cautioned against a gendered approach to feminist capacity development so that the interplay between the private and the public spheres of people's lives are brought to the forefront of discussing the necessary capabilities for overcoming disparities. The study drew attention to four contributions of feminist capacity development: (1) enabling the personal inside the notion of individual capacity; (2) supporting women organizing, and not organizing women; (3) stimulating learning and well-being of society as a whole, not just among women; and (4) trying new roles, often with a basis in leadership. These four contributions show that gender equality matters to the core capabilities envisioned by capacity development strategies and assessments. Some examples were cited from a few countries but realistically, the authors recognized that the work just started and learnt as more capacity development efforts come under the gender lens. The literature; thus, evidences studies in isolation and call for empirical studies to examine the impact of capacity building on women who are beginning to take on roles which are not gender determined so as to contribute to the society and the development process of the economy.

The Study

The study aims to examine the impact of capacity building on women entrepreneurs in Odisha from a gender perspective. More specifically, the demographic profile, motivation, problems faced and the impact of capacity building on women entrepreneurs was studied.

Methodology

Sampling Techniques and Sampling Procedure

Purposive sampling was used for the study and the sample size was 106. To achieve the objectives of the present study, the list of entrepreneurs who had already attended the programme and who have been at least one year in the business was obtained from the institutions like government institutions, district industrial centres, non-government institutions and nationalized banks engaged in capacity building of women entrepreneurs in Odisha.

Data Sources

Primary and secondary data was used to collect data for the study. The secondary data was used to clarify concepts and in this context the books, journals, periodicals, magazines, internet browsing was extensively reviewed. Primary data was collected through different tools – open-ended interview, structured questionnaire to collect data from 106 women entrepreneurs

Data Analysis

The data collected was processed with the help of SPSS. Descriptive and statistical methods were used for the presentation of the data. The responses were tabulated and then transferred into tables. The relevant materials obtained from primary and secondary sources were analysed to unfold the various dimensions relating to the central theme of the study. Data from the questionnaires were coded, investigated for authenticity, analysed and presented in useful outputs, such as frequency tables to draw conclusions and to make recommendations for the development of women entrepreneurs.

Data was collected from the following institutions from Odisha:

1. Centre for Youth and Social Development (CYSD)
2. Swayamshree Micro-Credit Services (SMCS)
3. Rural Development Self-Employment Training Institute (RUDESTI)
4. Udyog Vikas (UV)

Centre for Youth and Social Development (CYSD)

The Centre for Youth and Social Development (CYSD) is a non-government, non-profit civil society organization working for the development of the deprived and marginalized sector in Odisha, one of the most backward states of India. Since its inception in 1982, CYSD has come a long way. Starting with mobilizing social change with the help of local change agents, it has evolved into an 'enabling' institution having specific skills in participatory research and competencies in development management at various levels. CYSD's approaches to promote and strengthen peoples' institutions undertake micro-level planning, strengthening capacities, facilitating support, and a pro-poor advocacy, converges with the mainstream development programmes.

Swayamshree Micro-Credit Services (SMCS)

Promoted by CYSD to provide credit, financial training and support to promote micro-enterprises, the Swayamshree Micro-Credit Services (SMCS) is a not-for-profit micro finance institution in Odisha which focuses on SHG-driven livelihood promotion. The objectives include the provision of proximate, flexible, and sustainable services for the poor to have access to a range of financial as well as other complementary services and products appropriately designed to open up new opportunities for them to improve livelihoods, increase income, develop assets and capacities, create new space and identities, thereby promoting their economic and social well-being and empowering them to take control over their lives.

Rural Development Self-Employment Training institute (RUDSETI)

Rural Development and Self-Employment Training Institute (RUDSETI), a unique initiative in mitigating the problem of unemployment was taken way back in 1982 jointly by Sri Dharmasthala Manjunatheshwara Educational Trust, Syndicate Bank and Canara Bank. Providing solutions to the unemployed youth aspiring to take up self-employment sets RUDSETI apart among training/entrepreneurship development institutes. The following services are provided in an innovative and cost effective manner, with a spirit of service:

- Creating awareness on self-employment/entrepreneurship
- Developing motivation and positive attitude
- Training to acquire hard skills and soft/life skills
- Handholding for establishment and successful running of enterprise
- Linkages with banks for financial assistance

The training modules of RUDSETI have been accepted as standard modules by the Ministry of Rural Development, NIRD, SIDBI, NABARD, Department of Industries and Commerce, KSWDC, etc. Training modules of RUDSETI are so designed that the Entrepreneurship Development is achieved through Human Resource Development. RUDSETI offers more than 60 types of Entrepreneurship Development Programmes (EDPs) in various avenues. All the programmes are of short duration intervention ranging from one to six weeks.

Udyog Vikas (UV)

Udyog Vikas (UV) is an organization supported by the Government of Odishaa (Department of Industries), Small Industries Development Bank of India (SIDBI), Xavier Institute of Management (*XIM*), Bhubaneswar, Small Industries Service Institute (*SISI*), Cuttack, National Bank for Agriculture and Rural Development (*NABARD*), All India Radio and Doordarshan (Regional and National). The Institute is registered under the Societies of Registration Act XXI of 1860 bearing No. 21389/193 of 2001 at IGR, Cuttack and Odisha.

The services provided by them are:

- Providing self-employment to urban and rural unemployed youth.
- Enterprising culture building to promote enterprise culture in the Indian society by reaching out, information, educating, motivating and training mindsets of the people of Odisha in general poor, unemployment youth in particular.
- Enriching the skill by training and hands on practical works
- Providing income generation opportunities to the women folk
- Providing marketing linkage for the products of the entrepreneurs
- Providing hand-held support to new entrepreneurs
- To organize various trainings and campaigns for creation of awareness, identification of opportunities, harnessing the potential
- Enriching the skill by training and hands practical works
- Women empowerment to empower the women by specially assisting them in startup of their enterprise/income generating units of their own, thus

broadening their outlook on Literature, Anthology and related educational and cultural activities.

- Small enterprise promotion and development encouraging youths, triggering them by media and further driving them towards enterprises through awareness camps, personal counseling, training on business management and skill.

The Results

The data that was collected from the respondents was analysed in terms of the profile, opinions/perceptions on the various dimensions of the study. The demographic profile of the respondents is given in Table 1. The table reveals that majority of them (53.8%) belonging to the age group of 40–49 years were married (76.4%), had education up to graduation (44.4%), with very few women having professional qualifications (12.3%). Most of them were housewives (64.6%) and had the support of the family (68.0%). Women themselves initiated the business idea (57.5%) and a majority of them were into feminine activities in terms of enterprise and were sole proprietors. They started with their personal savings (28.4%) and also borrowed from the bank (27.4%). It is but natural for women to think of entrepreneurial career late in their life as they have to satisfy the societal norms of marriage and convincing the family.

Table 1

Demographic Profile of the Respondents

Particulars	*Classification*	*Number*	*Percentage*
Age group	20–39	29	27.4
	40–49	57	53.8
	50–59	20	18.9
Marital status	Married	81	76.4
	Single	16	15.1
	Widow	9	8.5
Educational qualification	Primary	2	1.9
	Secondary	10	9.4
	Higher Secondary	32	30.2
	Graduation	47	44.4
	Post-Graduation	15	14.2
Professional qualification	Certificate	15	14.2
	Diploma	6	5.7
	Degree	13	12.3
	Not applicable	72	68.0
Respondent doing immediately before starting the business	Student	9	8.9
	Unemployed	23	21.7
	Employed	4	3.8
	Housewife	68	64.6
	Another business	2	1.9

Cont'd...

...Cont'd

Types of family	Nuclear family	85	80.2
	Joint family	21	19.9
Family members support	Yes	72	68.0
	No	34	32.1
Form of support	Manual help	33	31.2
	Emotional support	40	37.8
	Financial help	26	24.6
	Advice	7	6.7
Initiated this business idea	Myself	61	57.5
	My husband	35	33.6
	Other family members	8	7.5
	Friends	1	.9
	Taken over already established business	1	.9
Type of enterprise	Beauty parlour	15	14.2
	Painting and handicraft	5	4.7
	Car filling/petrol pump	1	.9
	Gems and artificial jewellery	7	6.6
	Clay pots	1	.9
	Food preservation units	2	1.9
	Boutique	12	11.3
	Educational intuition	6	5.7
	Garment shop	6	5.7
	Brass-bell metal & appliqué work	5	4.7
	Stationary shop	9	8.5
	Detergent makers	3	2.8
	Screen painting	1	.9
	Office stationary shop	1	.9
	Food processing unit	8	7.5
	Jute product manufacturing	11	10.4
	Paper cover bag – envelope and file-making	2	1.9
	Snacks shop	2	1.9
	Utensil & silver ornaments shop	1	.9
	Web designing	1	.9
	Fitness centre	2	1.9
	Interior decorator	1	.9
	Restaurant	1	.9
	Pharmacy store	2	1.9
	Food catering	1	.9
Forms of ownership	Individual proprietorship	105	99.1
	Partnership	1	.9
Nature of enterprise building	Part of house	42	39.6
	Separate building	64	60.4

Cont'd...

...Cont'd

Time spent in business	Up to 4 hours	–	–
	4–8 hours	75	70.8
	8–12 hours	28	26.5
	Above 12 hours	3	2.9
Main source of start-up funding	Personal saving	30	28.4
	Family	14	13.3
	Borrowed from relatives or friend	9	8.5
	Borrowed from bank	29	27.4
	Micro-finance inheritance	24	22.7

Motivation

Motivation for women to start business was inherent in them. Income generation and supporting the family (76.4%) along with leading an independent life (58.3%) were the motivating factors to start their entrepreneurial journey. Thus, they can be categorized as forced entrepreneurs with focused objective in starting businesses.

Table 2

Factors Motivating them to Start the Business

Factors motivating them to start business	*Number*	*Percentage*
Desire to be self-employed and to become independent	62	58.5
Income generation and to support the family	81	76.4
Had an interest in the line of work and to exploit an opportunity	57	53.8
Had training and entrepreneurial qualification in the business area	56	52.8
Encouragement from family and friends to go into a business	41	38.7
Threat of losing job	26	24.6
Unemployment	42	39.6
Freedom from supervision	43	40.6
Sudden death of earning member in the family	3	2.8
No other income source	42	39.6
Relatively favourable policy environment	28	26.4

(Multiple responses from the respondents and hence the total does not add to 100.)

Problems Faced by Women Entrepreneurs

The moment an entrepreneur conceives the idea to start his/her own unit; he/she has to work hard against heavy odds. The problems of industries whether in small, medium or large sectors, are almost similar but their nature and scope vary. In the case of women entrepreneurs the problems gets compounded because certain problems have gender dimensions attached to it. The management of domestic commitment and child care support are the two issues where women have to play a more active role. This coupled with the narrow vision of the society in still accepting women in a separate entity as an entrepreneur makes the life of a women entrepreneur all the more difficult.

In order to find out the constraints/challenges women entrepreneurs face, an attempt was made to examine the problems (Table 3).

Table 3

Constraints/Challenges

Resistance from husband/family at time of start	32	30.2
Dual duties	68	64.2
Male dominance	54	50.9
Lack of experience	53	50
Identifying the available resources	68	64.1
Lack managerial quality	38	35.8
Less support from bank	52	49.0
Lack of working space	72	67.9
Cut throat competition	96	90.5
Indifferent attitude of customers	39	36.8
Lack of travelling mobility	55	51.9
Lack of negotiation and bargaining skill	22	20.8
Problem with accessibility of place of work	32	30.9
Hesitation of male labour to work under lady boss	53	50
Collection of payment	36	33.9
Lack of negotiation and bargaining skill	12	11.3
Not aware of legal formalities	79	74.5

(Multiple responses from the respondents and hence the total does not add upto 100.)

Cut throat competition, lack of awareness about legal formalities, lack of working space followed by the resource crunch and the dual duties restricted women from entering in to business. From a gender perspective, it is evident that women are not involved in major economic decisions and, hence, knowledge of legal matters understandably constrains them. Added to this, competition in the post globalization era, presupposes performance with quality thus, restricting women to enter into business. Education and exposure of women poses a problem to know about the schemes/projects for funding from government and other sources, which get compounded by the household responsibilities of women.

Impact of Capacity Building Programmes on Women Entrepreneurs

The impact of capacity building on women is seen in terms of its impact on individual level, physical level, marketing level and technical level.

Individual Factors (Table 4): Individually, women benefitted through their participation in the capacity building programme (77.4%). It helped them in getting financial assistance (72.7%) and in some the programme increased their awareness levels (71.7%).

Table 4
Individual Factors

Has your business in any way improved after you participated in the training	82	77.4
Increased awareness	76	71.7
Helped turn hobby into business	32	30.2
Helped in understanding of the nitty and gritty of law and regulation related to business	57	53.8
Help in getting financial assistance	77	72.7
Help to perfect oneself	32	30.2
Enhanced quality of products	19	17.9
Increased professionalism	42	39.7
Take decisions	22	20.8
Help to know own weaknesses	19	17.9
Know how to tackle problems	24	22.7
More customer-oriented	38	35.9
Helped in finding new markets	35	33.1
Increased investment	39	36.8

(Multiple Responses and hence the total does not add to 100.)

Physical Factors: Women could avail loans from the bank (60.4%) and could also get the needed raw material (43.4%) in terms of the physical factors (Table 5).

Table 5
Physical Factors

Availability of raw material	46	43.4
Availability of modern technologies	14	13.3
Adequate technical support for machinery utilization	22	20.8
Availability of labour, particularly skilled labour	37	34.9
Availability of loan from the bank	64	60.4
Assistance from government initiatives by funding of loans and granting of subsidies	21	19.8
Availability of working capital	5	4.7

Marketing Factors: 50.9 per cent per cent of women entrepreneurs have improved in negotiating and bargaining skill, 39.6 per cent per cent of women entrepreneurs got adequate information on changing markets (Table 6).

Table 6
Marketing Factors

Good market facility	23	21.7
Good transportation facility	19	17.9
Good demand for the product/service in that area	34	32.0
Adequate information on changing markets	42	39.6
Improvement negotiation and bargaining skill	54	50.9

Technical Factors: 71.7 per cent of women entrepreneurs have mentioned that they have improved in keeping proper books of account which is major task in business activities; 61.4 per cent of women entrepreneurs have registered their industries. Lack of business background makes women technically weak and it is here that they look for technical competence through capacity building (Table 7).

Table 7

Technical Factors

Adequate skill	48	45.3
Selling new products/services	39	36.8
Adequate training	48	45.3
Easy to manage employee	22	20.7
Extend business to other town or cities	13	12.3
Registration of industries	65	61.4
Provide working space	56	52.9
Enhanced in keeping proper books of account	76	71.7

Conclusion

An attempt has been made in this paper to investigate the impact of capacity building on women entrepreneurs. It is an established fact that more and more women are seeking economic opportunity and self-determination through enterprise creation. First and foremost, the issue of poverty particularly affecting women from economically and socially marginalized group and second, the broader issue of human rights violation affecting all groups of women are the two major problems which confront women in the context of the globalization of the economy. Thus, the challenge in this century is to work towards the economic, social and political development. The assumption is not that women do not have any capacity and that it therefore needs to be 'built' from scratch rather, women learn each day through the very process of struggling for survival, security and autonomy. However, women's learning can be enhanced if appropriate facilitation though external intervention is done at the appropriate time. In this connection, the concept of capacity building contributes through training and networking initiatives as a possible route to building courage and confidence among women.

The study clearly brought out the need for formal education and exposure of women for successful entrepreneurial journey. The family support also provides the much needed support in enterprise creation. It is established that women do have the necessary life experience and life skills to understand and manage businesses. Getting into the *male preserve* of business like the IT industry, pharma and manufacturing, etc. requires skill and orientation of a different nature, which appears to be lacking among the Odisha women entrepreneurs. Agencies engaged in capacity building need to keep this in mind while designing capacity building programmes for women in regions reflect traditional cultures as in Odisha. As a corollary to this, women are forced to depend on their personal savings, to enter into small businesses. Capacity building programmes should invite financial institutions, banks and other escort services not only to throw light on the available schemes for borrowing, but also to educate them on the basic financial literacy. Motivationally, the inherent advantage of a woman centres around the family and support to the family. Hence, capacity building can also highlight the mechanisms of work life balance and managing the competition through networking and exposure. Since, entrepreneurial development is an offshoot of the entrepreneur with the environment, capacity building programmes must aim at creating such an environment so as to involve women as equal partners in the development process of the economy.

References

Abimbola, O.H., Emmanuel, C.O. and Ahmadu, F.O. (2007). 'Women Entrepreneurship in Nigeria: Challenges and Prospects for Quality of Life', *Gender and Behaviour*, 5(1): 1,089–1,102.

Abor, J. and Biekpe, N. (2006). 'SME's access to Debt Finance: A Comparison between Male-owned and Female-owned Business in Ghana', *The International Journal of Entrepreneurship and Innovation*, 7(2): 105–112.

Affholder, J. and Box, D.M. (2004). 'Struggles of Female Entrepreneurs, Allied Academics International Conference', *Proceedings of the Academy of Entrepreneurship*, 10(1).

Ahl, H. (2006). 'Why Research on Women Entrepreneurs Needs New Directions', *Entrepreneurship: Theory and Practice*, 30(5): 595–621.

Anna, L., Chandler, G., Jansen, E. and Mero, N. (2000). 'Women Business Owners in Traditional and Non-traditional Industries', *Journal of Business Venturing*, 15(3): 279–303.

Baeva, M. (2004). 'Export: Challenge to Bulgarian Women Entrepreneurs', Club of Women Entrepreneurs and Managers. Bulgaria: Montréal.

Berger, A.N. and Udell, G.F. (1998). 'The Economics of Small Business Finance: The Roles of Private, Equality and Debt Markets in the Financial Growth Cycle', *Journal of Banking and Finance,* 22(6–8): 613–673.

Bolger, Joe (2000). 'Capacity Development: Why, What and How', *Canandian International Development Agency, Occasional Series*. Vol. 1(1).

Bureau of Statistics Lesotho (2004). Gender Statistics Report, Demographic, Labor and Social Statistics, Lesotho: Maseru.

Business Line, 10 May 2004 and 5 June 2002; <http: //www.bisnetindia.com/ficci/general/ficci-awards/ficci-awards.pdf>; and *The Hindu*, 17 May 2004 and 17 June 2002.

Buttner, E.H. and Moore, D.P. (1997). 'Women's Organizational Exodus to Entrepreneurship: Self-reported Motivations and Correlates with Success', *Journal of Small Business Management*, 35: 34–46.

Cannon, T. (2002). *Enterprise: Creation, Development and Growth*, UK: Butterworth.

Carter, N.; Gartner, W.; Shaver, K. and Gatewood, E. (2003). 'The Career Reasons of Nascent Entrepreneurs', *Journal of Business Venturing*, 18: 13–39. 1991.

DAC Network on Governance, 'The Challenge of Capacity Development: Working Towards Good Practice', February 2006.

Eade, Deborah (2005). *Capacity-Building: An Approach to People Centered Development*, UK and Ireland: Oxfam UK and Ireland. 30–39.

Eade, Deborah (2007). 'Capacity Building: Who Builds Whose Capacity?' *Development in Practice*, Vol. 17(4/5): 630–639.

ENERGIA/United Nations Development Programme. (2006). 'Economic Empowerment of Women through Small Business Enterprises, Gender and Sustainable Energy', Enhancement for Employment Project in Nepal Report.

Fukuda-Parr, S., Lopes, C., Malik, K. (eds). (2002) (UNDP). *Capacity for Development: New Solution to Old Problems*. London: Earthscan Publication Ltd.

Georgellis, Y. and Wall, H. (2004). 'Gender Differences in Self-Employment', Working Paper, The Federal Reserve Bank Saint Louis, http: /research.stlousfed.org/wp/1999/1999-008.pdf. [Date of access: 5 October 2008]

Ghosh, P. and Cheruvalath, R. (2007). 'Indian Female Entrepreneurs as Catalysts for Economic Growth and Development', *The International Journal of Entrepreneurship and Innovation,* 8(2): 139–148.

Greene, P.G.; Hart, M.M.; Gatewood, J.E.; Brush, C.G. and Cater, N.M. (2005). 'Women Entrepreneurs: Moving Front and Centre', *An Overview of Research and Theory*, Boston, MA: Boston University.

Hildebrand, Mary E. and Merilee S. Grindle (1994). 'Building Capacity: Challenges for the Public Sector', Harvard University, November 1994, http: //ec.europa.eu/enterprise/entrepreneurship/support_measures/training_education/doc/mini_companies_en.pdf

Ibeh, Ena-Mary (2009). 'Factors Affecting Performance of Women Entrepreneurs', *Journal of Women's Entrepreneurship* 46 *and Education,* 1–2, 39–50.

IFAD (2007 a). Country-Specific grant to the International Labor Organization for the Skills.

ILO (2002). Women and Men in the Informal Economy: A Statistical Picture.

Jalbert, S.E. (2000). Women Entrepreneurs in the Global Economy. [Web:] http: //www. cipe.org/programs/women/pdf/jalbert.pdf. [Date of access: 24 October 2009].

Kantor, P. (2001). Promoting Women's Entrepreneurship Development based on Good South African Programmes: Some Experiences from North to South, SEED working paper no. p. International Labor Office. Geneva.

Katepa-Kalala, P. (1999). Assessment Report on 'Women and Poverty and Economic Empowerment of Women. [Web] http: //www.uneca.org/ eca_resorces/publication/women. [Date of access: 22 November 2007]

Kock, A. (2008). A Framework for the Development of Women Entrepreneurship in the Ekurhuleni District, Potchefstroom: North-West University. (Unpublished MBA mini-dissertation).

Kuratko, Donald, F. and Hodgetts, Richard M. (2009). *Entrepreneurship in the New Millennium*, 6th Edition, Ohio, USA: Thomson South-Western.

Lafontaine, A. (2000). Assessment of Capacity Development Efforts of Other Development Cooperation Agencies. Capacity Development Initiative, GEF-UNDP Strategic Partnership.

Lawson, S. (2008). 'Women Hold Up Half the Sky', Goldman Sachs Global Economics, Paper No. 164, 2, 4 March. The Goldman Sachs Group, Available at: http: //www2.goldmansachs.com/ideas/demographic-change/women-hold-up-half-of-the-sky.pdf. Last accessed on 31 August 2008.

Loza, J. (2004). 'Business-Community Partnership: The Case for Community Organization Capacity Building', *Journal of Business Ethics*. 53(3).

McKinsey and Company (2001). *Effective Capacity Building in Non Profit Organisations*, Venture Philanthropy Partners, 36.

Mehra, Rekha (1997). 'Women, Empowerment, and Economic Development', *Annals of the American Academy of Political and Social Science*, Vol. 554, The Role of NGOs: Charity and Empowerment. *The Annals of American Academy of Political and Social Science*. 136–149.

Mirchandani, Kiran (1999). 'Feminist Insight on Gender Work: New Directions in Research on Women and Entrepreneurship', *Gender, Work and Organization Journal*, Vol. 6(4).

OECD (1995). 'Developing Environmental Capacity: A Framework for Donor Involvement'.

Parker, R. (1993). Another Point of View: A Manual on Gender Analysis Training for Grassroots Workers, New York: UNIFEM.

Rathakrishnan, L. (2008). 'Capacity Building of Women Though Tiny Industries' in L. Rathakrishnan (ed.) *Empowerment of Women through Entrepreneurship*, New Delhi: Gyan Publication.

Rathore, B.S. and Chhabra, Rama (1991). 'Promotion of Women Entrepreneurship Training Strategies', *SEDME*, 18(1) March: 1991.

Revivo-Steiner, M. (2006). Women Entrepreneurs: A Growing and Promising Phenomenon, School of Management, Ben Gurion University of the Negev.

Romijn, H.A. (1989). 'Entrepreneurship Training for Small Business in Developing Countries: Some Issues', *Economic and Political Weekly*, Vol. 24 (8): M8–M14.

Setty, E.D. and Moorthy, P. Krishna (2007). *Women Empowerment through Entrepreneurship Development*, New Delhi: Anmol Publication.

Taneja, S. (1990). 'Problems, Perspective and Status of Women Entrepreneurship in North-east Region', Proceeding of 8th National Convention of Women Entrepreneurs, organized by National Alliance of Young Entrepreneurs, New Delhi.

Teskey, G. (2006). 'Capacity Development and State Building: Issues, Evidence and Implications for DFID', Governance and State Development Group, UK, Department for International Development.

UNDP/UNDOALOS (1994). Report on the Consultative Meeting on Training in Integrated Management of Coastal and Marine Areas for Sustainable Development, Sassari, Sardinia, Italy, 21–23 June, 1993, United Nations Development Programme and Division for Ocean Affairs, United Nations, New York.

UNDP/UNDOALOS, 1994, Report on the Consultative Meeting on Training in Integrated Management of Coastal and Marine Areas for Sustainable Development, Sassari, Sardinia,. United Nations Development Programme and Division for Ocean Affairs, United Nations, New York, Italy, 21–23 June 1993.

Universalia (1999), 'Capacity Development: Definitions, Issues and Implications for Planning, Management and Evaluation'.

Vallejo, S.M. (2006). 'Are We Meeting the Challenges for Capacity Building for Managing Ocean and Coasts?' Balboa, Panama.

Verheul, I., Van Stel, A. and Thurik, R. (2004). Explaining Female and Male Entrepreneurship across 29 Countries. SCALES Working Paper, May 2004.

Watkin, Kevin (1995). *The Oxfam Poverty Report*, Oxford, Oxfam.

Welter, F. (2004). 'The Environment for Female Entrepreneurship in Germany', *Journal of Small Business and Enterprise Development*, 11(2): 212–221.

10

Gendered Division of Domestic and Child Work in Dual Earner's Marriage

A Question of Women Agency and Choice

RAMNEET KAUR

Abstract

Marriage is an institution which is fundamentally about gender relations and contributes to one's sense of being masculine and feminine by creating environments for expression of masculine and feminine identity. In marriage, men and women express their gender identity by performing their socially constructed gender roles – men in public sphere through their instrumental role of provider of the family in the outside world, and women in private sphere through their expressive role of housewife within the home. This gendered division of spheres becomes the basis of dividing the domestic tasks between the men and women in marriage. Though women have crossed the divide between the private worlds of home and moved into the public world of work and assumed major roles in running the home but they still have the division of domestic responsibilities in traditional manner suggesting that men do not revise their assumption regarding the distribution of domestic and child care responsibility even when their wives become employed. This paper argues that despite work and earning, women face the gendered division of domestic tasks. This paper has explored how the patriarchal social structure constrained the women choices: making it difficult for them to negotiate their situations and pressurized them to adjust and accept themselves to the choices and options society gives them.

Keywords

choice, gender roles, public private divide, patriarchy, power, socialization, domestic and child care tasks, marriage, multiple roles

Introduction

Kimmel asserts that in marriage husband and wife have their own sphere of responsibilities. His domain is outdoors and her domain is always indoors-kitchen. This make women tend to see the housework as necessary for family maintenance while men tend to see their participation in housework in terms of only helping. Moreover, the question of who serves to whom is closely·

connected with the power relationship between the spouses in marriage. In this paper, I have argued that the power relation between the men and women do not change despite women being working and earnings for the family. I have argued that the power imbalance which results from the gendered division of domestic tasks made it difficult for the women to exercise and express their choices due to which they continue to bear the unequal burden and play multiple roles to fulfil entire domestic and child care responsibilities in marriage.

The study was conducted in year 2012 in randomly selected areas of west Delhi. Through qualitative approach the random sampling was done and semi-structured (personal) interviews were conducted. As many as 100 married women following professions such as doctors, nurses, school teachers, bank employees, and beauticians were contacted at their respective work places for about five–six months. The women belonging to diverse professions were selected to see whether the education and income level makes a difference on division of domestic tasks in marriage.

Feminist approach was adopted because it starts from the women's experiences (Maynard, 2008). Harding asserts that all knowledge is socially situated and some of these objective social locations are better than others as starting point for knowledge. According to Harding, one's social situation enables and sets limit on what one can know. Some social situations are critically unexamined, the dominant ones are more limiting than the others and what makes this situation more limiting is their inability to generate the most critical questions about the received belief. Further, women's lives can provide the starting point for asking new, critical questions not only about their lives but also most importantly the casual relations between them. Starting from women's lives, we can generate questions about why women are assigned caring/emotional work and men the head work (Harding, 2005).

The paper is divided in four sections. Section one: provides the conceptual understanding of gender roles in patriarchal society. Section two: provides the insights from the field. This section examines the narratives from the field showing the gendered division of domestic and child care tasks among the dual earner marriages. Section three: questions the women agency and show how the women choices are regulated by their social circumstances. Section four: offers a conclusion of the study.

Section One: Conceptual Understanding of Gender Roles

Patriarchy is the power of the fathers, a familial social, ideological, political system in which men by force, direct pressure, or through ritual, tradition, law, language, custom, etiquette, education, and the division of labour-determine what part woman shall or shall not play, and in which the female is everywhere subsumed under the male (Whitehead, 2002).

Patriarchal ideology sustains the legitimacy of men's authority over women which have consequences on power relations between the spouses in marriage (Chapman, 2004). The balance of power between husband and wife is influenced by their preconception about marital roles (Blood, 1969). Patriarchal principles at every social and cultural level naturally helped to determine the roles seen as appropriate for each sex (Capp, 2003). A role can be defined as a set of prescriptions and proscriptions for behaviour-expectations about what behaviour are appropriate for a person holding a particular position within a particular social context (Kessler and McKenna, 1978).

Gender roles are social norms that dictate what is socially regarded as appropriate female and male behaviour (Knox and Schachet, 2008). Home and private life are generally held to represent the feminine world of the personal and emotional, the specific, the domestic, and the sexual while the public world of work set itself up as opposite of all these things; it is rational, abstract, ordered concerned with general principles and of course masculine. These structural distinctions, work and home, public and private, are made so routinely that it seems to be self-evident; how the things are (McDowell and Pringle, 1992). In marriage these gender created public and private spheres have very different implications for men and women lives (Rayaprol, 1999).

The division of tasks (labour or work) refers to the process through which domestic tasks are assigned on the basis of sex (Wharton, 2005). The *traditional role socialization* constitute the foundation of gender division of housework and fix the role patterns in which internalized attitudes, beliefs, norms, and values are expressed (Trivedi, 2009). Division of tasks between men and women is manifested in gender roles which direct women and men behaviour and attitudes in accordance with these roles (Trivedi, 2009). As traditionally women are expected to bear responsibilities related to domestic field which are socially culturally assigned to them and to provide services which are asked for. This flow of services from women to men in the marriage is the result of social norms, values, attitudes, and beliefs which regulate housework by gender (Trivedi, 2009). In this way division of domestic tasks is based on power relation between the spouses where while there is a strong social sanction and support to idea that wife should perform the domestic duties (Scanzoni, 1935), the husband has power to select what he will do and won't do in the house (Dryden, 1999).

Section Two: Gendered Division of Domestic and Child Care Tasks: Some Field Observations

In marriage the question of who does or who does not do chores is the bone of contention in a relationship (Mansfield and Collard, 1988). Marriage is a gendered institution in which duties and privileges are assigned on the basis of societal traditions, expectations, and norms (Chapman, 2004). Pat Mainardi argued that division of spheres that provides traditional housework as women work was a reflection of male domination, not the expression of some feminine biological predisposition toward laundry or dishwashing. Women did housework and child care because they had to and men did not do the housework because they could get out of it (Kimmel, 2000). It's not simply that house work is designated as women's work but that for women to engage in it and men not to engage in it is to draw on and exhibit the essential nature of each. Therefore, what is produced and reproduced is the material embodiment of wifely and husbandly roles derivative of womanly and manly conduct which produced the dominant and subordinate statues of the sex categories (West and Zimmerman, 2002).

As Reid and Smith (1986) argues:

> Wives who work full time outside the home while carrying the larger share of domestic and child care task may well complain about having to assume an unfair burden. The husband may argue that from a traditional perspective her wife obligation is to care for home and children and not to work. Her employment is a burden she chooses to assume; if she feels this unfair she can stop working. The wife may replay that she has as much right to work as her husband, who should be obliged to share the load at home.

As Folbre (1994) argues, 'if you do not do housework, you are not good mother, so, I do not have to be good father'. 'If you do a man's job outside home you cannot be real women inside the home'.

Even if women is the sole earner of the family because husband willingly does not work he waits for her to come and do the entire domestic and child care work because he does not consider domestic work his duty at all. The traditional sex specific division of domestic tasks has not changed in the families of working women because husband still expects his wife to assume the burden of domestic responsibility because domestic sphere is considered to be domain and functions of womanhood. The wife responsibilities and duties for routine home and family care are 'not reduced by working' (Nassbum, 1999). Even if they have servants it is only her responsibility to 'supervise servants to ensure things are done properly' and look after the general management of household affairs. Women were charged with the responsibility of effecting the smooth operation of household and providing an appropriate level of comfort for its members (Chapman, 2004).

If women are allowed working it does not signify a change in cultural norms and values, as men did not want her to change their attitude towards their roles and statuses at home is concerned and dislike their traditional responsibility being neglected (Knox and Schacht, 2008). Women were permitted to work on the condition 'that they can work only when housework and family routine are not affected by it. Women can work when they can manage both work and family simultaneously.' So, their work outside the home is acceptable only in so far as they can accommodate the requirements of their work inside the home (Mansfield and Collard, 1988).

Marriage is precisely a gendered and unequal division of tasks, with most wives working more hours a day than their husbands in a subordinate role. Even when women are full time employed, they are required to provide far more better service than if they were not employed, in order to justify having a job (Delphy and Leonard, 1994). This makes wife bound up to be an earning and serving wife whose privilege to work outside the house depend on goodwill of husband which she can only maintain if she is also serving him as better as a housewife (Knox and Schacht, 2008).

This makes wives to create circumstances where their jobs encroached as little as possible on their domestic life (Mansfield and Collard, 1988). This makes women tend to choose occupations that are compatible with their family needs. Women also limit their aspirations for career advancement, reduce their behavioural and psychological involvement in work, adjust their work schedules for family reasons, and turn down opportunities for career development and growth that would interfere with their family responsibilities (Greenhaus and

Parusuraman, 1999). 'Women sacrificed promotions because they have to give time to family.'

Further, partner's orientation towards bearing and rearing children had a powerful impact on women work and family choices due to which woman's rather than that of man employment is interrupted, if not radically altered by the birth of children (Evans, 2009). Women took chunk out of her career in order to look after children as she carried the major responsibility for household affairs even working as many paid hours as husband because the traditional specific task for married women in society is to bear and rear children (Hardyment, 1994).

It is because all the responsibilities of child are on only wife while there is no effect on men's routine, which makes wife leave paid employment or work part time to become principal caregiver while the husband continues his work full time. 'Some started working only when children had started going to school. So that they don't have any problem in managing kids and work. To ensure they don't have any gap or break in their career so they started late.' With her first pregnancy, wife leaves the paid employment and after the last child enters the school the wife rejoins her job but still carries a disproportionate share of domestic tasks and in addition the lion's share of work in caring for the children (Smith and Reid, 1986). Women participation in her work remains crucially affected by birth of children. It is certainly the case that women return to work after birth of first child, but with the birth of subsequent children the likelihood of women remaining in full time employment decreases women responsibility of domestic tasks and child care is therefore, a result of deliberate or unvoiced prejudice concerning the sexual division of labour (Evans, 2009).

The women are trying to negotiate their situation by making adjustment and compromises with their career so that they do not face the work and family conflict. This work-family conflict situation puts the wife under constant pressure to sacrifice her career for the sake of her husband career or for the sake of her children, as strain to manage everything at once (Rice, 1983). Since both rearing a child and having a career have been traditionally viewed as full time occupations, it is not surprising that many career women wonder if they have to choose between them (Smith and Reid, 1986). This is because the movement of women from home to work place has not been accompanied by a comparable movement of men back into the home (Kimmel, 2000). Thus, the domestic responsibilities prevent them from getting jobs which pays them as high as of men; it then becomes rational for person with lower economic prospect to become domestic worker, and further restricts the prospects (Bradley, 1994).

Hochschild argues women are working in many shifts. Women have a job in first shift, then at home another set of work demands in the form of house care and children as second shift and finally, there is the third shift, involving the expense of emotional energy by a spouse or parent in dealing with various issues in family living (Knox and Schact, 2008). In this way, being subjected to dual demands of home and works; women are liable to face crises of adjustment that may cause stress and strain (Kaila, 2005). As one respondent said, 'I have to wake up early to prepare my husband for his work and children for school, then I come to hospital, in lunch time to go to pick my children and drop them home, give them food and come back and after going home till late night I work and make sure all things are kept ready for the next day. It's really hectic.'

The women continue to perform the lion share of second shift which put an enormous strain on marriage. The balancing of work and family pulls working women in different directions which is bound to make them feel frustrated (Kimmel, 2000). But men are still reluctant to increase their participation at home even though their wives experiences high levels of work and family role stress through increased work and family conflict (Greenhause and Parusuram, 1999). The double shift worked by women was accompanied by the replication of wholly familiar patterns of the concentration of power and privileges in the male hands (Evans, 2009). The multiple role strain is a major source of overload for the employed women especially in a society that prescribes certain expectations and behaviours for women's roles that are often contradictory.

'No matter whether you come early or late you should bear all house and child care responsibilities, not your husband, and you should serve him.' Women expressed that they were fated to do the housework or wash dishes (Thapan, 2003). In this situation, family harmony remains intact only when wife, though has external status corresponding to that of husband, does not try to change the prescribed hierarchy in the family, when she accept the position of husband as superior and subordinate herself to his authority in the traditional way, when she sharply differentiates between her achieved externals status and her ascribed family status and when husband cherishes the same patriarchal expectations. In this case husband does not feel threatened in his superior husband role, he can even look at the high external status of his wife with benevolence and pride (Mies, 1980). In this way, marriage acts as a minor version of whole network of inequality between men and women which exist in the society (Mansfield and Collard, 1988).

Section Three: Question of Women Choice and Agency

Thapan asserts that even if women do exercise her agency, it is not always possible to be sure of the extent to which this will obtain results they want (Thapan, 2003). According to Gerson, though both women and men experience work and family conflicts but they confront different choices/options. Women may make choices in response to various circumstances but not every woman is equally well situated to respond by making choices. The constraints in their social environment limit the range of possible options and channelled motivation to select one option from among this range. In this sense, work and family decisions of these women were reactions to the socially structured contexts they faced (Gerson, 1985). This suggests a negative relationship between work and family would be stronger for women than men (Greenhause and Parusuraman, 1999) due to which women though may not give up their career, but they have to give up success greater than their husband. It is the women who have to take the risks, sacrifice more, and compromise career-ambitions in attempting to make dual-career pattern operative (Bell, 1983)

Gerson (1988) argues that women are often confronted with ambiguous structure that often requires them to choose among the number of desired goals. Women work and family decisions are inextricably linked; choices in one sphere depend on the opportunities, incentives, and constrains posed in the other. Whether women opt for work, motherhood or some combination of the two, she must accept the costs of what is forgone as well as benefits of what is chosen.

Gerson (1988) asserts:

> The forces that shape options, and channel actions, motives and beliefs system are often hidden from conscious awareness...women respond in contextually sensible ways to their environment without full conscious awareness of the structural forces impinging on them or the overall logic of their choices, just as they may be unaware of subconscious psychodynamic pushes and pull.

In marriage, couples rarely make decisions about the division of domestic responsibilities and are governed by structural realities around which their relationship is built and which have already moulded their expectation through the process of gender role socialization. Allan argues in marriage some social practices are so embedded that they are rarely questioned and therefore do not have to be deliberated upon to make any decision. Women due to their gender role socialization find it difficult to make choices or attempt for changes because they feared that asking for something they want may harm their relationship and this make much harder for them to step over the threshold for asking and try to negotiate (Bacock and Laschever, 2003) because negotiation is conceived as a situation where conflict and competitions are important but they may not be the comfortable place for women because it puts them in opposition to others. So, women in order to protect and foster their relationship may feel uncomfortable in negotiating and attempt fewer negotiations to influence the decisions of opposite negotiator.

This gendered divide in domestic tasks reflects the power relation between the spouses which involves the process of bargaining, negotiation, and compromising (Smith and Reid, 1986). Though Ramu opines that wife's contribution to family economy does result in a certain degree of flexibility between the husbands and wives in exercise of power and authority because for him economic resources are an objective force in renegotiating the balance of power between spouses; greater the resources either spouse has, greater will be his or her marital power. If economic resources are basis of strength to negotiate for greater marital power then employed women are in an ideal position to do so but it has not yielded uniform and universal change in domestic relations (Ramu, 2003).

Though education and income are very important determinant and influencing factor for women status in marriage but it does not necessarily leads to change in the position of women in marriage or their pattern of division of domestic tasks. Though it generates sort of power for the women but then it's not the same for every women because all women have their own distinct situations and circumstances. Her employment does not always allow her freedom or independence (Graham, 1985) because women find that 'our societal system constructed in a way that it creates difficulties in having equal sharing of tasks' therefore they have adopted themselves to the situations. This acceptance reflects women's lack of negotiation power in marriage because of which they are not able to get their demands and decisions implemented and therefore adopted and accepted themselves to their situations. For them to maintain marriage is more important therefore, to keep peace, and avoid arguments they subordinated themselves in marriage. Thus, it can be argued that women have accepted their circumstances and made choices which though may not be their choices but the choices which their socially structured situations have put towards them as their only available options in a patriarchal society. Thus, marriage entails an unequal relationship between men and women.

Conclusion

It can be concluded that the traditional gender divides between the roles and responsibilities of men and women are still operating in marriage. It does not matter what the working hours or the work situation of women is or whether women are coming later than their husbands or the husband and wife are coming at the same time. In all these situations it is wife who takes the major responsibility for looking after domestic work while husband may help occasionally or in certain circumstances like when wife is ill. Similarly, whether it's about caring, rearing, teaching, supervising, attending parent-teacher meeting and so on, it is women who have the major responsibility because the child well-being is still considered as being mother's responsibility.

The domestic work situation needs to be re-examined if one wants to understand the experiences of women because men and women roles and experiences in marriage are different and differently evaluated. Though the education and income are very important factors for negotiation in marriage but I argue that beyond a point it could not be used as an instrument of negotiation. The patriarchal structure and its socially constructed bondages in the name of societal norms, culture, socialization, plays an important role in regulating the conduct of couples and determining which tasks are to be performed by whom in marriage. It is this socialization and cultural bondages which makes difficult for the women to exercise their choices and forced them to accept and adapt themselves to their circumstances. This makes hard to expect the notion of equality and makes their marital relationship hierarchical and unequal.

References

Allan, Graham (1985). *Family Life, Domestic Roles and Social Organization*. New York: Basil Blackwell.

Bernard, Capp (2003). *When Gossips Meet, Women, Family, and Neighbourhood in Early Modern England*. New York: Oxford University Press.

Chapman, Tony (2004). *Gender and Domestic Life, Changing Practices in Families and Households*. New York: Palgrave Macmillan.

Christine, Delphy and Leonard, Diana (1994). The Variety of Work Done by Wives, in *The Polity Reader in Gender Studies* (ed. Blackwell Publishers), Cambridge: Polity Press.

Carolinem, Dryden (1999). *Being Married, Doing Gender: A Critical Analysis of Gender Relationships in Marriage*. London: Routledge.

Greenhaus, Jeffrey H. and Parasuraman, Saroj (1999). 'Research on Work, Family, and Gender: Current Status and Future Directions', in Gary Powell (ed.) *Handbook of Gender and Work*. London: Sage.

Harriet, Bradely (1994). 'Gendered Jobs and Social Inequality', in *The Polity Reader in Gender Studies*, Cambridge: Polity Press.

Harding, Sandra (2005). 'Rethinking Standpoint Epistemology: What is 'Strong Objectivity'?' in Ann Cudd and Robin Andreasen (eds) *Feminist Theory: A Philosophical Anthology*, , Malden: Blackwell Publishing.

Hardyment, Christina (1994). 'The Domestic Mystique', in *The Polity Reader in Gender Studies*, Cambridge: Polity Press.

Kathleen, Gerson (1985). *Hard Choices, How Women Decide about Work, Career, and Motherhood*. Berkeley: University of California Press.

Kaila, H.L. (2005). *Women, Work, and Family*. Jaipur: Rawat Publications.

Kimmel, Michael (2000). *The Gendered Society*. New York: Oxford University Press.

Kessler, Suzanne and Wendy, McKenna (1978). *Gender: An Ethnomethodological Approach*. Toronto: John Wiley and Sons.

Knox, David and Schacht, Caroline (2008). *Choices in Relationships, An Introduction to Marriage and the Family*, 9th ed. Australia: Thomson Wadsworth.

Linda, Babcock and Laschever, Sara (2003). *Women Don't Ask, Negotiating and the Gender Divide*. Princeton: Princeton University Press.

Mary, Evans (2009). *Gender and Social Theory*. Jaipur. Rawat Publications.

McDowell, Linda and Pringle, Rosemary (eds.) (1992). *Defining Women, Social Institutions and Gender Divisions*. London: Polity Press.

Mies, Maria (1980). *Indian Women and Patriarchy, Conflicts and Dilemmas of Students and Working Women*. New Delhi: Concept Publishing Company.

Mansfield, Penny and Collard, Jean (1988). *The Beginning of the Rest of Your Life? A Portrait of Newly-Wed Marriage*. London: Macmillan Press.

Maynard, Mary (2008). 'Methods, Practice and Epistemology: The Debate about Feminism and Research', in Sara Delamont and Paul Atkinson (eds) *Gender and Research*, Vol. 3, *Feminist Methods*, London: Sage.

Nancy, Folbre (1994). *Who Pays For The Kids? Gender and the Structures of Constraint*. London: Routledge.

Nassbaum Martha (1999). *Sex and Social Justice*. New York: Oxford.

Ramu G. (2003). 'Single Dual Earner Couples: Economic Status and Marital Power', in Sharmila Rege (ed.) *Sociology of Gender: The Challenges of Feminist Sociological Knowledge*, Delhi: Sage.

Rayaprol, Aparna (1997). *Negotiating Identities, Women in the Indian Diaspora*. Delhi: Oxford University Press.

Rice, Philip (1983). *Contemporary Marriage*, Boston: Allyn and Bacon.

Robert, Bell (1983). *Marriage and Family Interaction*, 6th ed. IIlinois: The Dorsey Press.

Robert, Blood (1969). *Marriage*, 2nd ed. London: Collier-Macmillan.

Scanzoni, John (1935). *Sex Roles, Women's Work, and Marital Conflict: A Study of Family Change*. Toronto: Lexington Books.

Smith, Audrey and Reid, William (1986). *Role-Sharing Marriage*. New York: Columbia University Press.

Thapan, Meenakshi (2003). 'Marriage, Well-Being, and Agency Among Women', in Caroline Sweetman (ed) *Gender, Development, and Marriage,* Oxford: Oxford University Press.

Trivedi, Tanuja (2009). *Domestic Women Workers*. New Delhi: Jnanada Prakashan.

West, Candace and Don, H. Zimmerman (2002). Doing Gender, in Sarah Fenstermaker and Candace West (eds) *Doing Gender, Doing Difference, Inequality, Power, and Institutional Change*, New York: Routledge.

Wharton, Amy (2005). *The Sociology of Gender, An Introduction to Theory and Research*. Malden: Blackwell Publishing.

Whitehead, Stephen (2002). *Men and Masculinities, Key Themes and New Directions*. Malden: Blackwell Publishing.

11

Role of Tribal Women in Family Economy

A Case Study of Three Tribal Dominated Villages of Central Madhya Pradesh

NEELU RAWAT

Abstract

Female participation in labour market is an indicator of economic growth, reciprocally well economic growth means greater opportunity of jobs and thus more female participation in economy. This paper is study of three tribal dominated villages of central Madhya Pradesh. Traditionally, tribal women had an important role in family economy through collecting forest products and firewood etc. and selling to the nearest market to earn their livelihood. Their contribution in family economy has its own utility, their income cope the failure of family economy, as the 'added worker' hypothesis says that when unemployment increases and men lose their jobs, wives may enter the labour force in order to compensate for the loss of family income. Women participation in economy is a prerequisite for a developed economy but it faces many challenges like illiteracy of women, social norms, unpaid work, etc. The objective of the research are – to know the tribal women participation in economic activities, and how they manage time and labour and what is the income of that participation, to analyse the social impact (both positive and negative) of this participation on family and on tribal women themselves. This is a case study of three tribal dominated villages of central Madhya Pradesh.

Keywords

tribal, firewood, livelihood, participation, family economy

Introduction

Historically the social, economic and cultural institutions of tribal community are integrated in such a deep manner that it is difficult to isolate them from each other. These are inter-related and mostly economic activities are constructed, conditioned and legitimized on the basis of socio-cultural activities, similarly socio-cultural activities are constructed, conditioned and legitimized on the basis of economic activities. Both economic and non-economic activities are formed and functioned on the basis of local natural animate or inanimate objects. After industrial revolution of England, a concept of maximization of benefit and production had emerged which changed this natural object as natural resources. This maximization of output and benefits became pre-requisite for well-being of mankind and tribal world also came under its influence. Before the arrival of East India Company, tribes of India were in constant contact with several indigenous and non-indigenous traditions and civilizations. So the process of acculturation of tribes of India may be old, but with the arrival of British, its motive, content and frequency definitely increased and expanded. Christian missionaries, logging of wood for administration and commercial purposes with classification of forests and formulation of provisions to manipulate forest for colonial interest, creation of middlemen from among tribal and non-tribal natives are the processes that affected tribal economy besides Hinduism and Islam as non-British processes. In this way this process of acculturation between tribal and non-tribal traditions resulted in breakdown of tribal autonomy in material and non-material culture, a new and alien way of life imposed on them whose part became elements of tribal culture. Efforts had been made in pre-British days to stop this exploitation by local lords at the institutional level but these efforts could not stop this process of exploitation.

After Independence this marginality of tribes was recognized by the state and the civil society bodies which led to formulation and implementation of different acts, provisions, policies and schemes to protect and promote the human rights of tribal mass. With the efforts of several civil society organizations, individual philanthropists and social reformers through protest movement capacity building oriented efforts emerged for their development. Tribal indigenous knowledge, customs and tradition, seasonal out migration, etc. also played an important role in encountering the process of pauperization and marginalization of tribes. Outcomes of these processes, limitation, socio-political barriers with reference to developmental programme and economic policy have been researched and discussed by a number of scholars. Finding unveils a mixed picture of tribal development, it says that the process of class formation among them is very slow, only few of them have availed the benefits of development process and majority of them are lagging behind.

There are 75 primitive tribes in the country whose socio-economic condition is much below the condition of average tribes. Those tribes who have availed institutional benefits, only few of them have been able to improve their socio-economic status but mostly they depend on outside intervention, so it can be said that the process of development and implication on selected tribe is not sustainable. Now, the local level resources decreased in such a manner that it is unable to fulfil the basic needs of native themselves. This is diminishing the tribal cultural heritage and lifestyle of tribe is being in process of change. Tribes are adopting food habit, dress pattern, language and religious practices of others. Hence, it can be said that while going through process of national integration and institutions led development programme has led tribal to lose their cultural heritage without any economic gain in sustainable manner.

After 1991, globalization came as a new factor to threaten the tribal economic and cultural heritage. Multi-national companies started expanding their reach to remote tribal areas to establish their companies. Many scholars believe that globalization is anti-tribal because of formation and expansion of consumer culture, expansion of market force, etc. and that tribes are going to lose their economic and cultural identity. Rehabilitation and displacement are attacking the natural resource heritage and indigenous economic activities, even with promise to maintain sustainable development, there is a gap between promise and implementation because it is difficult to displace or rehabilitate in same economic and cultural terms. Tribal women are historically involved in economic activities by collecting forest wood and earning to meet day-to-day needs or in other forms like agricultural activities. But in contemporary India it can be seen that many factors in name of development are affecting the economic and cultural identity of tribes.

In this era of globalization, where we talk about 'global village', we should keep in mind the socio-cultural and economic heritage of tribe and should maintain their natural characteristics because in Indian Constitution there is a right to maintain culture, so tribal economic and cultural identity should not be attacked in name of development. Exclusive growth and sustainable development don't promote development of one at the cost of another. This study focuses on economic activities of tribal women.

Objectives: More specifically the study will be conducted to achieve following broad objectives:

1. To know the tribal women participation in economic activities, and how they manage time and labour and what is the income of that participation.
2. To analyse the social impact (both positive and negative) of this participation on family and on tribal women themselves.

Methodology

Methodology is an important section of any research because whether in natural science or in social sciences, without a proper methodology, we cannot make the research fruitful in lack of proper formulation of work plan. An attempt has been made to follow a proper method, tool and techniques to bring objectivity in the study.

Madhya Pradesh

The state of Madhya Pradesh was created in November 1956 by merging the state of Madhya Pradesh, Vindhya Pradesh and Bhopal with Bhopal as its capital. The present Madhya Pradesh came into existence on 1 November 2000 after bifurcation of Madhya Pradesh into two states, the newly one as Chhattisgarh from it. The state is divided into seven social and cultural zones and each zone has its own social and demographical features. The state is predominantly rural because as per 2011 Census 72.37 per cent population of total population lives in villages, in rural areas. It ranks first in all states and union territories in India having 1,53,16,784 total tribal population. In total tribal population 77,19,404 are male and 75,97,380 are female. The state constitutes 21.1 per cent tribal population of total population. Bhil, Gond and Korku are the major Scheduled Tribes in the state. Bhil is the most populous tribe having a number of 4,618,068 (Census, 2001) constituting 37.7 per cent of total ST population and gond is the second largest tribe with a population of 4,357,918 (Census, 2001) constituting 35.6 per cent. Gond have major concentration in Chhindwara, Betul, Mandla, Seoni and Shahdol district. The study is based on Gond tribe of three villages of Betul district.

Betul

Betul district belongs to Narmadapuram Division of the Central Provinces and is situated between 21°22' and 22°23' N and 77°10' and 78°33' E on the Satpura Plateau. It is bounded on the north by Hoshangabad, on the west by Harda and Khandwa districts and the Amrawati district of Berar, on the south by the Amrawati district and on the east by Chhindwara district. It is spread in 10,043 sq km with having 1,328 inhabited and 111 forest villages. Its population size is 15,75,362 (Census, 2011) i.e. 2.16 per cent of Madhya Pradesh population. Most of the population of Betul lives in villages constitutes 80.3 per cent of total population and their prime source of livelihood is agriculture. Classification of land in the district is shown in Table 1:

Table 1

Land Use Pattern of Betul District

Type	*Area in sq km*
Forest	1,139.76
Land not available for agriculture	259.43
Other non-agriculture land	467.98
Agriculture land	8,175.84
Total sown area	5,547.99
Double cropped area	5,547.99
Total	10,043.00

Source: District Groundwater Information Booklet 2009.

Features which encouraged to choose this district for study:

1. Historically the district is tribal dominated i.e. 42.3 per cent of total population in which largely Gond and Korku reside in Betul villages with their distinct features.
2. Nearly 39 per cent of the area in the district is under forest. Although the district has deteriorating health status, these forest areas provide ample opportunity for tribal women to generate economy. They collect and market firewood from these forest to meet their day-to-day needs.
3. Sex ratio of the district is relatively better, while the state has 930 women per thousand men the district has 970 women per thousand men (Census, 2011) is shown in Table 2.

Table 2

Demographic Profile of Betul District

		Total	*Rural*	*Urban*
No. of Households		3,29,832	2,61,879	67,953
Total Population	**Person**	**15,75,362**	**12,66,211**	**3,09,151**
	Male	7,99,236	6,40,358	1,58,878
	Female	7,76,126	6,25,853	1,50,273
ST Population	**Person**	**6,67,018**	**6,38,348**	**28,670**
	Male	3,33,166	3,18,925	14,241
	Female	3,33,852	3,19,423	14,429

Source: Madhya Pradesh Census 2011.

Shahpur Development Block

There are 10 Development Blocks in Betul District in which four blocks have more than 50 per cent tribal population viz. Chicholi, Shahpur, Bhainsdehi and Bhimpur. This study was conducted on Shahpur Block. As far as Shahpur is concerned it is spread in about 592 sq km with 132 inhabited and 40 Gram Panchayat. Pathai, Nishana and Bhagtandhana are the three villages of Shahpur Development Block where study was conducted is shown in Tables 3 and 4.

Table 3

Demographic Profile of Three Villages

Village	*Household*	*Persons*	*Male*	*Female*
Pathai	201	1,174	577	597
Nishana	115	672	334	338
Bhagtandhana	56	338	172	166
Total	372	2,184	1,083	1,101

Source: Census 2011.

Table 4

Betul District ST Female Population

Area	*Population*	*Per cent of Total Female Population*	*% of Total Female ST Population*
Rural	3,19,423	51.0	95.6
Urban	14,429	9.6	4.32
Total	**3,33,852**		

Source: Census, 2011.

Sample Size

This study was carried on three villages of Shahpur Development Block of Betul district i.e. Pathai, Nishana and Bhagtandhana. Women of Gond tribe of these villages was sample for the study. Taking note on small size of total households 50 per cent households (as per Census of India, 2001, because the fieldwork was carried in 2008) were selected by random sampling for better representation. In this way data were collected from 186 households in which 100 households, 58 households and 28 households were selected from Pathai, Nishana and Bhagtandhana village respectively and semi-structured interview schedule were applied on these households for primary data collection.

Tools and Techniques

Semi-structured schedule was applied for data collection from main respondents. Interview guide was used for other respondents and panchayat representatives. Group interview, observation and informal interaction were adopted as other tool and technique.

Findings

The studied villages are tribal dominated and particularly the 'Gond' tribe constitutes above 90 per cent of total population. As far as their economic life is concerned, it has significantly changed, both at the family and at the village level, over the time. Earlier, it revolved around forest and farm work but institutional interventions in a continuous manner and NGO intervention has brought a significant changes. Their main source of livelihood is now agriculture and wage work especially in government led development schemes. Women participation in agriculture work and wage work is noticeable but their main concentration has been traced in firewood collection and a significant number of tribal women are engaged in firewood collection and its marketing.

Women of both Gond and Korku tribe are involved in firewood collection and it is done on regular basis. Most of them are illiterate and in the age group of 20–40 years. Ocassionally, female child of the age group 12–14 years also subordinate her mother during school holiday and some of the physically capable older women are also involved in this activity. They collect firewood from nearby forest and sell it to the nearest town Shahpur. Shahpur is a small town with having several tea-shops, hotels, offices, schools, health centres, bus stand, *thellawala* and government employee. Besides, there are also some households of retired persons and farmers. Most of these households and shop of different types, including tribal hostel, depend on firewood, supplied by these tribal women, for cooking purpose. These women carry firewood bundle on head and supply during both morning and evening hours. In the evening they supply less firewood in comparison to the morning hours. Weight of individual bundle is around 30–32 kg and the cost of each bundle is around ₹ 30–35 each. They sell it at Shahpur and whatever income they have they immediately spend it on meeting basic requirements such as rice, pulse, edible oil, soap, detergent powder, tobacco, *bidi* and so on. In this way these women contributing their family in earning livelihood. To know the quantity of firewood sold in a day and number of women involved in firewood collection and its marketing, an observation on 22 November 2008 and 23 November 2008 was carried by me. Details are given in Table 5.

Table 5

Number of Women involved in Firewood Collection and Marketing and Quantity of Firewood Sold in a Day

No. of Members in Group	*No. of Groups*	*No. of Firewood Bundle*	*Quantity of firewood (in Kilogram)*
22 November 2008			
5	23	66	1,815
6–10	6	50	1,375
11–15	1	12	330
16	1	18	495
Total	**31**	**146**	**4,015**
23 November 2008			
5	32	100	2,750
6–10	7	49	1,347.5
11–15	1	13	357.5
16	0	0	0
Total	**40**	**162**	**4,455**

Source: I observed and counted the firewood bundle on the mentioned dates.

Income and Expenditure from Firewood Collection

On an average a tribal woman earns ₹ 30–35 per day with the sale of one bundle of firewood and sometimes when they have any emergency to earn more than they earn ₹ 60–70 with selling two bundles a day. In this way the weekly income of these tribal women with one bundle of firewood is ₹ 210–245 and monthly income is ₹ 900–1,050. This income is hand to mouth and rarely any saving with this. These tribal women spend this income for two purposes:

1. Puchasing daily requirement
2. Purchasing things from weekly market

For daily requirement they purchase rice, pulse, edible oil, soap, detergent powder, tobacco, *bidi*, cosmetics and so on. If any member of the family falls ill then this income is spent on treatment and it increases the burden of the women for next day to collect more firewood to earn more money to cope with the deficit. Many of the female-headed households depend entirely on firewood collection and its marketing because they do not have land to cultivate. In an interview, a Gond tribe woman named Kala Dhurve, about 38 years old and having four children explained how she earns livelihood for their family. On 21 January 2009, Kala went to weekly market and purchased items which reflects how tribal women cope with basic requirements of family. Her purchasing details on that particular day is as shown in Table 6:

Table 6

Purchasing of Daily Needs by Kala Dhurve from Weekly Market

Items	*Quantity*	*Cost (in Rs.)*
Spices	150 grams	20
Salt	1 kg	5
Rice	5 kg	65
Burbati Dal	1 kg	28
Soyabean Oil	250 ml	13
Coconut Oil	100 ml	5
Nirma Washing Powder	1 packet	5
Bathing Soap (Nirma)	2 Piece	12
Jalebi (Sweet dish)	250 gram	10
Mixture	150 gram	5
Banana	1 Dozen	6
Egg	10 Piece	20
Total		**194**

Socio-Economic Impact

Firewood collection by these women clears the dry scattered wood from forest to prevent fire in summer, but at the same time green trees are being cut because the daily requirement of firewood cannot be fulfilled only through dry wood which is unfavourable for environment. Although it is source to earn livelihood for them but they suffer various types of social, psychological and physical problems. They cannot give proper time to family because they are busy in collection of wood the whole day. After getting tired at the end of the day, they use alcohol to relax themselves which increase alcoholism among them and it is an extra expenditure from their income which can be saved and can be used for better purpose. They also suffer from joint pain and several diseases with continuous hard labour in forest for many years. Children education is also indirectly affected because elder children stay at home to look after siblings as the mother is out for work and they do not go to school and female children stay at home for cooking food. Even the school-going children are irregular in school and sometime leave the school early to assist their mother in collection of firewood.

Conclusion

Tribal women of these three villages meet their daily requirements with the earning of firewood marketing, but it is a time-consuming job with much of labour requirement and income is very low which is not helpful in improving their socio-economic status. Markets for firewood are limited and buyers are also less in number, so they do not get the proper price of their firewood bundle, they have to sell it at the cheap rate decided by buyer. Forests are now only a source of income for them and the emotional attachment between them and forest is no more, so they are exploiting it at the highest level to earn their livelihood. This is resulting into degradation of forest of these areas. The spirit of hardwork of these tribal women can be utilized in some other work for their development without losing forest resources. Women participation in family economy is a prerequisite for development of both at individual level and country level but the challenges that are being faced should be eliminated. Some of the suggestions for their betterment are as under:

- Other source of income should be generated taking into account the available regional resources.
- Social forestry should be developed and these women should be included in its management.
- These villages have dams nearby, so occupation like fishing can be generated.
- These areas have rich production of maize and soya bean, so employment in this direction can be generated.

12

The Need for Gender Transformative Approaches in Nutrition and Livelihoods Interventions

The Bangladesh Experience

RAMONA RIDOLFI, MEREDITH JACKSON-DE GRAFFENRIED, MARIE SOPHIE SANDBERG PETTERSSON, FARIA SHABNAM, PAULA KANTOR AND AFRINA CHOUDHURY

Abstract

There is increasing recognition and evidence worldwide demonstrating that targeting women is not enough to enable sustainable gender-equitable outcomes of development interventions. Despite historical shifts in thinking around gender within the global development community and academic circles, the core assumption often remains that reducing gender gaps through targetting programme beneficiaries, or increasing the number of women beneficiaries in a project, equates to 'adequately' addressing gender issues. This approach is now being refined, and the need for Gender Transformative Approaches (GTAs) that go beyond targeting women to engage with gender relations within households and communities is gradually being accepted by development practitioners. Yet, few interventions worldwide have put this approach into practice, and even fewer have documented how to do so. This paper, written in partnership by HKI, EEP/Shiree and World Fish, builds the case for such approaches, first by sharing the results of a nutrition activities mapping exercise that identified gaps in nutrition programming related to addressing gender disparities and reaching adolescent girls. This paper then presents a conceptual approach to addressing the underlying causes of gender inequality in a transformative way and provides examples of applied ways to integrate GTAs in nutrition and livelihoods interventions across Bangladesh, involving all main decision-makers and power-brokers within the household and community.

Keywords

gender equality, women's empowerment, nutrition, livelihoods, normative change, Bangladesh, poverty reduction, food security, gender mainstreaming

Introduction

Maternal and child undernutrition remain a significant development challenge in Bangladesh. Considerable investments have been made to reverse existing rates of undernutrition through both nutrition specific programming and other programming that includes nutrition components. However, these efforts risk falling short of their aims because they do not address a key underlying causes of the problem – gender inequality.[1] This paper argues for the use of Gender Transformative Approaches (GTAs) as the means to integrate gender in nutrition and livelihoods programmes, since they better address the complexity of gender relations, and engage with the multiple institutions and actors that create and maintain gender inequality. A review of applications of this approach in Bangladesh with the aim of motivating other agencies to adopt, test and refine them, and share the resulting learning, is included.

The Link between Nutrition and Gender in Bangladesh

Despite significant reductions in both extreme and moderate poverty over the past two decades in Bangladesh, the rate of undernutrition for children under five is among the highest in the world, with maternal and child undernutrition as a leading contributor to 45 per cent of preventable child deaths, as well as irreversible, lifelong consequences for a child's physical and cognitive development (Finucane et al., 2011). The 2012 Food Security and Nutrition Surveillance Project (FSNSP) (HKI and BIGH, 2014) in Bangladesh found that 41 per cent of women of 19–49 years of age are of short stature (<150 cm), placing them at a risk for complications during childbirth, while 30 per cent of girls 10–18 years of age are stunted (compared to what is expected in a well-nourished population). Furthermore, over 60 per cent of women and adolescent girls aged 10–49 years do not consume adequate micro-and macronutrients (HKI and BIGH, 2012, 2013). Specifically, rates of anaemia, a key health indicator for women, especially during pregnancy, are high: according to 2011 Bangladesh Demographic Health Survey (BDHS), 42 per cent of women aged 15–49 years are anaemic. Furthermore, anaemia rates are higher in pregnant and lactating women, often resulting in increased risk of premature delivery and low birth weight (NIPORT, 2012).

Adolescence is a time of intense growth second only to infancy. During adolescence, individuals can gain 15 per cent of their ultimate adult height and 50 per cent of their adult weight (SCN, 2006). However, in Bangladesh, adolescent health for girls is put at risk by the high rates of child marriage and early pregnancy. The country has the second highest rate for girls married under 15 and third highest for under 18, with respectively 29 per cent and 65 per cent of women currently aged 20–24 years reportedly married before the age of 15 and 18, respectively (UNICEF, 2014).

Undernourishment among adolescents, pregnant girls and women contributes to an intergenerational cycle of undernutrition, which affects society as a whole. Children are more likely to be of low birth weight and to remain undernourished throughout their lives if their mothers were malnourished prior to and during pregnancy (UNICEF, 2012; Mehrotra et al., 2011: 132 and UN ACC/SCN, 2002). Undernourished mothers face greater risks during pregnancy and childbirth, and adolescence itself is a risk factor in pregnancy. Maternal malnutrition has been proven to be directly correlated with faltering nutritional status and growth retardation in children, low birth weight, high infant and child morbidity and mortality rates and, notably, high maternal mortality rates (UNICEF, 2012).

The 2011 BDHS (NIPORT, 2012) data found that 41 per cent of children under 5 in Bangladesh are stunted[2] and 36 per cent are underweight, compared to a global prevalence rate for stunting of 25 per cent (UNICEF, 2012). Stunting is directly related to persistent infections and inadequate dietary intake.[3]

While undernutrition is a complex problem caused by a variety of factors; women's low socio-economic status is increasingly recognized as a key determinant. For example, in times of food shortage, women and adolescent girls are usually the first to sacrifice consumption (FSNSP, 2013). Women's lack of voice and power in Bangladesh is further illustrated by the high prevalence of child marriage and early pregnancy; limited mobility to access healthcare, family planning, and markets; low decision-making power within the household; unequal intra-household food distribution, and gendered domestic roles that include sole female responsibility of household work. Specifically in Bangladesh, intimate partner violence (IPV) has been recognized as a leading cause of mortality and morbidity among women of reproductive age, as well as on the nutritional status of their children in Bangladesh (Ziaei, Naved and Ekström, 2012). Notably, a recent nationwide study showed that 87 per cent of women have been victims of domestic violence (BBS and UNFPA, 2011). These are all critical factors linked to women's limited opportunities and relatively poor nutritional status, with inevitable negative spillover effects on their children's own health and nutrition status. Highlighting these linkages, Sylhet Division in north-east Bangladesh has both the country's highest rates of stunting and the worst women's empowerment indicators (FSNSP, 2013).

Beyond negatively impacting women, women's lack of power has a negative impact on households and communities as a whole. The socially constructed gender roles of men and women interact with their biological roles to affect the nutrition status of the entire family and of each gender (UN ACC/SCN, 2002). Alleviation of gender inequality has been identified as one of the key interventions to protect children from both nutritional and developmental risks (Ruel and Alderman, 2013). In essence, women with poor nutrition are caught in a vicious cycle of poverty and undernutrition which translates to their offspring, who are predetermined by their mother's nutritional status to suffer from increased morbidity and lower productivity. Globally, undernutrition is estimated to reduce a nation's GDP by as much as 8 per cent (Bhutta et al., 2013). Thus, it is not just the individual, young, married mother, nor it is just her children and household, but society and the nation as a whole that bear the consequences of gender inequalities.

In turn, improvements in the nutrition of girls, adolescent females, and women may contribute to the relaxation of social and cultural constraints facing women as the advantages of investing in their human capital become apparent. 'Better nourished girls are more likely to stay in school and to learn more. They will miss fewer days to illness and be more attentive when in class. They will grow up to become more productive economically and more aware of the various livelihood options. They will become more empowered to make decisions in all spheres of activity, including parenting. They will have greater control over their sexuality-related choices – crucial for controlling family size and preventing HIV/AIDS' (UN ACC/SCN, 2002).

Notably, women's empowerment, including a greater say in decision-making around marriage and family planning, as well as gender-equitable intra-household food distribution, are essential requirements for improving overall nutrition status of poor households in Bangladesh. In recent years, the development sector has recognized the link between women's empowerment and better nutrition and health outcomes for individuals and households, resulting in a shifting dialogue and practice to integrate gender into nutrition and livelihoods programming. These gender integration efforts need to respond appropriately to a range of gender-specific risks, including how women and girls enter development programmes at a disadvantaged state of malnutrition.

The Lancet Series on Maternal and Child Undernutrition published in early 2008 identifies a series of effective, targeted nutrition interventions, which, if implemented at scale during the 1,000 days window of opportunity, could reduce the undernutrition-related mortality and disease burden by 25 per cent in the short term. This series recommends a set of nutrition-focused measures, usually integrated in standard nutrition programmes, and notably concludes that 'to eliminate stunting in the longer term, these interventions should be supplemented by improvements in the underlying determinants of malnutrition, such as poverty, poor education, disease burden, and lack of women's empowerment' (*The Lancet*, Volume 371, Issue 9610, Feburary 2008). Incorporating a focus on improving women's status into nutrition components will increase the likelihood that such interventions will reap more sustainable benefits for the next generation (UN ACC/SCN, 2002). Five years later, in 2013, the Lancet published a second series on the same topic, supporting a heavier emphasis on both women's empowerment and nutrition sensitive programming to better address undernutrition. Of the six pathways noted by Ruel and Alderman (2013) through which agriculture can affect nutrition, three of them centre on women: effect of women's social status and empowerment on their access to and control over resources, impact of women's participation in agriculture on their time allocation, and impact of women's participation in agriculture on their health and nutrition status.

Gender in Nutrition Programmes in Bangladesh

In 2013, the National Nutrition Services (NNS) of the Ministry of Health and Family Welfare (MOHFW) in Bangladesh requested a national mapping of nutrition-specific and nutrition-sensitive interventions, services and other activities across sectors, including development partners, civil society, private sector, academia and research organizations, and government (MOHFW).[4] The objective was to provide a comprehensive overview of nutrition-related programming to identify gaps, priority areas and opportunities for complementary activities to inform planning and decision-making for potential scale-up of nutrition services. The results demonstrate which actors are working in nutrition-related activities, where they are working, what they are doing, and for how long activities are planned. Twenty-one nutrition intervention categories, determined by the NNS Operational Plan were examined, including a myriad of nutrition-sensitive issues, from prevention and control of Vitamin A deficiency, to food security and livelihoods programmes.

In all, 210 organizations working on 183 projects were included in the dataset, which was collected and analysed by HKI. Given the focus on maternal and child nutrition and the 1,000 days window of opportunity, it is encouraging that over 50 per cent of projects address maternal nutrition, infant and young child feeding (IYCF), food security and livelihoods, and water, sanitation, and hygiene (WASH), usually together in one project. However, though Bangladesh faces the third highest child marriage rate in the world and a corresponding 30 per cent teenage pregnancy rate (NIPORT, 2012), coupled with alarming malnutrition for children under 5, projects still do not focus on adolescent and pre-pregnancy nutrition. Approximately one-fifth of projects (21%) include activities aimed at adolescent girls or adolescent girls as a specific target. Frequently, this entails iron and folic acid supplementation (IFA) and/or deworming to reduce or prevent anaemia and only occasionally involves messaging and education on nutritional needs, optimal meal frequency, adequate diet, and dietary diversity.

Considering the persistently high rates of child marriage in the country, it is clear that many pregnant and lactating women for which over half of projects are providing nutrition education are adolescents. However, programmes that provide nutrition education and services prior to pregnancy are few and far between, especially in early adolescence.

Apart from the lack of attention to the unique (and urgent) nutritional needs of adolescent girls as separate from pregnant and lactating women, it appears from responses to the mapping that most nutrition-related programming in Bangladesh may not prioritize measures to ensure interventions are gender-sensitive and lead to gender-equal outcomes. Organizations responded to open-ended questions on programme design, activities, objectives, and indicators for nutrition-related projects and the information was later categorized. Only eight per cent of projects mentioned gender-based approaches. Based on evidence that livelihood interventions can enhance women's decision-making power, mobility, and other aspects of empowerment, it would be expected that programmes with a livelihoods component would also include specific activities aimed at achieving these outcomes. Yet, there is a notable lack of reported gender awareness in programme design among the projects surveyed in this mapping exercise.

Another gap uncovered by the mapping is exclusion of the whole household (e.g. husbands, parents, and in-laws) when attempting to improve nutritional status of pregnant and lactating women and children under 5. For decades, projects aimed at improving the nutrition of women and children have focused on providing nutrition education to women under the assumption that knowledge translates into the ability to change behaviour. In more recent years, the development sector has recognized that this approach does not adequately address external factors, such as gender dynamics within the household, which enable women to put their knowledge into practice.[5] Although long-term, longitudinal case studies in Bangladesh have documented changing gender norms around what makes a woman 'smart' or 'good', specifically finding changes in women's mobility and ability to move in the public sphere as a result of health and development programming, researchers are careful to note that this shift is bounded by a change in what is considered a suitable and legitimate reason for leaving the house (Schuler et al., 2006). Furthermore, being educated and 'smart' (e.g. aware of oppression and human rights, as described by participants in Schuler et al., 2006) does not automatically result in empowerment within the household. Women may have influential roles outside of the home, but still can be relegated to subservience inside the home.

Development and health programmes and policies can and do contribute to improvements in gender equality and equity (Schuler et al., 2006). The door-to-door family planning programme and behaviour change campaign in the late 1990s in Bangladesh stimulated increased awareness and demand for contraceptives. Women, who had before relied on their husbands to bring medicines to them and had not been aware of family planning, became educated on the benefits, along with their husbands. When the programme temporarily stopped, demand remained and going to the doctor for contraception was seen as a legitimate reason to leave the house (Schuler et al., 2006), presumably because husbands understood the benefit to the family. This newfound reason for mobility influenced mobility for other reasons, such as going to the market. Likewise, livelihood and nutrition programming can serve as an entry point for addressing disempowerment at the household level. Including all members of the household in education and awareness raising of the benefits of activities such as allowing women to earn income and make decisions with the money, considering women's opinions in household decisions, ensuring women have access to optimal nutrition, and better sharing of domestic work will result in greater nutritional gains for the entire household.

In sum, the 2013 NNS mapping project, along with the broader body of evidence from Bangladesh, found three interrelated yet distinct gaps in current nutrition-related programming: lack of consideration of gendered power relations and women's low relative status in programme design, lack of focus on nutritional needs and status of adolescent girls as a category apart from pregnant and lactating women, and absence of a household approach to addressing malnutrition in women and children. The findings provide a foundation from which to discuss approaches to transforming gender norms within the context of addressing malnutrition and improving livelihoods.

The Need for Gender Transformative Approaches: Beyond Women to Gender Relations

Programmatic frameworks which attempt to integrate gender, without questioning gender-based power relations, represent a limited 'add women and stir' approach (Beneria, 2003) which does not lead to gender-equal empowerment. In the last three decades, support has emerged for a more 'holistic' embrace of poverty as multidimensional, encompassing factors of 'social deprivation' and incorporating less tangible aspects of well-being such as self-esteem, self-respect, power, belonging and participation (Johnsson-Latham, 2004b), cited in Chant (2007), all of which are relevant to the gender dimensions of poverty (Chant, 2007). This approach recognizes that people meet their survival needs not only through monetary income, but through a variety of social, economic and political resources. Access to these resources affects women's agency in re-negotiating their roles in production and reproduction with implications for the larger patriarchal order (Kabeer, 2003). This thinking is central to the evolution of 'livelihoods' approaches to poverty analysis, which draw on concepts such as 'entitlements' and 'capabilities'. According to Amartya Sen's Capability Approach, poverty must be seen as the deprivation of basic capabilities rather than merely as the standard criterion of law of income (Sen, 2001). Sen points out that different people have different opportunities for converting income into quality of life, thus the connection between income and capability is both variable and deeply contingent on the characteristics of the respective individuals and the environment in which they live, both natural and social (Beneria, 2003). In relation to this, widespread research has suggested that there are systematic inequalities within households and attempts to estimate poverty that overlook inequalities within the household therefore provide an incomplete picture. This is particularly in relation to women's experience of poverty relative to that of men within the same household (Kabeer, 2003) given the different social and gendered norms they are subject to determining their respective obligations and responsibilities as care-takers or breadwinners.

Similarly, programmes aimed at improving nutrition outcomes at the household level in Bangladesh have, until recently, mainly targeted women with nutrition education. However, until socio-cultural gender norms are transformed, these programmes will have limited success because women's knowledge and other resources may remain unused and undervalued by women themselves and others in their family and community. This is because women and men operate within a multidimensional system of social relations that influence what is acceptable and appropriate for them to be and do. This means that although women are educated and equipped with assets, their husbands or in-laws may continue to decide what women and children are allowed to eat and when, whether women can leave the house and contribute to family income, whether they can control and manage the productive assets they gain through project participation, or apply information they obtain through interventions.

Furthermore, women also may accept existing boundaries on their actions and opportunities as normal. Thus, activities aimed at raising awareness of gender inequalities and their consequences should consider that, in a given culture, women may hold the same expectations as men of 'what makes a good woman'. For example, HKI's qualitative research in north-west Bangladesh found that the practice of providing smaller portions of choice foods to women was often driven by women themselves, with men sometimes unaware of the practice because they normally eat separately (HKI, 2014).

An overarching lesson learned from social protection, livelihoods, and nutrition programmes globally is that 'targeting women does not automatically ensure gender equality' (Holmes and Jones, 2010). Notably, a key challenge faced by many development programmes is the assumption that the transfer of economic resources to, or awareness raising with women alone will automatically translate into their empowerment in the household and beyond. For instance, making women official owners of productive assets without ensuring that others recognize their ability to manage and operate them, may merely sustain women in their existing situation. It can also increase their vulnerability if they end up as bearers of the risk and burden of engaging in these interventions without directly benefitting from them.

Few programmes seem to prioritize transforming intra-household gender relations, as exhibited by the responses for each project included in the Bangladesh nutrition activities mapping. Yet these very issues must be addressed to enable progress towards women's empowerment in a sustainable and effective way. This necessitates going beyond simply 'adding women and stirring' to focusing on improving the gender dynamics that prevent existing nutrition and livelihoods interventions from contributing effectively to processes of women's empowerment. This includes focusing on improving women's control over assets and information rather than simply their access to them, and ensuring their equal role in household decision-making around expenditure of earnings, food distribution, family planning, marriage of children, and more. An approach that addresses these issues is crucial to ensure equal allocation of household resources (including food) to enable equitable intra-household benefits. Central to each of these issues is establishing with spouses and other family members the value of women's contribution to the household and their wider capabilities to contribute to household livelihoods. Effective approaches also foster communication and negotiation skills among household members, demonstrating the link to better economic, health, and life satisfaction outcomes.

Gender inequality needs to be addressed within, as well as beyond, the boundaries of household units. Unless factors such as 'secondary poverty' within households are recognized, then efforts to empower women through income generating activities (IGAs) may well come to nothing. We need to look beyond women to gender relations – the roles of men as well as women and how they interact. It is not possible to move gender systems far towards equality without broad social consensus in favour of gender equality – and that consensus must include men and boys (Connell, 2003). Men and boys are, in many ways, gatekeepers for gender equality. Research has repeatedly shown that patterns of gender inequality are interwoven with social definitions of masculinity and men's gender identities. To move towards a gender-equal society often requires men and boys to think and act in new ways, to reconsider traditional images of manhood, and to reshape their relationships with women and girls. Men and boys are most likely to support change towards gender equality when they can see positive benefits for themselves and the people in their lives.

In relation to this, while it may seem more urgent and sometimes easier to target women in female-headed households with livelihoods and nutrition interventions as there are less intra-household gendered barriers, it is still essential to focus on empowering the majority of women who live in male-headed households (Chant, 2003). Women in male-headed households also face serious risks (including male dominance, domestic violence, and restricted mobility, sole responsibility for household work, and restriction from earning income). In short, men's departure may in some ways enhance the economic security and well-being of other household members, and even if women may be poorer in income as heads of their households, they may feel more socially empowered (higher control and access) and less vulnerable to violence and restriction (Chant, 2003). Furthermore, women in male-headed households may one day become female heads themselves, whether from choice, abandonment or being widowed. Thus, the need to become economically empowered and financially independent is just as important for women in male-headed households as it is for female household heads. They also make up the majority of households, so if societal change is desired, a focus needs to be made on all households.

Unequal social and political circumstances, driven by the intersection of gender and social norms, patriarchal divisions within the household and women's unrecognized double burden of productive and reproductive work, leave women with unequal capabilities. If women do not participate on equal terms in household decision-making due to intra-household inequalities and unequal power relations, their preferences will not be reflected in resource allocation outcomes, such as asset and cash transfers, leading to intra-household distributional failure. Frequently, men's privileged bargaining position allows them to command an even larger share of resources than they bring to the household as most income is turned over to them as the final decision-makers. Along with reducing the resources available to other household members, irregularity in financial contributions can lead to serious vulnerability and 'secondary poverty' among women and children.

To realize long-term improvements in family health, nutrition, and women's status, new approaches to gender integration that address the underlying causes of gender inequality are needed. These approaches, called gender transformative approaches (GTAs), go beyond the targeting of women (and sometimes men), to analyse and foster transformation in the norms, attitudes and practice that underlie the roles and responsibilities of men and women within the existing social system. They differ from accommodative gender integration approaches which analyse gender roles and relations but then work within and around them to achieve project objectives (www.igwg.org). Key characteristics that distinguish GTAs from other efforts to integrate gender into research and development interventions include (Kantor, 2013):

- Development of a deep understanding of people in their context and the way social inequalities intersect to affect choices and outcomes.
- Engagement with different actors across scales, including both women and men, in recognition of the way that social inequality is created and maintained through their attitudes and practices.
- Action to address unequal power relations.
- Action that fosters iterative cycles of critical reflection and action as a means to challenge oppressive norms, behaviours and structures.

The way forward for improved gender equality outcomes through agriculture and nutrition programmes should be the institutionalization of

GTAs. It is often said that gender needs to be 'integrated', or 'mainstreamed' within the programme, but this is usually translated into technical approaches that target women to fill gaps in access to resources within existing social contexts, thus reinforcing inequalities. Furthermore, an attempt to 'integrate' gender into programme activities lacks cognizance that gender is already integrated into the everyday lives of programme beneficiaries. Existing gendered roles and responsibilities not only govern even mundane choices, but will determine how a programme is incorporated into the existing cultural schema. Transforming what is known and thought about gendered roles and responsibilities is essential to programme sustainability and socio-cultural change.

GTAs are based in a more conceptually robust understanding of gender as a social construct, embedded in how societies define women's and men's roles and relations and the distribution of resources (Risman, 2004; Martin, 2004). Gender infuses all aspects of women's and men's daily lives through how it shapes what is acceptable and appropriate for them to be and do. This means gender affects how women and men conceive of themselves and their capabilities; how women and men interact and relate to others within the framework of social expectations; and how opportunities are structured and resources are distributed within institutions like the market and the state. Discriminatory social institutions are the root causes of gender inequalities and 'reflect and reproduce underlying gendered power relations' (Cerise and Francamilla, 2012). In explicitly recognizing this, GTAs differ from other gender mainstreaming approaches in their definition of the problem underlying gender inequality and, therefore, in the solutions put forward to foster change. They engage with the complexity of gender to support women and men to act on the norms, attitudes, and wider structural constraints that limit their opportunities and outcomes and see the institutional context as a key barrier to equality, justice, and the achievement of global development outcomes (Kabeer, 2012; Chant and Sweetman, 2012; Razavi, 2009; Okali, 2012). Social change in the interests of women and other marginalized groups is the goal, in order to expand the types and quality of life and livelihood choices available and acceptable to women and men, and therefore these groups' entitlements to participate in and benefit from development processes in ways that they define and value. This process of challenging and changing the social context within which women and men earn their living involves engaging with power relations and entrenched norms, which are often legitimized by strong cultural traditions and beliefs. While there is bound to be resistance, there is scope for change, and men and women themselves need to be the primary agents of that change (Mayoux, 2007) to achieve gender equality and women's empowerment.

GTAs also seek to foster change in individual capacities (knowledge and skills), attitudes, agency and actions; the gendered expectations embedded within relationships between people in the home, in groups and organizations; and institutional rules and practices. The interconnected and cross-scale nature of the changes underlies the complexity of the challenge involved in fostering transformative change. For example, family member mindsets may need to shift in order to facilitate a change in women's and men's accepted roles, such as in domestic work or paid work outside of the home. Community opinion leaders and local service providers can stymie or support progress through how strongly they hold on to norms and attitudes that limit women's access to opportunities, such as by upholding mobility constraints. Community norms may influence the willingness of families and individuals to step outside of what is expected of them due to fear of the consequences of not conforming. Private sector actors may be blind to women as economic agents, and bypass their needs and interests in design and dissemination of technologies.

Development actors cannot impose gender transformative changes upon individuals, communities or societies from the outside. Therefore, a willingness to engage in gender transformative change processes needs to emerge from among those who will bring about and experience the changes – in the families, communities and local and national institutions composing a given society. Development actors have a role in sparking such processes through providing information, linking people to networks or demonstrating through role models or other means that change is possible. One key challenge for the uptake and application of GTAs in agriculture is to not see them as separate from more 'technical' interventions, and vice versa. A main hypothesis related to GTAs is that through implementing them hand in hand with technology-focused, livelihood enhancing interventions, optimal results from both are achieved (AAS, 2012). This marrying of the social and technical requires rethinking how technical interventions, such as around nutrition and livelihoods, are delivered (i.e. the process) and to whom, and planning how purely social interventions can be sequenced and layered with technical ones so that the integrated package incorporates the core characteristics of GTAs. Examining whether and how integrated packages of social and technical interventions foster gender transformative change across contexts and social groups, and whether and how these changes lead to improved agricultural and nutrition outcomes, is a central research agenda for GTAs in the agricultural sector. A range of mechanisms might foster the consciousness necessary to trigger critical questioning of the social status quo, participatory action research[6], including farmer field school approaches, is one mechanism that has shown success in catalyzing change in social relations through building confidence in and demonstrating the capacities of marginalized groups (Friis-Hansen et al., 2012; Humphries et al., 2012). Adult learning approaches focusing on social issues also can be incorporated into nutrition and agricultural technology training, and delivered to families and communities, as a means of linking technology and nutrition knowledge transfer to a critical analysis of the social barriers at the family and community levels that affect the use of the knowledge.

GTAs require the understanding that gender is part of our lives, and that socio-economic disparities, including access to appropriate nutrition, healthcare and production, are caused by how gender relations are framed within a socio-cultural context. By seeking to act upon the social context, GTAs try to identify ways of shifting discriminating gender norms that hinder women and men's abilities to define and achieve development goals. The downside of trying to shift gender norms is that the process is slow and results may not be visible and measurable in the short term. However, identifying a theory of change with realistic milestones that demonstrate progress towards gender transformative outcomes can justify the investments and provide the feedback needed to document successes and refine approaches. Changing attitudes requires time, but this approach is expected to ultimately perform better in sustaining positive changes that will benefit both women and their families.

Case Studies of Gender Transformative Approaches from Bangladesh

EEP/Shiree

EEP/Shiree is the Economic Empowerment of the Poorest Programme. It is also known as 'Shiree' – the Bangla word for steps – as it aims at 'Stimulating Household Improvements Resulting in Economic Empowerment'. It is a Government of Bangladesh initiative supported by UKaid (DFID) and the Swiss Development Cooperation. EEP/Shiree aims to help one million people lift themselves out of extreme poverty. EEP/Shiree uses the challenge fund model and finances partner NGOs focused on the extreme poor – targeting the bottom 10 per cent of the population. Through its partner NGOs, EEP is currently engaged in supporting over 3,00,000 extreme poor households – more than one million people.

To address enduring malnutrition among the extreme poor in Bangladesh, in September 2012 EEP/Shiree integrated nutrition interventions into its programming. The nutrition component followed a standard three-tier structure:

- Drug delivery (micro-nutrients, de-worming and anti-helminthic drugs).
- Behaviour change counselling (both individual household level counselling and in courtyard sessions on basic nutrition messages) led by over 2,200 female Community Nutrition Workers, Community Pushti Kormis (CPKs).
- Social mobilization with key community stakeholders (village leaders, religious leaders, traditional birth attendants, school teachers, etc.).

These standard nutrition interventions (besides the social mobilization) were provided to primary target groups: pregnant women, lactating mothers, children under two years, children aged 2–5 years and adolescent girls. However, after a year of observing the impact of this standard nutrition intervention, EEP/Shiree realized it was missing a gender component. Targetting women and girls with nutrition awareness did not empower them to apply their new learning in the absence of a supportive environment in their households and communities.

Vast gender inequalities had been observed among EEP/Shiree households at baseline. One-third of all parents said they believed sons to be more important than daughters in education and nutrition. And, one-third of all households gave more food to male earning members (EEP/Shiree, August 2014). The conclusion is that without gender equality and women's empowerment, malnutrition persists. Gender discrimination and vulnerability to 'secondary poverty' will continue among women and girls.

In 2014, EEP/Shiree mainstreamed gender into their nutrition component by providing training to the female CPKs: to become gender and nutrition change-makers in their communities, delivering gender and nutrition behaviour change messages through using flipcharts with entire beneficiary households and communities (including women, men, adolescents, in-laws) both in collective courtyard sessions and individual household counselling. The EEP/Shiree partner NGO Nutrition and Livestock Officers and CPKs, all received a two-day gender training involving role play exercises, interactive group work and storytelling to encourage them to address gender issues related to extreme poverty among households and communities.

Besides the standard Nutrition Modules on maternal, child and adolescent nutrition (e.g. breastfeeding, age appropriate complementary feeding, reproductive health, menstrual hygiene, maternal nutrition, nutrition in adolescent period), five additional, but directly nutrition-related, gender modules were incorporated: Stopping Child Marriage, Family Planning, Equal Healthcare, Equal Food Distribution and Sharing Household Work. A flipchart toolkit was designed based on a combination of field observations, M&E and research findings, and learning from best practices on other gender mainstreamed nutrition programmes in Bangladesh (HKI, Plan, Care, BRAC, 2013).

By combining Gender and Nutrition Behaviour Change Counselling with core programmatic efforts at empowering women in gender-transformative income generating activities (i.e. involving marketing and mobility outside the homestead), EEP/Shiree managed to establish a comprehensive model for women's empowerment ensuring sustainable gender-equal livelihoods.

Nurturing Connections

Although it is established that women's empowerment is an important factor in improving the effectiveness of food security and nutrition programmes, many development interventions target only resource and skills transfer to women, or posit that specifically targeting women will empower them and improve agricultural, nutritional and health impacts. Additionally, evidence about agricultural interventions' impact on women's assets is limited (Meinzen-Dick et al., 2011), and there is little documentation of specific interventions that are effective in challenging intra-household power relations imbalance and improving both the nutrition and food security of the family (Quisimbing and Roy, 2013).

To address intra-household power relations and improve nutrition, HKI tested a new GTA last year, through the Nurturing Connections curriculum. Inspired by the peer-based 'Stepping Stones' approach to addressing HIV/AIDS and sexual health in Africa, the curriculum is a series of participatory, non-formal learning sessions through which participants acquire communication, assertiveness and problem-solving skills to challenge intra-household inequalities among their peer groups first, and then in a mediated, community-group setting at the end of each thematic series of activities.

Nurturing Connections draws on approaches developed through HKI's homestead food production interventions, which have been used over decades of programming in Bangladesh to empower women in improving nutrition. It includes 10 facilitated sessions. In each session (of approximately two-hour durations), stakeholders are involved in as games, role-plays, drawing exercises, so and other activities that enable even the least literate to participate. Through these sessions, participants are encouraged to recall personal experiences with discriminating practices and behaviours that can lead to undernutrition, and unpack and discuss them to improve family relations and ultimately the nutritional status of the household.

HKI pilot-tested the curriculum in 2013 in 40 communities in the Nilphamari district, north-west Bangladesh, as part of the Oxfam-Novib supported Building Equity in Agriculture and Markets (BEAM) project. With a focus on the Char (Riverine Island) areas of north-west Bangladesh, BEAM targetted young women, whose mobility, decision-making and nutrition access were greatly constricted in the project areas. Nurturing Connections complemented a package of interventions aimed at empowering women economically, such as HKI's signature homestead food production programme and women's small-scale income generating activities. Project end line results showed that the proportion of women who reported having a say in decision-making over child care increased by 64 per cent. Additionally, women reported having increased support from their husbands in many household tasks, from cooking to water collection and cleaning, allowing them to get sufficient rest during pregnancy and dedicate the time they needed for breastfeeding.

CSISA-BD and AIN

In Bangladesh, various research and development projects target women with agricultural technologies that aim to reduce the technology adoption gap between men and women and bring about women's empowerment. In many cases, technologies are designed that accommodate the needs of women and have the potential to enhance productivity, especially of the homestead production system over which women usually have more access and control. However, a recent study[7] (Morgan et al., 2014) of two such women targetted aquaculture technologies[8], disseminated through two WorldFish projects, Cereal Systems Initiative for South Asia in Bangladesh (CSISA-BD) and Aquaculture for Income and Nutrition (AIN), has found that technology interventions that target women alone may not necessarily enhance women's contributions to aquaculture outcomes and the benefits they derive from them. This discrepancy between expected and actual outcomes arises because women and men, exist in a multidimensional system of gender relations which influence women's ability to: adopt technologies, gain and apply knowledge and skills to adapt them, achieve anticipated production and consumption outcomes and share equitably in their benefits. Therefore a different intervention approach was needed that responded to these nuanced social and power relationships and provided the tools, knowledge and skills for productivity gains, as well as addressing the underlying causes of gender inequality. Results from the study have informed the design and trial of a new aquaculture technology dissemination approach in two villages of CSISA-BD's Faridpur hub. Keeping in mind the time constraint and productivity driven nature of these projects, the technology package has been redesigned to combine technical aquaculture training with gender consciousness raising exercises derived from HKI's Nurturing Connections manual. Families are involved from the beginning of the intervention and the training is modularized to interact with the different stages of the production cycle and address any social and gender issues that may arise as a result of applying new knowledge. Changes in production and in knowledge, attitudes and practices (both technical and social) are being monitored among participating women and their spouses through survey research methods and process documentation. Initial findings show positive changes in levels of confidence including voicing opinions and being heard and valued in aquaculture decisions. The incentive of gaining technical livelihood-relevant knowledge has made it acceptable for women to participate as the knowledge brings value to the family. In 2015, the gender integrated homestead aquaculture training approach will be adapted, based on learning from the pilot, and implemented at scale. The aim is to evaluate the potential of new transformative extension approaches, including that of Participatory Action Research, to deliver more lasting and equitable outcomes than conventional technology delivery methods.

Conclusion

Interventions should foster the recognition that women and girls are valuable – as mothers, citizens, rights holders and economic contributors. Women's empowerment should not be pursued only as a fixed-point tool to improve the nutrition status of children and themselves, rather it should be pursued as a journey and as vital in its own right.

Although many development programmes are making an effort to focus on women living in vulnerable conditions, transferring assets to them for their own economic empowerment or educating them about gender-equal nutrition to reverse discriminating behaviour is extremely difficult in the context of unequal gender relations. Basing a project intervention on the premise that women alone, with tools or information, can change the patriarchal society they were socialized into throughout their lives, is dangerously flawed. Women do not operate in a vacuum, and for women to empower themselves they need an enabling environment where their empowerment is valued as key to long-term well-being, progress, and development of the society as a whole. Selecting female beneficiaries does not ensure their empowerment if other members in the household or community are the main decision-makers whose approval is needed to change unequal intra-household food distribution or the traditional 'male bread-winner – female caretaker' model. Hence, NGOs should engage all household and community members, both men and women, in project intervention training and orientation sessions, be they related to livelihoods or nutrition.

Moreover, if empowerment is understood to involve extending 'the horizons of possibility, of what people imagine themselves being able to be and do' (Cornwall and Edwards, 2010, cited in Scott, 2012) while also enabling them to realize these aspirations in their everyday lives, then clearly more work needs to be done to create the conditions within which empowerment processes can occur. This involves shifting away from thinking and acting within the gender normative framework and challenging the gendered perceptions of all development actors, across the project cycle. By providing necessary skills training and awareness raising to a range of relevant actors, women can be enabled to choose to enter traditional male spheres; to become breadwinners and entrepreneurs, managing their own businesses, finances, and accessing market linkages. Such livelihoods interventions will lead to socio-economic empowerment that is both equitable and sustainable.

It is essential to change mindsets of donors, implementers, husbands, sons, in-laws, village leaders, community members and women themselves. The case study examples from Bangladesh included in this paper show that with mobilization efforts and awareness raising by change makers and challenging traditional gender norms, this is possible. Transforming gender norms is transforming society.

Notes

1. Call to Action: Nutrition in the Post-2015 Development Agenda, http://thousanddays.org/wp-content/uploads/2013/09/Nutrition-in-the-Post-2015-Agenda-Key-Messages.pdf
2. Stunted means low length or height for age, meaning that the person is not achieving 'linear growth potential'.
3. Ibid.
4. Conducted by HKI in 2013, in collaboration with the National Nutrition Services (NNS) of the Ministry of Health and Family Welfare, Government of the People's Republic of Bangladesh (GOB), and funded by USAID through the Food and Nutrition Technical Assistance programme (FANTA-III) of FHI360.
5. Quisumbing, A., and Meinzen-Dick, R., 'Closing the Gender Gap', in 2012 Global Food Policy Report, http: //www.ifpri.org/gfpr/ 2012/women-agriculture.
6. For more details on PAR, please visit: http: //www.worldfishcenter.org/resource_centre/AAS-2013-27.pdf
7. Funded by the CGIAR Research Programme (CRP) on *Climate Change, Agriculture and Food Security (CCAFS)* and the CRP on Aquatic Agricultural Systems (AAS).
8. The two technologies were the pond polyculture with horticulture technology and cage aquaculture.

References

Abu-Saad, Kathleen and Fraser, Drora (2010). *Maternal Nutrition and Birth Outcomes*. UK: Oxford Journal.

Bangladesh Bureau of Statistics (2010). Report of the Household Income and Expenditure Survey.

Bangladesh Bureau of Statistics and UNFPA (2013). Report on Violence against Women Survey.

Beneria, Lourdes (2003). *Gender, Development and Globalisation*. London: Routledge.

Sen, Binayak; Menon, Purnima; Akhter, U.; Ahmed, Fatema and Chowdhury, Parveen (2010). *Food Utilization and Nutrition Security*, Bangladesh Food Security Investment Forum.

Care, Akhoni Shomoy (2012) Mid-Term Review Report.

Care, (2006) *From Policy to Practice: A Good Practice Guide to Gender Mainstreaming*, October 2006.

Cerise, S. and Francavilla, F. (2010). *Tackling the Root Causes of Gender Inequalities in the Post-2015 Development Agenda, Paris:* OECD Development Centre.

CGIAR (2012). Research Program on Aquatic Agricultural Systems, Gender Strategy Brief – A Gender Transformative Approach to Research in Development in Aquatic Agricultural Systems, CGIAR Research Program on Aquatic Agricultural Systems. Penang, Malaysia.

Chant, Silvia H. (2003). *Female Household Headship and the Feminization of Poverty: Facts, Fictions and Forward Strategies*. London: LSE.

Chant, Sylvia H. (2007). *Gender, Generation and Poverty: Exploring the Feminisation of Poverty in Africa, Asia and Latin America.* Elgar: Cheltenham.

Chant, S. and Sweetman, C. (2012). 'Fixing Women or Fixing the World? 'Smart economics', Efficiency Approaches, and Gender Equality in Development', *Gender and Development*, 20(3): 517–29.

Connell, R.W. (2003), The Role of Men and Boys in Achieving Gender Equality, United Nations Division for the Advancement of Women (DAW) in collaboration with International Labor Organization (ILO) Joint United Nations Programmes on HIV/AIDS (UNAIDS), United Nations Development Programme (UNDP), Expert Group Meeting on 'The Role of Men and Boys in Achieving Gender Equality', Brasilia, Brazil, 21 to 24 October.

EEP/Shiree, State of the Extreme Poor Baseline Report, August 2014.

Gill, Kirrin; Patel, Payal; Kantor, Paula and McGonagle, Allison (2012). Invisible Market: Energy and Agricultural Technologies for Women's Advancement, International Centre for Research on Women.

Goodarz, Danaei; Finucane, Mariel M.; Lin, John K.; Singh, Gitanjali M.' Paciorek, Christopher J.; Cowan, Melanie J.; Farzadfar, Farshad, Stevens, Gretchen A., Lim, Stephen S., Riley, Leanne M. and Ezzati, Majid (2011). National, Regional, and Global Trends in Systolic Blood Pressure since 1980, [on behalf of the Global Burden of Metabolic Risk Factors of Chronic Diseases Collaborating Group (Blood Pressure)] February 4.

Friis-Hansen, E. and Duvesgok, D. (2012). 'The Empowerment Route to Well Being: An Analysis of Farmer Field Schools in East Africa', *World Development*, 40: 414–427.

Helen Keller International (HKI) (2014). Affordable Nutritious Food for Women, Formative Research, unpublished document.

Helen Keller International (HKI) and BRAC Institute of Global Health (BIGH) (2012 and 2013). State of Food Security and Nutrition in Bangladesh.

Holden, G.W. (2003). 'Children Exposed to Domestic Violence and Child Abuse: Terminology and Taxonomy', Clin Child Fam Psychol Rev., Sep: 6 (3): 151–60.

Holmes and Jones (2010). 'Social Protection Programming: The Need for Gender Lens' Access at: http: //www.odi.org.uk/resources/download /4944.pdf

Humphries, S., Classen, L., Jimenez, J., Sierra, F., Gallardo, O. and M. Gomes (2012). *Opening Cracks for the Transgression of Social Boundaries: An Evaluation of the Gender Impacts of Farmer Research Teams in Honduras,* World Development 40: 2078–2095.

Inter-agency Gender Working Group (IGWG), Gender Continuum Categories, www.igwg.org/igwg_media/.../GendrContinuumCategories.doc

International Centre for Diahorreal Disease Research, Bangladesh, ACPR and Plan International Bangladesh (2013). Child Marriage in Bangladesh: Findings from a National Survey.

IDS (2011). Admissible Evidence in the Court of Development Evaluation: The Impact of Care's SHOUHARDO Project on Child Stunting in Bangladesh, IDS Working Paper, 2011, No 376, 2011.

Kabeer, N. (2003). *Gender Mainstreaming in Poverty Eradication and the Millennium Development Goals: A Handbook for Policy-Makers and Other Stakeholders*. London: Commonwealth Secretariat.

Kabeer, N. (2012). 'Women's Economic Empowerment and Inclusive Growth: Labor Markets and Enterprise Development', (working paper) *SIG* WP 2012/1: Ottawa: IDRC.

Kantor, P. and Apgar, M. (2013). Transformative Change in the CGIAR Research Program on Aquatic Agricultural Systems, Penang, Malaysia. Program Brief: AAS-2013-25.

Kantor, P., Transforming Gender Relations: A Key to Lasting Positive Agricultural Development Outcomes, CGIAR Research Program on Aquatic Agricultural Systems. Penang, Malaysia. Brief: AAS-2013-12.

Martin, P.Y. (2004). 'Gender as Social Institution', *Social Forces*, 82(4): 1249–1273.

Mayoux, L. and Mackie, G. (2007). *A Practical Guide to Mainstreaming Gender Analysis in Value Chain Development*, International Labor Office. Addis Ababa: ILO.

Meinzen-Dick, R.; Behrman, J.; Menon, P. and Quisimbing, A. (2011). 'Gender: A Key Dimension Linking Agricultural Programs to Improved Nutrition and Health', in S. Fan and R. Pandya-Lorch (eds) *Reshaping Agriculture for Nutrition and Health*, 135–144, IFPRI.

Mehrotra and Colleagues, India Human Development Report, 2011.

Morgan, M.; Choudhury, A.; Sultana, N.; Braun, M.; Beare, D.; Benedict, J.; Rajaratnam, S.; and Kantor, P. (2014). 'Understanding the Gender Dimensions of Adopting 'Climate-Smart' Smallholder Aquaculture Innovations', CCAFS and AAS Working Paper (in process).

NIPORT (2007). Mitra and Associates, Bangladesh Health and Demographic Survey.

NIPORT (2012). Mitra and Associates, Bangladesh Demographic and Health Survey, Measure DHS.

Nutrition Surveillance Project Bulletin (2006). The Burden of Anaemia in Rural Bangladesh: The Need for Urgent Action, No. 16.

Okali, C. (2012). 'Gender Analysis: Engaging with Rural Development and Agricultural Policy Processes', Working Paper 026, Future Agricultures Consortium, Brighton: IDS.

Quisimbing, A. and Roy, S. (2013). How Do Intra-Household Dynamics Change When Assets Are Transferred to Women? Evidence from BRAC'S 'Targeting the Ultra Poor' Program in Bangladesh. IFPRI Discussion Paper.

Quisumbing, A. and Meinzen-Dick, R. (2012). Closing the Gender Gap, in 2012 Global Food Policy Report. Accessed at: http: //www.ifpri.org/gfpr/2012/women-agriculture.

Razavi, S. (2009). 'Engendering the Political Economy of Agrarian Change', *Journal of Peasant Studies*, Vol. 36(1): 197–226.

Risman, B. (2004). 'Gender as a Social Structure: Theory Wrestling with Activism', *Gender and Society*, Vol. 18(4): 429–450.

Ruel, Marie T. and Alderman, Harold, (2013). 'Nutrition-Sensitive Interventions and Programmes: How Can They Help to Accelerate Progress in Improving Maternal and Child Nutrition?' *The Lancet*, 382 (9891): 536–551.

Ruth, Oniang'o and Edith, Mukudi (2002). Nutrition and Gender, In Nutrition: A Foundation for Development, Geneva: UN ACC/SCN.

Schuler, Sydney R.; Islam, Farzana; Boender, Carol; Islam, Md. Kahirul and Bates, Lisa M. (2006). 'Health and Development Policies and the Emerging Smart Women in Rural Bangladesh: Local Perceptions', Working Paper #286, *Women and International Development*, Michigan State University.

Scott, L. (2012). 'Contested Relationships: Women's Economic and Social Empowerment, Insights from the Transfer of Material Assets in Bangladesh', UNU-WIDER, WP/002. Accessed at: http: //www.wider.unu.edu/publications/working-papers/2012/en_GB/ wp2012-002/

Sen, Amartya (2001). *Development as Freedom*. New Delhi: Oxford University Press.

Standing Committee on Nutrition, Adolescence, news #31, United Kingdom, 2006.

Talukder, R.K. (2005). 'Food Security, Self-sufficiency and Nutrition Gap in Bangladesh', *The Bangladesh Development Studies*, 35–62.

The Maternal and Child Under Nutrition Study Group (2008). 'What works? Interventions for Maternal and Child Under nutrition and Survival', *The Lancet*, 371 (9610): 417–440.

United Nations Children's Fund (UNICEF) (2012). Programming Guide: Infant and Young Child Feeding.

UNICEF (2014). The State of the World's Children 2014 in Numbers: Every Child Counts.

World Food Programme (WFP) (2005). MOFDM, Food Security in Bangladesh.

WFP, Bangladesh Nutrition Strategy 2012–2016.

World Health Organisation (WHO) (2002). Complementary Feeding of Young Children in Developing Countries, in WHO Complementary Feeding: Report of The Global Consultation.

WHO (2001). Guiding Principles for Complementary Feeding of the Breast-Feed Child.

Zieai S., Naved, R.T. and Ekström E.C. (2012). Women's Exposure to Intimate Partner Violence and Child Malnutrition: Findings from Demographic and Health Surveys in Bangladesh', in *Maternal and Child Nutrition*, Dacca: Blackwell Publishing Ltd.

13

Impact of Natural Disaster on the Coping Strategies of the Women

Kedar Valley in Rudraprayag District of the Central Himalayas, Uttarakhand

ANNPURNA NAUTIYAL AND R.K. MAIKHURI

Abstract

In Uttarakhand, the meager resources of livelihood and unproductive rained agriculture forced male migration to the plain areas for employment and, in their absence women not only looked after the domestic work but also agriculture. Due to women's immense contribution in agriculture they are considered axis of the hill economy. But as agriculture and animal husbandry is not productive, women also depend on remittances sent by the migrated male members. Unfortunately this chain of sending remittances was broken by the unprecedented natural tragedy that struck Uttarkhand during 16–17 June 2013, particularly in the Rudraprayag district in Garhwal Himalayas. Male members of several nearby villages in the age group of 14–60 years who had gone to Kedarnath for earning their livelihood by working in hotels, small eateries, running mules, their own shops, working as priest in Kedarnath temple were swept away by the massive flood along with a large number of pilgrims. It had a very disastrous impact particularly on the villages of Ukhimath block of District Rudraprayag which lost most of the young and able bodied men leaving behind the widows, old people and children. It has created real problems for women as they have to cope with the absence of their husbands and male children and overcome the sociological and psychological pressures of the loss of their family members, generate income to run the household and oversee the day-to-day and other expenses like marriage of the girls, etc. They have also to look after the old people and also to think about the coping strategies. In view of the above, the present paper aims to study and analyse the impact of natural disaster of June 2013 on the coping strategies of the women of Rudraprayag district in Uttarakhand Himalayas.

Keywords

Uttarakhand, Central Himalayas, Rudraprayag, Kedarnath Yatra, natural disaster, coping strategies

Disasters: Types and Effects

Disasters are the antithesis of human development because of their capacity for inducing extensive damages, death and destruction, affecting the recovery of infrastructure, education, health and income-generating processes. A disaster is a function of the risk process: it results from the combination of hazards, conditions of vulnerability and insufficient capacity or measures to reduce the potential negative consequences of risk (UNISDR, 2004). The strong population growth, unplanned human settlements, rising pollution, environmental degradation and poverty assists the transformation of natural hazards into natural disasters and enhances the magnitude of vulnerability. The destruction of bridges, roads and buildings by natural disaster like earthquakes and floods not only affects people's livelihoods but also capacities of movement, communication and work. The number and severity of disasters particularly hydro meteorological disasters, which includes cyclones, floods, hurricanes, etc. is increasing as a result of climate change or extreme events. It is estimated that in 2009, there were 335 natural disasters worldwide which killed 10,655 persons, affected more than 119 million others and caused over US$ 41.3 billion economic damages (Ferris, 2010). According to some other estimates from 1999 to 2008, floods have affected nearly one billion people in Asia, whereas in Europe it affected 4 million people, in America 28 million and in Africa 22 million and its overall impact was massive. Over the last 30 years, floods and landslides in South Asia have caused more than 65,000 deaths (Shrestha and Takara, 2007). The people in a large number suffer in parts of north-east India, south-central Nepal, central and southern Pakistan, Bangladesh and China every year because of the high population density. In China, approximately 130 million people are exposed to flooding every year and about 2,000 people die in floods every year. Though the flood prone parts of China produce 70 per cent of the industrial and agricultural goods but more than 8 million hectares of such land is flooded every year causing high economic loss. In Bangladesh, between 1998 and 2008, 86 million people were affected by natural disasters, primarily floods. In August 2010 in Pakistan, two weeks of intense monsoon rains caused major rivers to wash away roads, bridges and croplands, affecting 20.5 million people, killing over 1,700 people and displacing 6 million people (NCVST, 2009). Parts of Nepal are also vulnerable to seasonal flooding. India's North-East is also prone to constant flooding and in June 2013 large parts of Uttarakhand Himalayas were also affected by flash floods causing immense loss of people, property and infrastructure.[1] The natural disasters can be classified into following categories, as mentioned in Table 1.

Table 1

Categories of Natural Disasters

Disaster Generic Group	*Disaster Sub Group*	*Definition*	*Disaster Main Type*
Natural Disaster	Geophysical	Events originating from solid Earth	Earthquake, Volcano, Mass Movement (dry)
	Meteorological	Events caused by short lived/small to meso scale atmospheric processes	Storm
	Hydrological	Events caused by deviations in the normal water cycle or overflow of bodies of water by wind set up	Flood, Mass Movement (wet)
	Climatologically	Events caused by long lived meso or macro scale processes	Extreme Temperature Drought Wildfire
	Biological	Disaster Caused by the exposure of living organism to germs and toxic substances	Epidemic Insect infestation Animal Stampede

Source: The International Disaster Database Classification 2009, http: //www.emdat.be/classification.

Natural disasters are mostly seen as random 'acts of God' over which individuals have little control. Some disasters may be seen as the fault of those in decision-making positions and in some other cases, blame is directed at those who chose to live in high-risk areas, constructed houses in the river flood plain or did not take appropriate precautionary measures, such as purchasing insurance (Fothergill, 2003). The most apparent impacts of natural disasters can be seen in the form of loss of human lives, rise in physical disabilities, damage or destruction of infrastructure, loss of livelihood, housing, and facilities like water, sanitation, electricity, schools, health centres, crops and livestock (UNDP, 2008). Disasters do not affect people equally because inequalities in risk experience, sensitivity to risk, access to resources, opportunities and capabilities, put specific segments of the population in a disadvantageous position. Identifying universal patterns in the magnitude of the impacts is not easy but it is accepted by a large number of scholars that the poorest suffer most during the disasters (Neumayer and Plumper, 2002, Ferris, 2010). Since socio-economic status is a significant indicator of the physical and the emotional impacts in the pre- and post-disaster stages therefore, according to these studies, the poor are more likely to die, suffer from injuries, have higher material losses; emotional trauma; and face more obstacles during the phases of response, recovery, and reconstruction. The woman-headed households, the elderly, the unemployed, the illiterate or uneducated, the ill or handicapped people form the categories of the groups who usually experience low socio-economic status in the society suffer the grave impacts of disaster due to their lack of access to economic or human resources or knowledge (Masozera, Bailey and Kerchner, 2007). Though the natural disasters cannot be stopped and their occurrence is for most part out of control of authorities, but effective implementation of policy tools in the aftermath of disaster for improving prevention and risk-management strategies and mechanisms both at the household, sub-national and national levels may reduce the impacts of disaster considerably.

Effect of Disasters on Women

It is also generally accepted that disaster affects women differently than men. The Beijing Declaration and Platform for Action (1995) also highlights that environmental degradation and disasters often impact more directly on women. It is due to this reason that the Hyogo Framework for Action 2005 stressed that a gender perspective should be integrated into all disaster risk management policies, plans and decision-making process, risk assessment, early warning, information management and education and training. Women face different challenges and levels of vulnerability and are affected much more badly than men because of the difference in exposure to risk, risk sensitivity, awareness, response, physical and emotional impact, revival and rebuilding (Women and Natural Disaster, 2010). The biological and physical differences between men and women and pre-existing social norms and roles as well as new forms of gender discrimination in the aftermath of disaster also tend to enhance the impact of disaster on the women. While taking the case study of Pakistan during the earthquake of 2005 Neumayer and Plumper have pointed out that in 2005 earthquake in Pakistan which killed 73,000 people it was found that women were mostly at home when the earthquake hit and their adult male family members were working in the fields. This meant women were more apt to be injured by collapsing homes than their husbands and the UN agencies also reported a large number of paraplegics among Pakistani women after this disaster (Neumayer and Plumper, 2002). Elizabeth Ferris has also opined that women tend to have higher levels of depression than men after disasters. On the basis of the findings of the UNHR, workers in Pakistan who were running a welfare centre in Pakistan for victims of the 2010 floods, Ferris has noted that the majority of the women had been suffering from phobic or panic attacks, depression and anxiety after the floods because women were particularly more worried about the future uncertainties regarding employment, livelihood, and education of their children therefore their anxiety and tension were generally linked to losing homes and all the means of livelihood in the floods (Ferris, 2010).

Elaine Enarson (2000) has provided the following reasons for increase in women's insecurity after the disaster. First, women's economic insecurity increases, as their productive assets are destroyed. They often become sole earners, their household entitlements may decline, their small-businesses are hard-hit, they lose jobs and work time. Second, women's workload increase dramatically. They often take on more waged or other forms of income-generating work; engage in a number of new forms of 'disaster work and have expanded responsibilities as care givers. Third, women's working condition in the household and paid work place deteriorates, due to lack of child care and increased work and family conflicts. Fourth, women recover more slowly than men from major economic losses, as they are less mobile than male workers and often fail to receive equitable financial recovery assistance from the government or external donors.

Women are also found to be more vulnerable to disasters. Vulnerability is a condition that is determined by physical, social, economic and environmental factors or processes, which increase the susceptibility of a community to the impact of hazards (Women and Natural Disaster, 2010). Vulnerability is 'insecurity, and reflects 'the characteristics of a person or group in terms of their capacity to foresee and cope with, defy, and recover from the impact of a natural hazard.' It involves a combination of factors that determine the degree to which someone's life and livelihood is put at risk by a discrete and identifiable event in nature or in society (Blaikie, Davis and Wisner, 1994). Vulnerability refers to exposure to contingencies and stress and difficulty in coping with them. It has been noticed that women, children, elderly and person with disability are more vulnerable than the other sections to disasters. They are left behind in cases of emergency because they lack knowledge, mobility and resources. In some cases, a post disaster loss of livelihood pushes migration of men which forces women to head the responsibilities of the households and family. Sometimes men are killed, leaving behind their wives which brings more responsibilities on the shoulders of the women from looking after their children to performing other various social and economic activities. Against this background, this paper discusses the impact of disaster which struck the various parts of Uttarakhand in June 2013 on the people, particularly women.

The Context

The natural disaster was not only unprecedented from the point of view of the magnitude of destruction in terms of human life and infrastructure but also shaking the faith of the people as it hit all the four famous holy shrines namely Yamunotri, Gangotri, Badrinath and Kedarnath and also Hem Kunt Sahab; however, the scale of destruction in Kedarnath shrine and the Rudraprayg district was massive. In view of this, it becomes pertinent to evaluate the lifestyle changes and threats being faced by the people particularly women of the disaster affected areas of Rudraparyag district[2] in the aftermath of this disaster. It is a well-known fact that the disaster of June 2013 has left tally telling marks of severe destruction of infrastructure, misery and pain in these areas. However, with the recently repaired national highway the connectivity in the areas located at the road head has been restored and with the resumption of the Keadarnath shrine Yatra (tourism) and the influx of a small number of pilgrims the tourist activity has also started in 2013. The people dependent on the religious tourism, though, were not very happy with the pace of the *yatra* and the limited number of tourists but they have something to look forward even if they are not satisfied. This was necessary to put a healing balm on the wounds of the people affected by the disaster who have been suffering from the socio, psychological, economic, ecological and political impacts of the disaster.

Though connectivity and road network has been restored in the areas located at the main *yatra* route in Kedarnath shrine area but in the other adjoining areas still much needs to be done. A visit to the locations like Kalimath, Kabiltha, Kotma, Khonu, Kunjethi, etc. in other part of Kedar valley provided us with a realistic picture of the area and the situation after the disaster. Kalimath is a place known for religious tourism and Kabiltha is the birth place of the famous Sanskrit poet Kalidas where every year Kalidas's birthday is celebrated which is attended by the scholars from India and abroad but the road network and other facilities in these places are hopeless.[3] In Kalimath, the approach road to the temple of the goddess Durga which is visited by a large number of people, was washed away by the deluge of June 2013, therefore, a temporary bridge on the river was erected by the Public Works Department (PWD) with a cost of approximately ₹ 4 lakh but the bridge was so temporary that it could not withstand the heavy flow of water in the river in the rainy season. This is the only access point for the Kalimath temple which is a source of livelihood for a large number of priest families located at Kabiltha and Guptkashi. The temple was also damaged due to the flood; however, with the commendable work done by the Border Security Force (BSF), the facilities and somewhat normalcy seems to have returned in Kalimath. Though, the BSF has also constructed Panchayat Bhawan, Aagan Bari Kendra and a high school in Kalimath and provided solar lights to the people of Kabiltha, Kotma, Khonu, Kunjethi, etc. but this area seems to be as cut off from the mainstream as it was before the disaster. The nearest bank for the people of Kalimath, Kabiltha, Kotma, Khonu, Kunjethi, Chaumasi, Jal Talla, Jal Malla, Syinusu, Bunkhi is located at Guptkashi which is almost 10–15 km away from these villages of the lower Kedar valley. The nearest market is also Guptkashi, there are hardly shops and selling points which is also affecting the livelihood opportunities of the people. The area produces large quantity of citrus (locally called Malta) fruits but due to the lack of good market facility, the produce remains unable to fetch a good price and be the source of the livelihood. The growing menace of monkeys also keeps the villagers at the tenterhooks. The areas like Syinusu are not only remote but still lack a proper connectivity and connection. The facilities like hospitals and schools are either missing or in pathetic conditions. Some NGOs have also been working in the area but the people do not seem to be satisfied with their work. As these areas are rarely visited by the government officials therefore, the difficulties being faced by the people are not often highlighted. The condition of the disaster affected villages is not only making the surroundings sad but the non-fulfillment of the goal of self-sufficient villages is promoting migration of families from these villages in a large number.

The Study

This being the context, it becomes necessary to examine the opinions of people affected by natural disasters not only to have a firsthand account of their experience, but also to cross check on the efforts of government and other agencies involved in disaster management. This study collected the opinions of the people about the lifestyle changes, socio-economic conditions, level of satisfaction about their situation and other issues after disaster. A field survey was conducted in the villages of Kalimath, Kabiltha, Kotma, Khonu, Jal Malla, Jal Talla, Kunjethi, Chilond and Bedula in Ukimath Block of Rudra Prayag district. A total number of 59 people in the age group of 18 to 65 years were interviewed to know their opinions and perceptions. The primary data, thus, collected was content analysed in terms of demographics and opinions/perceptions on issues relating to the post-disaster management on a three-point scale and content analysed in a descriptive way. The issues related to the measures taken by the government, the laws of the land, and socio-psychological impacts of disaster and the level of satisfaction on the different issues relating to disaster management. In addition, their opinions on the disaster management policy, the impact of loss of family members on their source of livelihood along with the impact of the natural disaster on women was also collected and analysed in terms of frequency and percentages.

The Analysis

The data collected was analysed in terms of the demographics. The analysis revealed 46 per cent were women and 54 per cent were male, 7 per cent were unmarried and 93 per cent were married; 3 per cent were working in government jobs, 74 per cent in agriculture, 14 per cent were involved in private business, 11 per cent were involved in various other small jobs. In terms of education, 17 per cent were uneducated, 12 per cent had education up to primary level, 51 per cent intermediate level and only 20 per cent were graduates and post-graduates.

Table 2

Inactions of the Uttarakhand Government (in %)

S.No.	*Issues*	*Agree*	*Do Not Agree*	*Don't Know*
1.	Did not take effective measures for cleaning river Ganga	56	3	41
2.	Did not ban illegal quarrying of raw material on river bed	54	5	41
3.	Did not ban construction along the river banks and floor plain, river course/flood plain and landslide prone areas	80	5	15
4.	Did not pay attention towards disaster management	94	3	3
5.	Did not make attempts to reduce the inefficiency of the administration	82	3	15
6.	Did not make attempts to make people aware about disaster	100	0	0

Data was also collected on the measures taken/not taken by the government (Table 2). A majority shared the opinion that the government neither took effective steps for cleaning the tributaries of river Ganga, nor for banning quarrying on the river bed or construction of buildings on the river flood plain, or disaster management or the inefficiency of the administration. These issues played a very important role in aggravating the impact of the disaster on the people. With the surge of water in the river Mandakini, the houses constructed near to river course/flood plain were damaged to large extent causing immense loss. People were also annoyed with the inefficiency of the administration after disaster in assessing the situation and making attempts for effective disaster management. In fact for a considerable period the government itself was in dark about the impact of the continuous and heavy rainfall in these areas or the number of people trapped at various places like Kedarnath, Gaurikund, Rambara, Kalimath, etc. Almost (100%) respondents shared the opinion that the government did not formulate any attempts to make them aware about the disaster therefore, they were caught unaware of the repercussion of the heavy rainfall and the glacier melt above the Kedarnath temple. The government did not take the weather forecast about the heavy rainfall seriously and, thus, did not issue any advisory for the people as well as the pilgrims. As a result almost 10,000 pilgrims along with the local people who were trapped at Kedarnath temple and the nearby areas were washed away by the flash flood. The government neither made any attempts to restrict the number of pilgrims visiting these areas nor the people were prohibited to visit the Kedarnath temple amidst the heavy rainfall thus leading to the disaster (Table 2).

Non-Implementation of Laws

The flash flood of 16–17 June 2013, coupled with manmade factors, created havoc by killing almost 10,000 people and washing away property, also revealed that the laws made under the Disaster Management Act 2005 were not implemented by the state. This act required every state government to make a similar regulatory body as was appointed and proposed by the central government to prepare the action plan to mitigate the impact of the natural disaster. Actually the Disaster Management Act, which aimed for developing a continuous and integrated process of planning, organizing, coordinating and implementing measures to deal with any disaster and taking a prompt response to any threatening disaster was never considered seriously by the Uttarakhand Government. It is ironical that the disaster management act which proposed to enhance the capacity to assess the severity or magnitude of effects of any disaster on the people and property, taking quick measures for evacuation of the affected people, conducting rescue and relief work and also taking appropriate actions about the rehabilitation and reconstruction of the areas was neither taken seriously by the Uttarakhand Government nor any pressures on the state government for its proper implementation was imposed by the central government. Therefore, the state machinery was caught napping in the wake of the massive disaster. What could be more regrettable than the fact that the district Rudrprayag which was most affected by the disaster remained without a district magistrate for about two-three days because the sitting district magistrate had to be airlifted to the state capital due to health reasons.

In fact, Uttarakhand is one of the hapless Himalayan states of India which has always been prone to natural disasters but the administrative machinery of the state has not taken any lessons from the many natural calamities and tragedies that have taken place in the past. Besides the non-implementation of laws, the unplanned construction along the river banks and fragile hill slopes also helped to aggravate the impact of the disaster. Even Kedarnath shrine which is located at an altitude of 11,000 feet was not spared of the unplanned construction boom of the last two decades. The fast appearance of many luxurious resorts, holiday retreats, rafting camps, motels, multistoried buildings and other infrastructure indicate the growing trend. There were used to be notice boards on the roadside indicating that the construction on 100 metres on either side of the road was strictly prohibited but with the passage of time and multiple violation such warnings and notice boards have not only disappeared but has also become antiquity. It is a common knowledge that rivers can change their course anytime; therefore, as the rule of thumb, construction should not be allowed in largely populated areas along the river banks. In view of this the construction of structures on either side of the national highway from Rishikesh to Badrinath or Kedarnath is a sadly befitting example of authoritative apathy towards implementing construction rules. Otherwise, how can so many structures that hang on mere pillars come into existence? Even the government buildings have been made alongside the river bank. For example, at Srinagar which has a history of flooding, the SSB (Sastrasth Seema Bal), a paramilitary government organization, has been allowed to construct its huge buildings on the banks of river Alaknanda, which was also devastated in the wake of this flood. Similarly the lodges and hotels of the Garhwal Mandal Vikas Nigam (an Uttarakhand Government undertaking) constructed on the river banks in Kaudiyala, Rudraprayag, Tilwara, Chandrapuri, Rambara (near Kedarnath), Gaurikund and other such places were also totally wiped out following this tragedy. It poses a serious question that if the government itself shows utter apathy and allows construction in the river bed/flood plain then how can we restrain the private parties? Here lies the crux of the problem and that indicates towards the weak implementation of laws, lack of good governance, good leadership and will power of the authorities and leadership which has augmented the problems. Apart from the unplanned construction, the growing number of pilgrims visiting Badrinath, Kedarnath, Hemkund, Gangotri and Yamnotri shrines has not only added to the state's woes in terms of managing tourism and resources but to some extent the unrestrained and unregulated tourism was also responsible in compounding the impact of the disaster. Thus, the reckless deforestation, construction of buildings, dams, roads, settlements and other infrastructure, without taking into consideration the fragile ecology of this area, played a major role in this massive calamity and destruction caused by it. This is not only an eye opener but also a warning to mend ways if the humanity has to survive for a longer duration. Actually the scale of the June 2013 tragedy was so big that it would take years together for rebuilding and redevelopment of this area.

The Socio-Psychological Impacts of the Disaster

The socio-psychological impacts of the disaster could be witnessed clearly on the families residing in these villages that have lost their earning male members (who were at Kedarnath for earning their livelihood by conducting various small jobs on that fateful day). The left out women and the girls of such families have been suffering from the psychological problems of loneliness and insecurity. Their helplessness and worries about the future coping options are real. Since agriculture in this area is largely less productive and non-lucrative therefore, in the absence of guidance and training for growing cash crops and other livelihood strategies they have been finding it quite difficult to fend for their daily needs. As the source of income of most of the people and families was based on the Kedarnath pilgrimage, with the limited number pilgrims visiting the shrines, the economic capacity and capability of the people has been badly affected. With the efforts of the government, pilgrimage at the main route has started but for want of proper facilities and the difficult route, the number of the pilgrims visiting Kedarnath shrine and adjoining areas has drastically reduced which is also increasing the worries of the people. The level of satisfaction of the people with the different issues, their personal problems and socio-economic condition in the aftermath of disaster has been given in Table 3. As shown in Table 3, 91 per cent were found to be fully dissatisfied with their economic situation in the aftermath of the disaster because the source of income of the majority of the people was associated with the Kedarnath pilgrimage. This means that the destruction and the limited number of pilgrims visiting the shrines have affected their lifestyle adversely.

Table 3

Level of Satisfaction with Different Issues (in %)

S.No.	*Issue*	*Fully satisfied*	*Partially satisfied*	*Fully unsatisfied*	*Can't say*
1.	Functioning of the government/ administration after disaster	14	61	20	5
2.	Satisfaction with the personal situation after disaster	0	64	31	5
3.	Satisfaction with the economic situation after disaster	2	7	91	0
4.	Satisfaction with compensation	54	26	20	0

As the Table 4 shows, almost 100 per cent responded that they were affected by the disaster in some or the other form and 75 per cent people shared the opinion that the impact of the devastation increased due to the hydro-power projects that are being constructed on the various rivers. The cloud burst and heavy snow melt in the glacial lake right above 3 km of the Kedarnath temple swept away the small town, and damaged the wall of the temple and human beings and all that came into its path. Besides water, the stones, silt and mud that were brought out together created havoc in the areas located all along the rivers Alaknanda and Madakini. Most of the scholars and people agree that the devastation in the Garhwal Himalayas was much on the predicted lines and much of damage and loss to the property in down streams caused due to illegal construction along the river side. A report in the daily newspaper *The Times of India* highlighted that an environment assessment of the Bhagirathi and Alaknanda rivers by the Comptroller and Auditor General (CAG) of India three years ago had clearly warned of severe hazards both for ecosystem and stabilization of hill slopes along with the river bed. The CAG report conducted for performance audit on hydro-power development in Uttarakhand through private participation had alerted both the centre and the state government that mushrooming of hydro-power projects on the Alaknanda and Mandakini rivers were causing severe damage to the hills and also increasing the possibility of flash floods that could result into huge loss of life. The CAG's apprehension turned true when the massive floods killing thousands of people in Kedarnath and also sweeping away major towns and villages along the banks of river Alaknanda and Mandakini in June 2013 took place. The CAG report had pointed out that 42 hydro-power projects were in operation and 203 were under various stages of construction and sanction on Alaknanda and Mandakini rivers which meant that almost every km of the rivers was sold out and if completed there would be one power project every 5–7 km of the rivers. The report had also warned how deforestation due to these projects was damaging the hills and reforestation was highly deficient. The report had also given the example of Srinagar town 3 (also devastated by June 2013 flood) that the agency responsible for the power project was supposed to plant 1,15,700 trees around the construction site but it planted no seedlings/trees and took no measures to cope with the flash floods, though the project developers were aware that higher hills release large amounts of water from melting snow and glaciers and the bursting glacial lakes could cause flash floods with catastrophic consequences (*The Times of India*, 21 June 2013). The CAG's apprehensions were found to be true during the survey as the equipment, sites, and tunnels of the hydro-power projects were totally devastated by the surge of water not only in Rudraparayg but also in Kalimath, Kabiltha, Khonu.

Table 4

Impact on Socio-Economic Condition due to Natural Disaster (in %)

S.No.	*Socio-Economic condition*	*Yes*	*No*	*Can't say*
1.	Affected by the June 2013 natural disaster	98	2	0
2.	Excessive hydro-power project in hill areas of Uttarakhand responsible for increasing the impact of natural disaster	75	13	12
3.	Proper compensation to the families	54	26	20
4.	Timely assistance to the disaster affected people	27	73	0
5.	Relief provided by other states was received	58	42	0

The ecological effects of the disaster could also be found in the form of landslides and severely sinking roads and a large number of villages, thus making them totally unlivable. The deep cracks in the houses at the foundation level not only speak clearly about the extent of sinkage of the land but also of their being unsafe for people's residence. The people of such areas need to be rehabilitated urgently. The roads of these areas are in such a bad shape that the slightest rainfall makes the people fearful about the closure of the roads. The problems and destruction by the disaster has allowed the people of these areas to feel that there should be change in the disaster management policy for Uttarakhand. About 97 per cent favoured change in this policy, 69 per cent respondents opined that there was no effective disaster management policy in Uttarakhand; therefore, such policy needs to be developed and implemented. Almost 100 per cent respondents supported the idea of seeking suggestions from the people regarding policies of development for such areas which should be different as per the ecological, geographical and economic conditions of the area. It was also opined by 88 per cent people that despite having full knowledge of the disaster-prone areas, serious and timely attempts are not made by the governments to identify such areas or to relocate the people to other places which is not only unfortunate but leads to the loss of men and material (Table 5).

Table 5

Opinion about the Disaster Management Policy for Uttarakhand (in %)

S.No.	*Policy*	*Yes*	*No*	*Can't say*
1.	Major change in the disaster management policy is required in Uttarakhand	97	3	0
2.	Was there any effective policy for disaster management in Uttarakhand?	31	69	0
3.	Suggestions to be opted from the people for developing of new policies for hill area development	100	0	0
4.	There should be mountain specific policy considering the fragility and geological instability of the region	95	0	5
5.	Does government identify the areas prone to disaster	5	88	7

Though the people affirmed that relief material was provided to them in plenty by various agencies but, at the same time, it was also accepted that such relief has made the people defunct and lethargic by promoting lack of interest in taking up any new work or initiative for earning livelihood. Interestingly no one among the respondents was found to be earning livelihood through animal husbandry or MNREGA. The women who had lost their male members in this tragedy had been earning their livelihood through the monetary compensation provided to them by the government and as shown in the Table 6, a total of 56 per cent respondents accepted that proper compensation was provided to them. However, about 20 per cent women who reported that the disaster had killed their male members revealed that their life was totally changed with an added amount of loneliness. About 12 per cent women told that life seems to be totally useless and 14 per cent women accepted that it has also increased their social responsibilities. These women also admitted that though they have received compensation through which they can meet their day-to-day expenses but it was not possible to fill up the vacuum created in their lives with the loss of their husbands or sons (Table 6).

Table 6

Affect due to Loss of Male Members and Source of Livelihood Earning of Women (in %)

S.No.	*Livelihood Earning*	*%*	*Affect due to loss of male members*	*%*
1.	Through compensation	32	Life totally changed	10
2.	Through agriculture	9	High amount of loneliness	10
3.	Through animal husbandry	0	Life seems to be useless	12
4.	Through MANREGA	0	Increased social responsibility	14
5.	Through daily wages	10	All the above	54
6.	All the above	49	–	

As shown in Table 7, about 90 per cent women respondents accepted that the disaster has not only changed their lifestyle but also affected their education and health. About 76 per cent women accepted that there is a need to make different policies for their upliftment and solution of problems. About 80 per cent women opined that a separate disaster management policy for the women needs to be developed so that their concerns and anxieties are taken care off. About 61 per cent respondents accepted that work has not been done on the resolution of the fundamental needs of the people and 100 per cent respondents opined that as women have a better idea about the needs and development therefore, women's opinion should be taken before making policies for the hill areas.

Table 7

Impact on Women due to Natural Disaster (in %)

S.No.	*Impact on Women*	*Yes*	*No*	*Can't say*
1.	Change in the lifestyle of the affected women	90	10	0
2.	Effect on education and health of the women	93	7	0
3.	Need to make different policy for the upliftment and solution of problems of the affected women	76	9	15
4.	Need for a separate policy for disaster management for women	80	20	0
5.	Is work done on the fundamental needs of the people	39	61	0
6.	Before making policies for development of the hill areas opinion of the women need to be obtained	100	0	0

Conclusion

The above analysis makes it clear that the disaster has not only shaken the faith of the people but it has also made them aware about the causes and consequences. It has also produced an adverse effect on the women and their coping strategies as in the absence of many options available to the women who have lost their male members; their dependence on the compensation package for fulfilling their needs has been increased. But with the growing awareness they are now demanding their participation in the policy-making for the hill areas which is a good sign. Women are also voicing their concerns and aspiring for a larger involvement in the various schemes and development planning. However, the rebuilding of the area which is a tough task is yet to be done but for the rebuilding people's interest, awareness, sincerity and unity is essential.

Acknowledgement: The authors are thankful to the ICSSR, New Delhi, for the financial support provided for conducting the field work for this study. The authors are also thankful to Shri Girish Bhatt, project Assistant under the ICSSR Project, Department of Political Science, HNB Garhwal University, Srinagar, Garhwal, for providing help in data collection and analysis.

Notes

1. Uttarakhand consists of 13 districts which are distributed among the two hill areas Garhwal and Kumaun and some adjoining plain areas. Out of the 13 districts of Uttarakhand, the seven districts, namely Uttarkashi, Chamoli, Rudraprayag, Tehri, Dehradun, Pauri Garhwal and Haridwar are in Garhwal division and Pithoragarh, Champawat, Almora, Bageshwar, Nainital, Udham Singh Nagar are in Kumaun division. In Garhwal division, Haridwar and some areas of Dehradun and in Kumaun division, some areas of Nainital and Udham Sighh Nagar fall in the plain

areas. Tibet to the north, Nepal to the east and Himachal and Uttar Pradesh to the west border this area. Most of the hill region is made up of valleys and mountains that range from 1,200 to 3,000 metres in height and form a landscape of steep and often-terraced hillsides, snow clad mountains, forests and fast-running rivers in the valleys. Due to its typical geographical and strategic location it has been given Special Category Status by the Government of India. Actually only 13 per cent land in Uttarakhand is suitable for agriculture as steep and snow covered mountains and forests cover almost 66 per cent of the land area. Although the mainstay of the 75 per cent people is agriculture, yet agriculture is highly unproductive due to the small and scattered landholdings and lack of irrigation facilities. Moreover in the absence of many employment avenues the rate of migration of the male population is very high and has converted the hill economy in to 'money order' economy. Nearly 80 per cent population of Uttarakhand region is rural and most of the areas are not only economically backward but also different from the plain areas from the point of view of culture, language and political history etc. The world famous four holy shrines; Gangorti, Yamunotri, Badrinath and Kedarnath are also located in this area.

2. Rudraprayg district's total geographical area is 2,328 sq km. Uttarkashi to the north, Chamoli to the east, Pauri Garhwal to the south and Tehri Garhwal to the west borders this district. Rudraprayag District was established on 16 September 1997. The district has three blocks Ukhimath, August Muni and Jakohli. According to the 2011 Census, Rudraprayag district has a population of 2,36,857. The district has a population density of 119 inhabitants per sq km (310/sq mi). Its population growth rate over the decade 2001–2011 was 4.14 per cent and it has a sex ratio of 1,120 females for every 1,000 males making it the 6th highest in the country as per 2011 Census. It has a literacy rate of 82.09 per cent. Male and female literacy were 93.90 and 70.35, respectively.
3. Major town of Pauri District located on way to Kedarnath and Rudraprayag

References

Blaikie, P.; Cannon, T.: Davis, I. and Wisner, B. (1994). *At Risk: Natural Hazards, People's Vulnerability and Disasters*. London: Routledge.

Brookings Institution (2010). Keynote presentation, Women's Leadership Lunch, National Council of Churches Assembly, 10 November, New Orleans, Louisiana.

Enarson, Elaine (2000). Gender and Natural Disasters, Recovery and Reconstruction Department, Geneva, 1–53.

Ferris, Elizabeth (2010). *When Disaster Strikes: Women's Particular Vulnerabilities and Amazing Strengths*. New Orleans: Brookings Institution.

Fothergill, Alice (2003). 'The Stigma of Charity: Gender, Class, and Disaster Assistance', *The Sociological Quarterly*, Vol. 44(4) (Autumn): 659–680.

Hyogo Framework for Action (2005). World Conference for Disaster www.unisdr.org/2005/wcdr/.../Hyogo-framework-for-action-english.

Mąsozera, Michel; Bailey, Melissa and Kerchner, Charles (2007). 'Distribution of Impacts of Natural Disasters across Income Groups: A Case Study of New Orleans Ecological Economics', *Ecological Economics*. (63): 299–306.

Neumayer, Eric and Pluemper, Thomas (2002). 'The Gendered Nature of Natural Disaster: The Impact of Catastrophic Events on The Gendered Gap in the Life Expectancy 1981–2002', *Annals of the Association of American Geographers*, Vol. 97(3): 551–566.

Shrestha, M.S. and Takara (2007). 'Impacts of Floods in South Asia', paper presented at the meeting of the Asia and Oceanic Geological Society, Bangkok, 31 July-3 August.

The Beijing Declaration and Platform for Action (1995) Fourth World Conference on Women. http: //www.un.org/womenwatch/daw/beijing/platform/

UNDP (2008). Annual Report: Capacity Development: Empowering People and Institutions, 2008 www.undp.org/content/undp/en/home/.../undp_in_action_2008.html

UNISDR (2004). Terminology: Basic Terms of Disaster Reduction and Reducing Disaster Risk: A Challenge for Development, http: //www.unisdr.org

Vulnerability through the Eyes of Vulnerable: Climate Change Induced Uncertainties and Nepal's Development Predicaments. Institute of Social and Environmental Transition and Institute for Social and Environmental Transition-Boulder, Colorado for Nepal Climate Vulnerability Study Team, Kathmandu, 2009.

Women and Natural Disaster: A Regional Analysis on Asia and Pacific April, 2010, Social Development Division, United Nations Economic and Social Commission for Asia and the Pacific, United Nations, Bangkok pp 1–14.

14

Overcoming Glass Ceiling

Case Studies of Women in Corporate India

BULAN PAL

> Gender equality is more than a goal in itself. It is a precondition for meeting the challenge of reducing poverty, promoting sustainable development and building good governance.
>
> –Kofi Annan

Abstract

The term 'glass ceiling' is used to describe the invisible barrier that inhibits minorities and women from rising to the upper tier of the corporate ladder, regardless of their qualifications or achievements. The glass ceiling metaphor literally means invisible barriers ('glass') through which women can see elite positions but cannot reach them ('ceiling').

The study is a descriptive study aimed at understanding the factors that contribute to the formation of glass ceiling for Indian women in corporates and the means by which they can overcome it. Fifteen case studies of women who are working in corporates at various management positions have been selected through purposive sampling.

Some of the key findings reveal that glass ceiling is not a universal phenomenon but is person, industry and occupation specific. The study concluded that it is a societal phenomenon with various stakeholders involved in which women can overcome the glass ceiling and balance personal and professional lives at the workplace.

Keywords

women, glass ceiling, corporate, workplace, case study, qualitative

Introduction

Glass Ceiling: Definition

The term 'glass ceiling' was first coined in March 1984 by Gay Bryant, the former editor of *Working Woman* magazine. According to Bryant, after reaching a certain height in the corporate ladder women get stuck, some stays in that level, some starts their own venture and some goes back to raise their families.

David Cotter et al. (2001) defined four distinctive characteristics that must be met to conclude that a *glass ceiling* exists. A glass ceiling inequality represents:

1. A gender or racial difference that is not explained by other job-relevant characteristics of the employee.
2. A gender or racial difference that is greater at higher levels of an outcome than at lower levels of an outcome.
3. A gender or racial inequality in the chances of advancement into higher levels, not merely the proportions of each gender or race currently at those higher levels.
4. A gender or racial inequality that increases over the course of a career.

Cotter and his team found that glass ceilings are correlated strongly with gender. Both White and African-American women face a glass ceiling in the course of their careers. In contrast, the researchers did not find evidence of a glass ceiling for African-American men.

In most developing countries, since women do not have access to equal opportunities even at the grassroot level, the question of a glass ceiling does not even arise. In emerging countries like India and China, however, the women who have the opportunity to work and have a career, the glass ceiling they confront is similar in nature to those faced by their counterparts in the western world.

India, with a rich history of freedom for women guaranteed by the Constitution has a truly grim situation. In spite of more and more women entering the corporate board room, it continues to rank very poorly on the Gender Inequality Index (129 out of 146 countries). The Global Gender Gap Index of the World Economic Forum, too ranked India at 101 out of the 136 countries. Of the 1,112 directorships of 100 companies listed on the Bombay Stock Exchange, only 59 are held by women.

Table 1

Indian Political Environment

Name	*India*
2012 HDI Rank	136
2012 Gender Inequality Index Rank	132
2012 Gender Inequality Index Value	0.61
2010 Maternal Mortality Ratio	200
Adolescent Fertility Rate	74.7
2012 Seats in National Parliament (% female)	10.9
2006–2010 Population with at least secondary education (Female)	26.6
2006–2010 Population with at least secondary education (Male)	50.4
2011 Labour force participation rate (Female)	29
2011 Labour force participation rate (Male)	80.7

Taking a glimpse at the Indian political environment, one can witness that the world's largest democracy has only 11 per cent women representatives (61 out of 543 Members of Parliament) in the 16th Lok Sabha. The growth of women's participation has been minimal, a mere 6 per cent in 67 years of Independence, the First Lok Sabha had 5 per cent women Members of Parliament. These figures supported by multiple researches indicate the presence of an unseen barrier that prevents Indian women from rising to the upper strata of corporate ladder (Table 1).

These barriers prevent large numbers of women from obtaining and securing the most powerful, prestigious, and highest-grossing jobs in the workforce. Moreover, as an impact, more and more women feel they are unworthy to fill high-ranking positions as their superiors do not take them seriously or see them as potential candidates for advancement.

Research Methodology

This paper is a descriptive study aimed at understanding the factors that contribute to the formation of glass ceiling for Indian women in corporates and how they can overcome it themselves. Fifteen case studies of women, who are working in corporates in various managerial positions have been selected through purposive sampling. Semi-structured interviews were conducted with the participants. Each interview lasted for about 60 minutes and flowed in the form of a discussion. The respondents were asked:

- about their understanding of the word 'glass ceiling'
- whether 'glass ceiling' existed in the Indian corporates
- whether they felt its presence themselves or in any ones career in their environment
- the factors, according to them, contributing to its formation
- whether a woman can herself overcome 'glass ceiling' and
- means for overcoming 'glass ceiling'

Once the interviews were conducted, the recorded data was transcribed and analysed using Microsoft Excel. Thereafter, the data was thematically arranged, highlighting significant quotations which captures the essence of these women's experiences.

Findings

Factors Contributing to Glass Ceiling

Various factors were identified by the respondents which contributed to formation of glass ceiling. The perceptions of the respondents are given below:

- The women were aware about the existence of glass ceiling. Some had felt its presence in their workplace while others did not encounter it directly. However, they perceived that it was difficult to understand the extent of impact which glass ceiling had on their growth as there were multiple other factors playing a significant role in their career path which were not coloured by gender discrimination. For example, one's superior may be unhappy with an employee because she is applying for better opportunities. Here, even though relationship between the management and the employee (female) may turn sour, it is not the result of glass ceiling but more prominently corporate politics.

- Glass ceiling was not a universal phenomenon but it was person, industry and occupation specific. Women argued that they felt the presence of glass ceiling because of particular individuals in the workplace. These people had some hidden agenda or mindset inculcated out of societal or cultural baggage which acted as a deterrent to fair growth policy for women. The presence of occupational segregation – male jobs and female jobs – and such personifications created glass ceiling for women especially if she was working in the position of so-called 'male job'. Some industrial segments like manufacturing/heavy engineering were considered to be 'male organizations' compared to advertising/PR, etc. which were more female oriented.
- Due to gender inequality in education, acquiring the right skills was difficult for the girls. As the overall human development reflected the male dominance in outdoor work, women were always conditioned to be good mothers and dutiful wives. Thus, in a family with a boy and girl child, often the boy is given preference for acquiring education and proper skill set development over the girl who is trained in the household chores. Since, the stereotypical role segmentation prompted the male member to be the eventual bread earner while the female would be fulfilling familial duties, women's mentoring as a bread earner was never prioritized. Conservative social order resisted Indian women from breaking the shackles of age old traditions. Though, there is a gradual transition in the pro-women thought processes but we are still a long way to go to erase the existing gender inequality in education and training. Since proper education and training becomes one of the hygiene factor for career progression absence of this creates greater challenge for women and, hence, this contributes to the formation of glass ceiling.
- The perception that strong women were a pushover and soft ones were incapable promoted the emergence of glass ceiling. The respondents felt that due to societal discernment women have often been considered by their male counterparts, as pushovers or incapables. This lopsided judgment has resulted in the development of glass ceiling on many occasions. The benevolent behaviour has been misunderstood as softness and misfit in a tough challenging professional environment.
- Environment with high majority of men at the workplace was perceived to create glass ceiling. Any department where majority women employees reflected less glass ceiling effect compared to the one with majority of men. This situation was quite similar to the natural phenomenon of majority rules, even in a coalition government it is the major partner who dictates terms. One of the respondents commented:

  > Indian men cannot handle strong Indian women going up the ladder. Besides, they also consider the earning of a woman is a secondary income in the family and empathize with another man while considering for growth. This adversely affects the woman who has the same skills but lose out in the battle of genders.

- Absence of right mentors at various managerial levels was deduced as a major barrier to the growth of women. Mentors played an important role of a catalyst in career progression of any professional. Lack of women in top managerial posts, dearth of socializing time due to family commitments, stereotypes and norm in cross gender relationships were identified as some of the factors deterring proper mentoring of women employees. One of the respondents argued:

> If you have a nurturing mentor in the workplace nothing can stop a woman from growing. We are as good as our male co-workers but finding the right mentor at the right time is difficult.

The lack of support from the family members, especially post-marriage, resulted in the creation of glass ceiling at workplace. The stereotypical concept of division of labour releases the male partner from the responsibility of household chores and child care. From times immemorial women had been conditioned to marry, bear children and raise them. The purpose of education was to find a well-bred groom and increase the value of girls in the marriage market. Working and developing one's career was seen as a supplementary pastime which should not hinder family responsibilities in any manner. One of the interviewees felt:

> Whenever there is competition between a man and woman of equal talent for a single position, in most cases, the men get more time to devote and prepare, while I have to continue to balance between work and home.

At times, under family pressure and compulsion women have to leave their jobs in the pinnacle of their careers. As a result, many are unable to return to their profession while those who join the work force once again are forced to start at a lower position and lose out to their male counterparts in the face of tough competition.

Two very important aspects in corporate professionalism are flexibility in work hours and locational mobility. In high positions, leaders often have to be flexible in their work hours and are required to devote a substantial time in their professional world which becomes a challenge for women who also have to play a similar role at home. Things become more challenging when it comes to mobility and willingness to relocate to different locations to meet the demand of profession. One of the respondents said:

> If both the husband and wife are working and the husband gets transferred the wife either has to relocate sacrificing her job or look for the job in the new location or request the company to accommodate her in the new location which hardly is the case in a vice versa situation.

These were some of the experiences shared by the women during the interviews. They felt that their environment acted as a deterrent to their progress. Stereotypical perceptions of Indian professionals and decision-makers hinder women's growth. Lack of family support and social conditioning make it a lopsided bargain for the Indian women to prosper in the workplace. Yet, more and more women are fighting their way all through and breaking away the glass ceiling to reach high positions in the ever challenging and toughening corporate world. How do they do it? That's what I have tried to capture in the next section.

How Women can Prevent Glass Ceiling

The women felt that the prevalence of glass ceiling was a societal phenomenon which involved multiple stakeholders, however they could and had overcome the glass ceiling in different ways at various occasions in the career map.

Challenging the Status Quo

A woman must make challenging moves whenever she gets an opportunity. By challenging the status quo one takes the calculated risk which is an attribute of a leader and, thus, offers a possible way of overcoming a glass ceiling. It had been observed there was a set pattern which primarily contributed to the formation of glass ceiling – beginning with access to proper education and acquiring desired skill to lack of flexibility and mobility among women employees. All these stereotypes were encompassed in the perceived notion about women. For instance, women were seen as less flexible in their working hours due to their family engagements. So, wherever flexibility was required they had to demonstrate that quality to nullify the perceived notion. Similarly, if it was important to relocate to a new place for professional compulsion, one had to be able to address the requirement without sacrificing on professional front. A respondent working in the middle management noted:

> If my male counterpart is mobile and flexible and if the job demands so I also have to cope up with it.

> Another respondent shared:

> Last year, I got the opportunity to be a part of a very lucrative on-site posting for a year. My daughter was only three months at that time, but I did not want to lose out on the competition so I went abroad. Took my family along, my husband also requested for a transfer at his workplace and we went there and stayed for a year.

Maintaining Highly Professional but Amiable Relations at Work Place

In a male-dominated work environment the stereotypes, socialization practices and norms of cross gender relationships plays an important role. Thus, as one has to be very collaborative in order to positively attract other professionals in the environment, while simultaneously ensuring that the same is done in a professional manner to avoid misinterpretation.

> Working in a highly male dominated work environment and with so many parties happening all the time, I am very careful to be within my limits. Some women might say, why does a woman need to control? But I feel it is essential to avoid creating that barrier in my workplace. If I don't maintain an attitude, my colleagues will stop taking me seriously from the very next day. I feel it has worked for me because I have achieved a lot without being an object of gossip.

Balancing Personal and Professional Life

The respondents felt that one could overcome the glass ceiling by maintaining proper work life balance. Work life balance, being a relative term, varies in definition from person to person. The most important aspect highlighted by many was the switching off and switching on concept. As long as a person was able to ensure that any stress related to professional environment was unable to impact her family environment and vice versa, she had a better chance of breaking the glass ceiling. This task was relatively difficult for women to achieve because of their social expectation to carry out the lead role in family management, including child-rearing, compared to their male counterpart. In order to be successful in their career path they had to find ways to balance personal and professional worlds. Some achieved it by delegating and outsourcing certain tasks.

> Woman should stop attempting to be like a superwoman in both the worlds, set her priorities in life and get her actions aligned with those priorities. To reduce stress I have outsourced my household work. I have hired help for the cooking and cleaning. I merely supervise. I make it a point to give them annual raise and keep them happy. They are happy then I am happy. I have less things to bother and can concentrate whatever time I have at home on my daughters and my husband. That way I can give more time to my career too.

Finding the Right Mentors/Sponsors and Understanding the Difference between the Two

Mentors are the people who coach people in areas where they do not have deep knowledge. They provide professional support to develop their career. But they are generally not from the top management. Usually the latter does not have the time or specific knowledge to mentor effectively. They may be a sponsor. A sponsor is a senior level leader who is willing to advocate for someone and positively influence key decision-makers on your behalf. So one needs to identify and have mentors and sponsors to rise up the corporate ladder and break the glass ceiling.

Converting Family from being Area of Weakness to being an Area of Strength

Lack of family support, especially post-marriage may result in the creation of glass ceiling at workplace. With rising women education, freedom and increasing awareness, we are moving in a direction to reduce the gender inequality in sharing responsibilities within the family set-up. As women are earning almost in tune with their male counterpart, their independence and importance in family is on the rise. The respondents felt that women could now collaborate with their male counterpart to ensure the household responsibility was equally distributed so that they could concentrate on their professional careers too. Few respondents reported that the extended family comprising parents and relatives also rendered additional support in child rearing and other household chores. One of the women working at the mid-management level reported:

> Family support is extremely crucial and I ensured that I can make that as my area of strength before stepping out for a professional career. Before marriage, I told my husband and in-laws about my profession and passion to work. I was very clear that I wanted a career and I would expect their full co-operation in the same. I feel laying out my cards helped me a lot and I was able to continue as before.

Another respondent reported:

> My parents were never supportive of working women. Their only objective was to get me married. They felt that if at all I wanted to work I must become a teacher. But that was never my goal. So I took up a job in a different city and made my career. Thankfully, my husband is more understanding and supports me completely. I feel to avoid the glass ceiling one must choose one's life partner very carefully, otherwise it's a doom.

Bypassing the Glass Ceiling Where it Cannot be Broken

The respondents felt that at times it became very difficult and almost impossible to overcome a glass ceiling. In such situations, instead of wasting energy in trying to break the glass ceiling, it was better to explore ways of bypassing the glass ceiling. One had to see the larger picture, if it so happened that there was prevalence of glass ceiling related to the specific environment. It may be related to her colleagues, occupation or industry she must be ready to change and seek opportunity elsewhere. A switch to a different environment can be helpful. One of the women shared:

> If organically things become very difficult to overcome I try to bypass the same by taking a roundabout route. Whether it is within the family environment or in office. To succeed one has to be diplomatic.

Another reported:

> I was once at a job where I felt that my colleagues tried to push me away or ignore me and my boss said nothing. Initially, I could not understand their reasons for such behaviour but later realized I was being penalized because I was the only woman in the team. I resisted but then I got a very good opportunity and I moved. Now I am very happy in my current job. I am still the only woman in the team here but I don't feel the presence of a glass ceiling. Some people might say I ran away but I think this was a practical move.

Conclusion

> Male and female citizens, being equal in the eyes of the law, must be equally admitted to all honours, positions, and public employment according to their capacity and without other distinctions besides those of their virtues and talents, observed Olympe de Gouges.

The glass ceiling is present all over the world and the forces trying to keep women away from the work place possess certain typical stereotypical patriarchal ideas and attitude. The degree and intensity of these forces may vary by region, occupation or industry. In developing countries, religious, legal, and economic factors are particularly discriminatory towards women. However, with time, a gradual change can be witnessed among the younger generation with greater awareness of the presence of glass ceiling, especially in the corporate environment. With increased awareness, factors contributing to glass ceiling are being exposed and dealt with strictly. Women too are conscious about the possible ways glass ceiling may inhibit their career progression. They are confident about breaking the 'glass ceiling' themselves by challenging the status quo, balancing the personal and professional world, seeking the right life partner, prioritizing their professional career, acquiring requisite knowledge and skill set and adopting right mentor and sponsor. One can be hopeful that with these conscious efforts the glass in the man-made glass ceiling will become thinner and shorter and eventually disappear giving birth to a new era of gender equality.

References

Annan, K. (2004). 'Africa' s Green Revolution. A Call to Action'. Address at High Level Seminar on Innovative Approaches to Meet the Hunger Millennium Development Goal in Africa. UN Conference Centre, Addis Ababa.

Catalyst United States Glass Ceiling Commission (1993). Successful Initiatives for Breaking the Glass Ceiling to Upward Mobility for Minorities and Women Staff. http: //www.researchgate.net/publication/37157453_Successful_Initiatives_for_Breaking_the_Glass_Ceiling_to_Upward_Mobility_for_Minorities_and_Women.Accessed on: 15.07.2014.

Centre for Social Research (2009). Women Managers in India Challenges and Opportunities. New Delhi: Centre for Social Research. www.womenleadership.in/csr/Women-Managers-In-India.pdf. Accessed on: 18.07.2014.

Cohen, L.; Manion, L. and Morrison, K. (2007). *Management Research Methods in Education*, 6th Edition. London: Routledge.

Cotter, D.A.; Hermsen, J.M.; Ovadia, S. and Vanneman, R. (2001). 'The Glass Ceiling Effect', *Social Forces*, 80(2): 655–682. http: //www.vanneman.umd.edu/papers/CotterHOV01.pdf.Accessed on: 28.11.2014.

Gouges, O.D. (1791). 'Declaration of the Rights of Women'. http: //csivc.csi.cuny.edu/americanstudies/files/lavender/decwom2.html.Accessed on: 28.11.2014.

International Labor Office (1997). Breaking through the Glass Ceiling: Women in Management: Geneva: International Labor Organization.

Kakodkar, P. (2013). 'Defying the Glass Ceiling'. *The Hindu*, Nov 10, http: //www.thehindu.com/todays-paper/tp-business/defying-the-glass-ceiling/article5337046.ece Accessed on: 15.07.2014.

Maheshwari, K., (2012), 'The Glass Ceiling impact on Indian Women Employees', National Conference on Emerging Challenges for Sustainable Business 2012.

Sitterly, C. and Duke, B. (1988). *A Woman's Place*. New Jersey: Prentice Hall.

Smith, J.C. (2007). 'Strategies for Breaking Through the Glass Ceiling' November 16–17, 2007. Excerpt from the Plenary Panel, North Carolina. http: //www.nyu.edu/frn/publications/advancing.women/Keynote%20fran%20white.html.Accessed on: 20.07.2014.

UNDP (2012). Breaking the Glass Ceiling in India, http: //www.undp.org/content/undp/en/home/presscenter/articles/2012/03/14/breaking-the-glass-ceiling-in-india/.Accessed on: 10.07.2014.

Wall Street Journal (2013). Five Ways to break through the Glass Ceiling, 14 August 2013. http://blogs.wsj.com/speakeasy/2013/08/14/five-ways-to-break-through-the-glass-ceiling/.Accessed on: 15.07.2014, http: //tejas.iimb.ac.in/ An iimb management review initiative: Glass Ceiling in India: A Reality for Women? with Hema Krishnan. Accessed on 15.08.2014.

15

The Changing Role of Indian Women in the Information Age

ANINDITA PAUL

Abstract

Women in India have traditionally held roles and responsibilities that are typical to the Indian household that concerns the domestic chores. Restricted access to the external world leads to restricted access to information. However, with the advent of Information Age, it has become possible for women to have better access to information through various ICT devices that were hitherto absent. This paper examines the impact of the information-age on the role of women in India. Data was collected from five Indian women from the Indian state of Kerala. The findings indicated that women have various roles in the Information Age. What has not changed is women's focus on family responsibilities. Rather, the information-age has empowered Indian women with information at her fingertips. The study has its implication in understanding the 21st century Indian woman. Organizations and businesses can re-evaluate and formulate strategies and schemes to target audiences that are women who are decision-makers or influencers of products and services.

Keywords

ICT, India, women, gender studies, social type

Introduction

The internet marketplace has inspired a need for understanding the information society. Though there has been massive investments in Information and Communication Technologies (ICT), the information society has largely remained silent on gender issues (Jansen, 1989). According to a recent report, the Indian mobile phone market is third in ranking in terms of subscriptions and 30 per cent of the world's mobile users live in India and China ('Global mobile statistics'). ICT has contributed to social change in India that has led to social inclusion. ICT has also enabled women to participate in new ways that redefine the traditional roles they have been playing. Hilbert recognizes women's use of ICT significant as they have been unequally treated in the past and these inequalities have transmitted to their use of ICT. He further called for the need to look at women's positive attitudes and natural abilities such as good communication skills and media capacities as positive qualities to overcome such transmitted inequalities of ICT use. ICT has also brought about changes in women's roles. Researchers have pointed out the increasing role of women in the country's economy due to ICT (Youngs, 2012). Nath (2001) elicited the importance of women in a developing knowledge society. He specially examined the role of ICT in providing avenues for women to contribute to knowledge and stress upon the use of ICT for effecting social change such as women empowerment and their increased participation. Subramanian and Saxena (2006) also point at the importance of mainstreaming gender into ICT policies and programmes in the Indian context.

This study is conducted in the state of Kerala which has a high sex ratio as well as a relatively high literacy rate for women ('Sex Ratio 2011'). The status of women in Kerala in terms of education and professional positions held has been reportedly high compared to other states of India ('Status of Women'). In order to look deeper into the lives of these women and their use of ICT for information seeking, an exploratory qualitative study was considered appropriate. Five cases of Indian women's use of ICT are discussed to further throw light on the various factors affecting each of their ICT use for information seeking.

Our study contributes to an understanding of how a more detailed study looking at specific aspects reflected in our study needs to be conducted. Various indicators and implications of their changing behaviour is discussed in the 21st century. The findings questioned some of the conjectures held by the authors about Indian women's current ICT use and helped in research directions of a subsequent study. Additionally, the study has implications on policy-making. With the increasing role of ICT in women's lives proper policy measures need to be taken that lead to higher ICT adoption resulting in higher ICT-mediated participation.

Literature Review

Gillard et al. (2008) studied gender in ICT research in developing countries. They pointed out the effect of globalization that has led to an increased women economic activity rate. They also mention how women have a major role to play in order to contribute to the international competition and global markets. A number of other studies have noted the stereotypes held about women (Youngs, 2012; Wei and Kramrae, 2012; Prakash, 2012) and also talked about the influence of the west on eastern culture (Youngs, 2012).

Some of the Indian stereotypes of women render them to be a burden, having less knowledge compared to the male counterpart, to be incompetent technology user and much more. Jain (2006) reviewed the UNESCO project about Indian women on 'Networking Rural Women and Knowledge' and found a substantial influence of ICT in empowerment of the women some of which involved gaining more respect in families and local communities, greater confidence in the job market, increased creativity, increased income and enhanced solidarity among women in the community. Such stereotypes may vary across urban, suburban and rural settings. To add to the existing social challenge due to these stereotypes held by women, there is a general notion of women's disability towards technology (Howcraft and Trauth, 2008). Prakash (2012) notes how women may consider themselves as technophobic as they are socialized to believe so. Statistics have shown the rise in ICT use by women across developed and developing countries (Figure 1).

Figure 1

Gender-Wise ICT use is Developed and Developing Countries

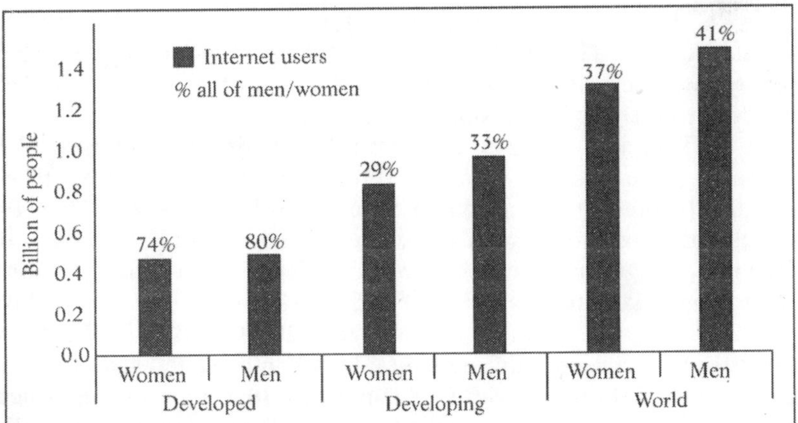

Source : ITU World Telecommunication ICT Indicators database
Note: Estimate

Source: http: //www.itu.int/en/ITU-D/Statistics/Documents/facts/ICTFactsFigures 2013.pdf

Few studies look at women's use of ICT. Johnson (2013) studied factors affecting Indian women's use of internet and noted that middle class Indian women were better equipped to access internet as compared to lower class Indian women owing to their differing priorities (survival being the priority for the later than literacy or better standards of living). Maghferat and Stock found that women behaved cautiously in choosing search sources. They decided either on sources, which they knew skilfully or when their use was assigned. In contrast, men seemed to be extremely self-confident and determined. Further, Lim and Kwon too found women's information behaviour on Wikipedia varying than that of their male counterparts. According to them, women had 'more cautious or conservative attitudes, emotions, and behaviours than their male counterparts' (219). In contrast, Halder, Ray, and Chakrabarty (2010) found that women who were university students accessed many resources when seeking information as possible, including primary, secondary and tertiary as well as in and out of their institute (formal and informal sources). In their study women seemed to have a high need for information, as well as a high search drive. With increasing exposure to technology and higher information needs, women seem to have overcome their technophobic attitudes and have willingly and suitably adapted to ICT.

Other studies have enquired how and what prompts women to adapt to ICT. Ghobadi and Smith (2011) used activity theory to understand how ICT has influenced in transforming eastern women's feminist related attitudes to feminist related behaviours. They postulated that if certain measures such as those that break the fear of technologies, create safe cyber environment and provide support for technology use are taken then ICT can play a major role in participating in 'Communities of Practice'.

Warner and Procaccino (2001) studied women's health information seeking and found that though women were active health information seekers and make use of information received about health, they had a low awareness of resources that provide health and medical information. There were also indications of weak search strategies to retrieve health information on the World Wide Web using ICT. Family and friends were found to be instrumental in seeking health information. The study also indicates the uncertainty in relying on internet repositories when it comes to crucial health information and also unfamiliarity towards available online health resources.

The environment plays a considerable role in shaping women's role. Quesenberry, Trauth and Morgan (2009) posited that environmental context complicates the pressure on a woman about work-life decisions. They also hint towards the negative stereotypes about a woman that lead her to strive more to prove her worth. Other studies have considered environmental influences when studying a woman's association with IT in formal and informal settings (Dunne, 2002; Kvasny, Trauth, and Morgan, 2009; Sarker et al., Pap. 2009; Trauth, 2011). Social and environmental factors may encourage or discourage a woman's information behaviour. It is possible that with adequate measures the inherent phobia or reluctance that has been observed in women in their use of ICT can be eradicated. Finally, women can also pose as strong intermediaries of information dissemination based on the positive stereotypes they hold such as their caring, approachable and sociable qualities. Such qualities make women more approachable to people who need help with ICT. Women can be intermediaries to others' information need. Urquhart and Yeoman (2010) call for an inquiry into women's use of ICT that gives rise to situations that can influence the 'knowledge node' to strengthen connections, or make new connections and also affect other connections. Though these studies look at women's use of ICT, more needs to be understood about Indian women's use of ICT in their domestic circle for personal purpose.

Method

This study follows the interpretive paradigm and is situated in an understanding of culture and gender in the Indian context. Patton uses 'Orientational Qualitative Inquiry' (Patton, 2001) to represent situations when explicit theoretical or ideological perspectives determine the conceptual framework to direct fieldwork and the interpretation of findings. The motivation for the study originated from an interest in the premise that ICT has the potential to liberate the female gender from its fettered past. Patton describes the 'reality-oriented qualitative inquiry' (95) as an approach that seeks to identify and correspond with the 'real world'. Much has been talked about generalization in qualitative inquiry (See Denzin and Lincoln 2013; Patton, 2001). An account of generalizability by Denzin and Lincoln may throw some light on the treatment of generalizability in the current study:

> No individual or case is ever just an individual or a case. He or she must be studied as a single instance of more universal social experiences and social

processes. The individual, Sartre states, is 'summed up and for this reason universalised by his [her] epoch, he [she] in turn resumes it by reproducing him- [her-] self in it as a singularity.' Thus to study the particular is to study the general. (48)

The current study aims to reach an in-depth understanding of how women use ICT in India for seeking information. The status of women has been lower than men across most regions in India. Women's ICT use in the 21st century may be affected by various factors such as economy, family characteristics, development, cultural roots, etc.

Participants

The five participants of the study were Indians from Kerala. All resided in Calicut but some were brought up in different towns of Kerala that are in the outskirts or other places. The participants of the study were identified through purposive sampling based on the demographics-tertiary graduates, aged early- to mid-30s, married, mothers, employed, users of ICT in the state of Kerala. Table 1 summarizes the profiles of the five participants.

Table 1

Participants' Profile

Age	*Members in family – by gender (M/F) and by age group (m-minor)*	*Family structure*	*Profession/ Industry*	*ICT Ownership*	*Lifestyle*
32	2M, 2F, 2m	Joint	Entrepreneur/ Hotel	iPod, iPad, Samsung Duo smartphone, Personal Computer	Upper middle class, fairly busy with work, not much domestic responsibility.
35	1M, 4F, 2m	Joint	Anaesthetist and Faculty /Medicine	iPod touch, Samsung smartphone, Laptop, Personal Computer	Middle class, busy lifestyle where she manages household responsibilities, family and work.
34	1M, 1F, 1m	Nuclear	Dentist and Entrepreneur/ Medicine	Smartphone, Laptop, Personal Computer	Middle class; busy mostly with work, not too busy with domestic responsibilities; does not have large social circle; home-centred lifestyle.
35	1M, 1F, 1m	Nuclear	Bookseller and radio-announcer/ Media and Publishing	Feature phone, PC	Lower middle class, busy during standard office hours; busy social life; spends time in hobbies (such as frequent tours, watching plays, learning and writing about dance), does not have many domestic responsibilities
33	1M, 1F, 2m	Nuclear	IT professional/ Education	Smartphone, Laptop	Middle class; busy with household and family responsibilities; hired domestic help to care for the minors.

Data Collection

All the participants were interviewed using semi-structured interviews of at least an hour. They were asked to keep a note of their ICT use. The researcher then followed up with the participants about their ICT use through phone calls. Data were collected from October 2012 to January 2013 and again from June to August 2013.

Data Analysis

NVivo10 was used to code the interview responses. Two coders coded the data. Different themes were identified across the participants. The authors own experience and understanding of the social, cultural and environmental aspects of the context being studied were also applied in analysis.

Findings

The findings from the five interviews suggest the different roles held by women in the Information Age related to their use of ICT. Though the study's focus is in and around ICT, the interviews sought to explore various factors such as attitude, upbringing, family, etc. that affected the participants' use of ICT. The participants provided insights into how women use ICT generally and the transformation it is bringing in their role as a family or a community member. The different themes of the women around ICT use found were – women as technology users and supporters, women as professional users, women as online learners, women as family care-takers, women as information nodes, women as decision-makers, women as online community-members. The following paragraphs cover each of the roles in detail.

Women as Technology Users and Supporters

The study hinted at the changing technophobic image of Indian women. Three out of the five participants – participants 1, 2 and 5 in this regard were particularly noteworthy. They showed exceptional diligence in their use of ICT not only for their personal purpose but also for helping others with their technology use and support. They were often consulted for information as well as for help related to checking e-mails, etc. Such a change in the image of Indian women as technically-savvy individuals is a major leap forward in the 21st century.

Participant 1, specially, was confident about her technology use. Some of the statements on her technology comfort included the following:

- 'I personally feel smart phones are much easier than the regular, the old phones that you have.'
- 'I don't think I have any issue getting on to a new device but by that I stay comfortable in an Apple environment than any other one, very recently I was trying HP tablet I thought it was slightly complicated you know.'
- 'I'm always online...you know, invariably every hour or something I would check my mail, you know or I would, you know if I have the time will just look around in the app store.
- 'I could say you know I'm more than eight hours a day I think, I should be, on the net.'

Both participants 1 and 5 used IT extensively for professional purpose that may have been a reason for their technology use for other non-professional purpose as well. For participant 2 who was in the medical profession, ICT use for professional purpose was not a necessity yet she was a comfortable ICT user like the other two participants 1 and 5. All the three participants were supporters of ICT use for other people as well. In the following two statements, Participant 1 expressed her image as a supporter for others:

- In a sense you know… I am the, you know, reference point for my family…'
- 'Like [what] is the train status and... I am like, come on guys get one for yourself, it's so simple you know.'

Further statements by the participants indicated that all of them considered ICT useful in their lives though with some degree of reservation. Participant 1 stated how she used the iPad as her primary device, the phone and the desktop came in that order of usage. She also shared how she kept articles of interest offline that she could read later in 'Adobe or PDF reader'. All the three participants, 1, 2 and 5, acknowledge the usefulness of ICT for their purpose without much reservations. Participant 1 at one instance mentioned how she was trying to overcome her addiction with e-shopping. Apart from accessing the Internet for information, the participants used ICT for listening to music, setting up reminders for birthdays or anniversaries, for transactions such as e-shopping or reporting building maintenance issues. Participant 3 and 4 had more reservations about ICT use and sought support from family and friends for accessing ICT. A major use of ICT for participant 3 was for communicating with her sister through Skype. Apart from that she did not really appreciate the Information Age in general and ICT specifically. Compared to her participant 4 was more appreciative of the Information Age and the conveniences that it has brought in the lives of people but she did not think that she is losing out on anything by not using ICT as much. Her need for information when she planned her tours were mostly fulfilled through her friends. Even bank related transactions were carried out through her friend's accounts.

From the ICT use and support of the participants, it is apparent that there is an overall acceptance of women's use of technology in the Indian society and women themselves have been able to overcome the stereotypes about technology use. Women has also been able to support others need with their ICT use. However, there could be some lag in the supporter image amongst women who have not yet used ICT to the same degree as supporters.

Women as Professional Users

Women have been able to utilize ICT for professional purpose as well, specially working women. All participants had some use of ICT for professional purpose but the use of ICT for professional purpose participants 1 and 5 was quite high. Most of their ICT use was for managing work, coordinating or using it for different work-related needs such as scanning, internet searches, clicking pictures or setting up reminders. ICT was also the most preferred means for communication using e-mails. Participant 1 had to work long distance for her family business. She had to travel frequently between cities to attend to business. ICT enabled her to be organized and be in touch over phone so she could work long distance as well as do other activities that are not related to work. She explains about her online usage:

> We have the mails that [are]...the reports that I will check in the morning and in the afternoon. And then the other mails that come that I will check them. It's mostly mails and responding to mails on one side of my internet and the other is when I'm free, if it's not work, I'm regularly shopping. You know I do a lot of online shopping, that's what I mean.

Most of her regular communication with her office was through email. She mentioned that she was somewhat addicted to checking her email. Besides e-mail she also relied on her phone where she has a to-do or 'getting things done' applications that she uses to plan her work out so it fits her daily routine.

Besides the above, she has also used Facebook mostly because of her business as they have a page for their hotel on Facebook. She also uses her phone to take pictures and has downloaded an app that can enable her to scan documents.

Participant 5 was from an IT background and worked as a programme manager in a telecom company posted in an educational setting. She used her laptop extensively for using Google to search information. In her words: '... if I see something in this notice board I'll take a picture and I'll come to office and read from here only and things like that.' She also uses her phone to take notes during meetings. She also uses the organizer for work-related reminders such as last date for payments, etc.

For participants 2, 3 and 4, the scope for professional use was very limited. Participants 2 and 3 were from the medical profession that did not require them to use ICT regularly; however, participant 2 used it for helping her colleagues at work from her home internet access by supplying them information on drug doses, lab investigations and normal values. Since the medical facility she worked did not have the proper infrastructure for seamless internet access, she was not able to access ICT for work purpose. She had, in fact, recently downloaded two applications on her phone that could be used even when offline to calculate the drug doses. Apart from the above, she has used ICT for its GPS capabilities that have been of help when she visited other cities for conferences.

Participant 3's use of ICT is limited to her office laptop, PC at home and her husband's smart phone. She did not use her own smart phone for internet at all. Her use of ICT was through the laptop at clinic that she used for mostly work-related needs such as searching for sellers of dental materials using Google search. Apart from that, she also looked for reviews of the dental materials but only when she had some issue with those. She reasons, '... our products are always ... selected or comes into the market after series of studies. So, those people who get things to my clinic they will be providing some papers or articles related to that, but still if I see some kind of issues that may appear I'll just seek for reviews.' Besides, such a use of ICT, participant 3 considers herself as an incompetent ICT user in her professional circle.

Participant 4 had the most restricted access to ICT, both at her house and in the office too. Her professional use was not as much compared to the other participants. She needed much help when she used ICT for journalism. She had to use the computer for checking work-related e-mail or searching for information for articles she writes for magazine. She also searched for online matter regarding topics for her article that was discussed in the online forums. The editor also used to give her other responsibilities like assisting with the emails and publishing tasks. A reason for her low ICT usage was because she did not have a PC on her desk at the small bookshop where she worked and neither had she an access to her home PC that was mostly occupied by the writer husband. To access a PC at work she had to go two shops away to the main office of the publisher, but she could not leave the shop unattended. So she could not access the PC during the bookshop hours. This, in fact, reduced her ICT use. Her mobile phone was also not very user-friendly for Internet access.

It can be inferred from the above that various factors affect the professional ICT user image of an Indian woman. Some of these factors are interest, comfort, knowledge, accessibility, relevance, attitude while some other are more professional as infrastructure, need and relevance to the profession.

Women as Online Learners

Learning is a goal that the participants have achieved with the help of ICT. Participant 5 specially has utilized ICT for updating her knowledge and learning new programming languages. She stated, 'I learned things from internet only, actually I learned web design from [ICT]. I learned other programming languages from [ICT].' Participant 5 has utilized the e-learning capabilities of the internet rather than enrolling in a formal programme. She states further, 'Whatever information I need, I am searching Google nowadays. Cooking, if I have some doubt I'll check in Google or in any other search engine.' The internet has enabled her to pursue her learning goals. Other participants, 2 and 5, also mentioned that they used the internet to learn new récipes.

ICT has enabled women to engage in learning whether it concerns upgrading her professional skills or pursuing a hobby. In some cases it also seems women might also engage in learning that involves conforming to traditional, expected roles. Overall ICT has provided a means for Indian women to fulfil their learning needs without having to commit to a substantial time or effort as they can resort to online learning from their daily regular routine and responsibilities.

Women as Family Care-Takers

Two of the participants have used ICT extensively for obtaining family-care information that relate mostly to health. ICT provided them a means to be well-informed about family care responsibilities. Participant 2 had an ailing mother-in-law at home and a minor son who had a protein allergy condition that drove her to seek information on the internet. She was able to find information on people with similar condition as her son. She stated, '...we don't have much allergy specialist here. So, even paediatricians don't know much about this (protein allergy).' She was also able to find information that her son's protein allergy may get over till he is 6 years old as she stated, '...in most cases it was, and kids get over this by 5, 6 years.' This information worked as a relief for her.

In a similar situation, participant 5 was able to find more information on the internet about her baby's infection. She was able to supplement information gained online with the information she got from the doctor. Apart from getting mere information she mentioned it as a great resource for medical information when she was not clear about the jargon used by the doctor. Rather than asking the doctor about it, which she felt would be wasting the doctors' time, she resorted to the internet. She stated, '[Online] opinions and all, it was there [in the internet]. So, I found it and I also understand, most of the doctors do not know these things one by one and they have other patients [so] they don't have time. So, in that Google search I found that it came from the Pampers, that [diaper for babies]. Actually we [buy] it from shops, [those] have [bacteria that cause the infection].' Through her access to online resources she was able to find the real cause of the infection that was helpful to her.

As a part of the family-care responsibilities, participants 1,2,3 and 5 have utilized ICT for looking up various online reviews of products and services that are helpful for purchase decisions either online or offline. During travelling three of the participants (1, 2 and 5) mentioned that they have utilized the GPS functionalities to find their way to restaurants, hotels or other places that have been a major help when moving around with family in new cities.

Another use of ICT that participant 3 mentioned was using it to check information for her husband. She used to check his email, look up conference related information for him and get other work that he would ask her to do for him since he was busy.

Women have had family-care responsibilities traditionally. With the availability of ICT they have been able to not only fulfil traditional roles expected of them such as being good at child care or at cooking but also fulfil new responsibilities such as helping others with their ICT use.

Another significant factor for a woman's ICT use for domestic purpose is the support she has by her family members as well as her friend circle. If there is adequate support who can help her with her information needs then a woman may not feel the need to adapt to ICT for her family-care needs. Similarly, in case there is adequate support from the friend circle or if they have inhibitions in using ICT due to her own attitude or because of factors such as fear, accessibility, affordability or infrastructure issues then she would rely on her friend circle rather than making any effort to use ICT. In collective cultures women may get away with not using ICT, however, much of their need or realization about the benefits of ICT may be.

Women as Information Nodes

Another role change for women was when they took up roles as information disseminator. Having full access to the Internet some of these women could get the information they require as well as help others who do not have access to the internet or who are digitally illiterate by supporting their information needs. In a sense these women are seen as the information nodes for their family and friends.

Participants 1, 2 and 5 are significant in that respect. Participant 1's friends and relatives have approached her for not only online information help but also information on technology-related queries. On one occasion she shared, 'this morning you know my uncle from home, he called up and because he wanted to know a friend of his … wanted to go to Udupi so he got [in touch with me] to just find out, you know, which are the trains that's there from Kannur to Udupi.' Since participant 1 spent a lot of time online and was known to be internet-savvy amongst her family and friends, she was seen as the information hub. She also realizes that she is better amongst her relatives and states, 'they [relatives] are quite ignorant about it [ICT] so I'm like you know the better one, you know.' She adds, 'On my own I don't think I know a lot, but [for] my folks … I'm kind of reference point for things.' She had quite a bit of knowledge about applications and would then share the information among her close friends. Participant 2 was not an ardent user of her smartphone for Internet access as participant 1 but she uses it to make calls to her friend circle.

Participant 5 has been an information node not only for her family members but also her neighbours and community. She states, '… in my family there is [not many] ladies who [have] technology knowledge. Usually they ask me…whatever doubts are there.' She goes on to add, '… my sisters …sometimes they will ask from which portal I get this information, from where I will get [that] information, …even my in-laws ask same questions, [about] information [on] Aadhar and all.' She also helped her parents with information about their pilgrimage. She stated:

> My parents wanted to go for the pilgrim, Haj and all. The information is available an the net, they don't know how to check it, they don't know how to [find out] whether they are selected or not [in] the government quota. They have applied for government quota and I used to check it regularly and sometimes if I don't inform them, then they will call me and remind me to check it on [a] regular basis, and they got it.

Regarding information help to her neighbours, she recalls one instance when they benefitted from it:

> One of my neighbours bought a computer [because] I only told them … there are three kids [who] are learning computer from the schools but they don't have [computer at home], so I told her mother that if you buy it at home and if they have a facility to, [I] mean, learn from it, most of the time they are spending in front of the TV only, so it will be useful for them. They bought it and it was useful for them also.

Besides this, she had also helped her neighbours in checking their e-mail. The neighbours entrusted her with their ID and password and she looked up their e-mails for them. Sometimes she also carried out online transactions for them when they also gave away their credit card related information to her for carrying out their transaction. Apart from this she recalled another instance when she helped out her tailor by suggesting the use of ICT. She stated:

> [The tailor has] a dress shop [where] various net pattern, various designs can [be designed] in Photoshop… and can be printed out and [stuck] on the wall. [When] people buy the material [they may] like these patterns or models, [and will order those]. [Earlier the patterns]…was drawn on a wall…I just gave them an idea and they also found that it will be helpful.

These women have been able to benefit people around them by sourcing information from the internet to them. They have also been able to help with knowledge about technology that was not seen as their forte. Women, hence, have been able to fit into the image of information nodes in the 21st century.

Women as Decision-Makers

Though there was a certain shift amongst women who are becoming self-dependent and adopting different roles, their image as a decision-maker in the family is yet to be established as per the interviews. Though they had access to ICT, it did not necessarily mean that these participants were comfortable in making decisions regarding household or family affairs any more than before. The women were able to provide support for decisions with information they found or searched online such as when participant 2 visited online websites to find the required information about a property or car that the family planned to purchase. As for participant 3 who was a scarce user of ICT at home relied on ICT for decision-making only for professional purpose such as equipment purchase for the clinic. For some of the purchase decisions, she consulted with her husband but for some other purchases she looked up product reviews before she went to the market with her husband. She was not able to make decisions about online purchases because she did not have full control over the credit card that she held jointly with her husband. As for participant 5, she also consulted her husband for decisions related to household or technology.

In summary, though these women were seen as professional working women who have been able to come out of the traditional image of the Indian women, they were not entirely independent decision-makers. It needs to be further investigated till what extent Indian women have been able to make decisions on their own and what barriers lay to their independent decision-making. Is ICT, or access to it, enabling these women to make decisions that were traditionally not made by them, would be interesting to know.

Women as Online Community Members

Women are generally seen to be emotional, having better soft skills and connect to people better. The online environment has provided a medium for women to overcome the barriers of their homes or limited circle. Women can participate in online forums on varied topics of interest and can be part of many virtual special interest groups. However, the participants did not seem to relate to online communities that well. A possible reason could be attributed to individual characteristic or attitude. Participant 1 was the most technology savvy amongst all the five participants but was the least active on social media. On the other hand, participant 4 was active in socializing but mostly offline and participant 2 was active both offline and online on Facebook but not as much on other forums where she visited for health related information. Participant 2 benefitted from the discussions of the online health forum when she found crucial information related to her family members' health. Participants 3 and 5 were not very active in virtual communities. Familiarity with groups might be a factor for Indian women when participating in online forums. They may be more active in close knit groups. Apart from this there are laggards who may not be knowledgeable about ICT as much to be able to participate well. However, with the rapid expansion and use of mobile chat apps, access to groups through online media has become a possibility. More study will elicit the various characteristics of women as online community members.

The study helped elicit the changing role of Indian women in the Information Age. Women are accepting ICT in their lives and the change that it is bringing about, in some cases slower than before. Women have started to use ICT to meet their various needs. Some women have not yet accepted their changing roles out of sheer denial of it. Adding to it the support provided by their near and dear ones has also kept them away from a direct use of ICT. The findings of this study is by no means exclusive but hint towards a need for more study into the various roles that women are adopting because of ICT in their lives. Government, businesses and social scientists can gain from such study in formulating policies, development programmes, marketing campaigns and studying the dynamic changing society.

Conclusion

The role of the Indian women in the domestic and social circle has changed with the Information Age. It is important to explore women's use of ICT especially now with increasing ICT penetration in India. This study attempts to look at the different role taken by Indian women in the Information Age by exploring in depth the various use of ICT in their daily lives. The themes found point to various roles that Indian women's use of ICT is bringing about. Some of these themes point towards increasing usage of ICT for fulfilling their different needs including e-commerce activities and supporting others as well as seeking support for their own ICT use; ICT use for professional purpose; ICT use for seeking family related information that involves healthcare; ICT use for self-directed online learning; ICT use for disseminating information from the web to others; ICT use for supporting decision-making related to family affairs and for benefitting community through their knowledge and use of ICT. There remains a dearth of studies on women's use of ICT that could help in gender mainstreaming of ICT policies and programmes. This study is in no way intended to be exclusive but seeks to provide some pointers of Indian women's use of ICT that is becoming an interesting phenomenon.

References

Denzin, Norman K. and Yvonna S. Lincoln (eds.) (2013). *Strategies of Qualitative Inquiry*, fourth edition. California: Sage Publications Inc. 43–59.

Dunne, Jennifer, E. (2002). 'Information Seeking and Use by Battered Women: A "Person-in-Progressive-Situations" Approach.' Library and Information Science Research, 24: 343–55.

Ghobadi, Shahla and Stephen Smith (2011). 'The Employment of Online Communities of Practice for Manifesting Feminist Behaviors among Eastern Women'. PACIS 2011 Proceedings.

Gillard, Hazel; Howcroft, Debra; Mitev, Natalie and Richaedson, Helen (2008). 'Missing Women' Gender, ICTs, and the Shaping of the Global Economy', *Information Technology for Development*, 14.4: 262–79.

'Global Mobile Statistics 2012 Part A: Mobile Subscribers; Handset Market Share; Mobile Operators'. 2012. Web. 2 February 2013.

Halder, Santoshi; Anjali Ray and P.K. Chakrabarty (2010). 'Gender Differences in Information Seeking Behavior in Three Universities in West Bengal, India', *The International Information and Library Review*, 42: 242–51.

Hilbert, Martin (2011). 'Digital Gender Divide or Technologically Empowered Women in Developing Countries? A Typical Case of Lies, Damned Lies, and Statistics', *Women's Studies International Forum,* 34(6): 479–89.

Howcroft, Debra and Eileen M. Trauth (2008). 'The Implications of a Critical Agenda in Gender and Is Research', *Information Systems Journal*, 18.2: 185–202.

Jain, Suman (2006). *ICTs and Women's Empowerment: Some Case Studies from India*, Department of Economics at Lakshmi Bai College, Delhi University.

Jansen, Sue Curry (1989). 'Gender and the Information Society: A Socially Structured Silence', *Journal of Communication,* 39.3: 196–215.

Johnson, Vinitha (2010). 'Women and the Internet: A Micro Study in Chennai, India', *Indian Journal of Gender Studies*, 17.1: 12.

Kvasny, Lynette, Eileen, Trauth and Allison, Morgan J. (2009). 'Power Relations in It Education and Work: The Intersectionality of Gender, Race, and Class', *Journal of Information, Communication and Ethics in Society*, 7.2/3: 96–118.

Lim, Sook and Nahyun, Kwon (2010). 'Gender Differences in Information Behavior Concerning Wikipedia, an Unorthodox Information Source?' *Library and Information Science Research*, 32: 212–20.

Maghferat, Parinaz and Wolfgang, G. Stock (2010). 'Gender-Specific Information Search Behavior', *Webology*, 7.2.

Nath, Vikas (2001). 'Empowerment and Governance through Information and Communication Technologies: Women's Perspective', *International Information and Library Review*, 33: 317–39.

Patton, Michael Quinn (2001). *Qualitative Research and Evaluation Methods*, third edition. California: Sage Publications Inc. 75–142.

Prakash, Nirupama (2012). 'Ict and Women Empowerment in a Rural Setting in India', in Rekha Pande and Theo P. van der Weide (eds) *Globalization, Technology Diffusion and Gender Disparity. Social Impact of ICTs.* Hershey, PA: Information Science Reference (an imprint of IGI Global), 15–24.

Quesenberry, J.L., Trauth, E.M. and Morgan, A.J. 'Understanding The 'Mommy Tracks': A Framework for Analyzing Work-Family Balance in the IT Workforce', *Information Resources Management Journal*, 19.2: 37–53.

Sarker, Saonee et al. (2011). 'The Role of Individual, Family-Related, and Organizational Factors in Shaping WLC in Offshoring Contexts: A Study of European and Indian IT Professionals.' PACIS 2011 Proceedings. Paper 162.

'Sex-Ratio 2011' (2011). The Official Web Portal of the Government of Kerala. 13.11.2013.

'Status of Women' (2001) ed. Public Relations Department: Kerala.gov.in.

Subramanian, Malathi, and Saxena, Anupama (2006). 'Gender and ICT Policies and Programmes in an Indian State', Global Encyclopedia on 'Gender and ICT', USA: IGI Publishers, 411–416.

Trauth, Eileen (2011). 'What Can We Learn from Gender Research? Seven Lessons for Business Research Methods', *The Electronic Journal of Business Research Methods*, 9(1): 1–9.

Urquhart, Christine and Alison, Yeoman (2010). 'Information Behaviour of Women: Theoretical Perspectives on Gender', *Journal of Documentation*, 66(1): 113–39.

Warner, D. and Procaccino, J.D. (2004). 'Toward Wellness: Women Seeking Health Information', *Journal of the American Society for Information Science and Technology*, 55(8): 709–730.

Wei, Zhang and Kramrae, Cheris (2012). 'Women, Big Ideas and Social Networking Technologies: Hidden Assumptions', in Rekha Pande and Theo P. van der Weide (eds) *Globalization, Technology Diffusion and Gender Disparity. Social Impact of Icts*, Hershey, PA: Information Science Reference (an imprint of IGI Global), 70–82.

Youngs, Gillian (2012). 'Globalization, Information and Communication Technologies and Women's Lives', in Rekha Pande and Theo P. van der Weide (eds) *Globalization, Technology Diffusion and Gender Disparity. Social Impact of Icts*. Hershey, PA: Information Science Reference (an imprint of IGI Global), 25–33.

16

Emotional Intelligence and Values

A Study across Gender in India

SOMA NANDI AND SRI MRINMOY ROY

Abstract

Individuals vary in their perception of the world around them and the difference in perception may be due to age, culture, sex/gender, attitude towards life, level and quality of education, socio-economic-political conditions, parenting style and many other factors. The level or quality of emotional intelligence of an individual influences his/her attitude towards life, output in life and also the value system. Emotional intelligence is the skill, ability, capacity of an individual to identify his own emotions, control them, to be aware of the emotions of others and also to manage them to attain harmony in life. Every successful individual, be in a particular profession or at home or at both should be high in emotional intelligence and possess a sound value system. Values are essential part of our life and the development of a nation depends upon the value system of its citizen. Our ancient Indian system of education has also emphasized upon the inculcation and development of values among the learners. Great Indian educator-philosophers like Swami Vivekananda, Sri Aurobindo and many others emphasized upon the development of values. The present study is a modest attempt to study the emotional intelligence and value orientation of various professional areas across gender in and around Kolkata.

Keywords

emotional intelligence, values, value orientation, gender

Introduction

Human beings are born with biological heritage into a psycho-socio-cultural heritage. These heritages are associated with changes and development both inside and outside the individual which in turn influences the adjustment in life and to life. The physical, mental, cognitive, moral development determines the extent to which an individual is successful in life. It is the developmental pattern which gives shape to the perception, thought processes, understanding of the world, feeling, emotions, personality, belief of an individual. A sound development of the above mentioned aspects determines the level of success in life, be it professional or personal.

The psychology of human being is a complex process and it is assumed that persons of a particular profession possess certain specific personality patterns that explain their inclination towards that particular profession. In this present day of tremendous knowledge explosion and technological advancement, general intelligence and education alone are not enough for survival, the need of the hour is the proper development of emotional intelligence along with a sound value system. The concept of emotional intelligence is not something new as review of literature shows that it was Charles Darwin who first emphasized it for the process of survival and adaptation of animals. E.L. Thorndike (1920), Wechsler (1940), Maslow in the 1950s have spoken about the enhancement and development of the emotional abilities of an individual for adjustment in life. The term emotional intelligence was coined by Salovey and Mayer (1990) who described it as a form of social intelligence that involves the ability to monitor one's own and others' feelings and emotions, to discriminate among them, and to use this information to guide one's thinking and action.

The term 'value' has been defined in various ways, as noun and also as verb. As a noun, value is regarded as something that is worthy or useful, as principles or standards of behaviour, one's judgement of what is important in life. As a verb, value is to evaluate, assess, estimate, and appraise someone or something to be important or beneficial.

Objectives of the Study

The main objectives of the study are:

1. To study the emotional intelligence and value orientation of college teachers, bank officers, government officers and IT personnel across gender in Kolkata.
2. To find out the difference between emotional intelligence and value orientation across gender and profession in Kolkata.

Null Hypotheses

The study proposes the following null hypotheses based on the objectives of the study:

H 1 There is no significant difference between emotional intelligence of (a) male and female college teachers (b) male and female bank officers (c) male and female government officers (d) male and female IT personnel.

H 2 There is no significant difference between value orientation of (a) male and female college teachers (b) male and female bank officers (c) male and female government officers (d) male and female IT personnel.

H 3 There is no significant difference in emotional intelligence of (a) the male group with respect to their profession (b) the female group with respect to their profession.

H 4 There is no significant difference in value orientation of (a) the male group with respect to their profession (b) the female group with respect to their profession.

H 5 There is no significant difference in emotional intelligence of the total group with respect to their profession.

H 6 There is no significant difference in Value Orientation of the total group with respect to their profession.

Methodology

Sample Selection

The sample consisted of college teachers, bank officers, government officers and IT personnel in and around Kolkata. Each group was divided into three sub-groups, the male, the female and the total group. The study employed 15 males and 15 females for each profession.

Tools Used

The study employs two tools:

I. An Emotional Intelligence Inventory by Mangal and Mangal (2004).
II. Personal Values Questionnaire by Sherry and Verma (2005).

Mangal Emotional Intelligence Inventory (MGTI)

This scale has been designed for use with Hindi and English speaking people in the 16+ age group. It consists of 100 questions pertaining to four areas of emotional intelligence, like intra-personal awareness, inter-personal awareness, intra-personal management and inter-personal management. The total time for administration is 30–40 mins, the questions are of yes/no type. As far as scoring is concerned, 1 mark is to be given for presence of emotional intelligence and zero for the absence of emotional intelligence.

Personal Values Questionnaire (PVQ-SV)

This scale has also been designed for use with Hindi and English speaking people in the 16+ age group. There are 40 statements with three responses, spread over 10 values – religious, social, democratic, aesthetic, economic, knowledge, hedonistic, power, family prestige and health. The mode of response and scoring are as most preferred (2), least preferred (0) and not preferred value (1). There is no fixed time limit for the administration of this test but so far as psychological tests are concerned, it is preferable to ensure a proper time so that the thinking of the persons undertaking the test do not get the opportunity to change.

Procedure

The study involved people of four professions – college teachers, bank officers, government officers and IT personnel in and around Kolkata. There was no fixed age group, the minimum age of the candidates involved in the study was found to be 25 years and the maximum age being 55 years. The scores obtained from the two tests were subjected to statistical analysis using Minitab 14 software. The mean (Mn) and standard deviation (SD) were calculated to describe the emotional intelligence and value orientation across gender and profession. Chi square were calculated to test the hypotheses formulated for the study.

Results and Discussion

For the convenience of interpretation of data and discussion, the findings are presented in different tables. Some abbreviations have been used for this purpose and they are – EmI (emotional intelligence), VO (value orientation), Mn (mean), SD (standard deviation), N (total number of cases), df (degrees of freedom), M (male), F (female), T (teacher), B (bank), G (government official), IT (information technology), TL (total) and P-value (probability value).

From Table 1 it is observed that the female group of the four professional areas are higher in emotional intelligence than their male counterpart; the bank and IT female group are higher than the other two female groups with respect to emotional intelligence. As far as the total groups are concerned, the bank and the IT group are higher than the total teachers and total government officials.

Table 1

Descriptive Statistics of the Sample with respect to Emotional Intelligence and Value Orientation across Gender and Profession (M=15, F=15; TL=30)

Groups	*EmI*		*VO*	
	Mn	*SD*	*Mn*	*SD*
TM	69.87	8.99	119.93	3.06
TF	70.07!	9.82	119.93	0.70
BM	64.38	9.38	119.54!	1.39
BF	74.33!	4.65	118.80	2.21
GM	64.87	11.27	118.33	2.16
GF	71.80!	9.15	120.60!	1.06
ITM	65.60	12.94	119.60	3.20
ITF	74.6!	3.77	118.33	1.95
TTL	69.97	9.25	119.93!	2.18
BTL	70.20!	8.70	119.20!	1.83
GTL	68.33	10.68	119.47!	2.03
ITTL	70.10!	10.42	118.97	2.68

With respect to value orientation, the bank and the IT male groups are slightly higher than the female groups; the government female group is higher than their male counterpart, the male and the female teachers possess the same level of value orientation as far as this sample is concerned. The total teacher, bank and government groups are higher in value orientation than the total IT group.

Table 2

H1: There is no Significant Difference in EmI of (a) TM and TF (b) BM and BF (c) GM and GF (d) ITM and ITF

Group	*Chi Sq*	*df*	*P-value*
TM and TF	23.568	14	0.052 (+)
BM and BF	10.271	14	0.742
GM and GF	27.101	14	0.019 (*)
ITM and ITF	19.602	14	0.143

From Table 2 it is observed that there is significant difference in EmI of TM and TF (at 0.05 level) and EmI of GM and GF (at 0.01 level), hence H1 (a) and (c) are rejected. There is no significant differences between EmI of BM and BF, ITM and ITF, hence, H1 (b) and (c) are accepted.

Table 3

H2: There is no Significant Difference in VO of (a) TM and TF (b) BM and BF (c) GM and GF (d) ITM and ITF

Group	*Chi Sq*	*df*	*P-value*
TM and TF	0.576	14	1.00
BM and BF	0.300	14	1.00
GM and GF	0.421	14	1.00
ITM and ITF	0.558	14	1.00

From Table 3, it is observed that there is no significant difference in VO of TM and TF, BM and BF, GM and GF, ITM and ITF. Hence H2 (a), (b), (c) and (d) are accepted.

Table 4

H3 (a): There is no Significant Difference in the EmI of the Male Group with Respect to Profession

Chi Sq	*df*	*P-value*
79.461	42	0.00

Table 4(a)

H3 (b): There is no Significant Difference in the EmI of the Female Group with Respect to Profession

Chi Sq	*df*	*P-value*
35.610	42	0.74

From Tables 4 and 4(a), it is observed that, there is no significant difference between EmI of the four male groups and also the four female groups involved in the study. Hence H3 (a) and H3 (b) are accepted.

Table 5

H4 (a): There is no Significant Difference in the VO of the Male Group with Respect to Profession

Chi Sq	*df*	*P-value*
2.087	42	1.00

Table 5(a)

H4 (b): There is no Significant Difference in the VO of the Female Group with Respect to Profession

Chi Sq	*df*	*P-value*
0.967	42	0.00

From Tables 5 and 5(a), it is observed that there is no significant difference between VO of the four male groups and also the four female groups involved in the study. Hence H4 (a) and H4 (b) are accepted.

Table 6

H5: There is no Significant Difference in the EmI of the Total Group with Respect to Profession

Chi Sq	*df*	*P-value*
119.231	87	0.012 (*)

From Table 6 it is observed that there is significant difference between EmI of the total group (at 0.01 level) with respect to profession, hence H5 is rejected.

Table 7

H6: There is no Significant Difference in the VO of the Total Group with Respect to Profession

Chi Sq	*df*	*P-value*
3.516	87	1.00

Finally, Table 7 it is observed that there is no significant difference between VO of the total group with respect to profession. Hence H6 is accepted.

In the present study, it is observed that the female group shows higher emotional intelligence than the male group, especially with respect to bank, government and IT officials. With respect to the teachers, the difference in emotional intelligence between the two groups is very slight. As far as the total groups of the four professional areas are concerned, the bank and the IT group are higher in emotional intelligence than the two other groups. Regarding the value orientation of the groups, a very slight difference is observed, the bank male, government female and the IT male are slightly higher than the others. As far as the total groups of the four professional areas are concerned, the total teachers, bank and government groups are slightly higher than the IT total group of the sample. Although there is a significant difference in emotional intelligence of the total groups involved, with respect to value orientation, there is no significant difference among them.

Conclusion

Emotionally intelligent individuals are expected to be well adjusted in all aspects of life as they can interpret and manage their own emotions as well as that of others. It is also believed that emotionally intelligent individuals have a sound value system (Higgs and Lichtenstien, 2011). Individuals with high emotional intelligence strive continuously for personal development, support the interest of others, possess clarity of intention, sustain positive values, listen and observe others' objective, challenge the status quo, take the longer view, convert negative inclinations into positive thought and can nurture a team. Professionally considered, there should not be any difference in the quality of emotional intelligence and value system, as these are individual qualities, inherent within an individual but the environment in which an individual is born and nurtured plays a significant role in the development of both aspects. An individual high in both is bound to be successful in life but again the definition of success is subjective; perhaps a person high in emotional intelligence has his/her own definition of success in life. Studies indicate that women are high in emotional intelligence than men (Ciarrochi, 2001) but both men and women approach problems with similar goals with different considerations. Women are more concerned with how problems are solved, for men it is an opportunity to demonstrate their competence, strength of resolve and commitment.

Limitations

The present study has some limitations, the sample size was small, rural areas were not explored, the level of qualification was not taken into consideration, years of experience, present designation, family background and parental qualification were not considered.

References

Ciarrochi, J. et al. (2001). Measuring Emotional Intelligence in Adults, *Personality and Individual Differences,* 31(7): 1105–1119.

Goleman, D. (1996). *Emotional Intelligence: Why it can Matter more than IQ*. New York: Bloomsbury.

Gupta, N.L. (2000). *Human Values in Education*. New Delhi: Concept Publishing Company.

Higgs, M. and Lichtenstien, S. (2011). 'Is there a Relationship between Emotional Intelligence and Individual Values?' An Exploratory Study', *Journal of General Management*, 37(1): 65–79.

Lopes, P.N.; Salovey, P. and Straus, R. (2003). 'Emotional Intelligence and the Perceived Quality of Social Relationships', *Personality and Individual Differences*, 35(3): 641–658.

Mangal, S.K. and Mangal, S. (2004). Mangal Emotional Intelligence Inventory, National Psychological Corporation, Agra.

Salovey, P. and Mayer, J. (1990). 'Emotional Intelligence', *Intelligence,* 17(4): 433–442.

Sherry, G.P. and Verma, R.P. (2005). Personal Values Questionnaire, PVQ – SV, National Psychological Corporation, Agra.

Thorndike, E.L. (1920). 'Intelligence and its Uses', *Harper's Magazine*, Vol. 140: 227-35.

Wechsler, D. (1940). 'Non-Intellective Factors in General Intelligence', *Psychological Bulletin*, Vol. 37: 444–45.

17

Gender and Physical Activity in Spanish Students

A Social-Cognitive Approach

ELENA RAMÍREZ-RICO AND EMILIA FERNÁNDEZ-GARCÍA

Abstract

Currently, girls have a less active participation models and even more sedentary than boys, a situation that perpetuates the gender inequalities in the physical activity scope. This minor involvement influences negatively on youth health and general wellness, since the acquisition of active lifestyles is an essential requirement for the adoption of a healthy lifestyle. The purpose of this study, from a gender perspective, is delving into the social-cognitive factors that may influence the relationship with physical activity, which will allow to identify important aspects to consider in intervention strategies to promote physical activity in the young girls. Through a descriptive design, the study explains and interprets with a sample of 1,642 students (50.9% girls and 49.1% boys) aged between 10 and 17 years old, a number of personal, psychological and cognitive influencing factors that can ensure involvement are analysed. The information was collected through surveys. The overall conclusions underscore the importance of social-cognitive perspective for the analysis of gender participation and involvement of women with physical activity. This perspective is set as important for understanding gender inequalities, confirming the negative influence of cognitive and social factors studied on the participation and involvement of women with physical activity.

Keywords

gender, physical activity, social-cognitive approach, school age

Introduction

The practice of physical activity of students in pre-adolescence and adolescence is insufficient and discontinuously performed (Armstrong and McManus, 1994; Hovell et al., 1999; Ramírez-Rico et al., 2013), increasing also this situation among girls in both primary (Crocker and Faulkner 1999; Shropshire and Carroll, 1998) and secondary education (Dowda et al., 2007; Ramírez-Rico,

2013, Fernández and Blández, 2006). This situation involves not to obtain the benefits that such physical activity has, which is proven in studies. At school age, the benefit of physical activity is associated, among other possible aspects, with the increase of self-esteem, a better school performance and sociability, and a better maturation of motor nervous system (Calfas and Taylor, 1994; Ministry of Education and Science and Ministry of Health, 2007). In the particular case of girls, there are studies which have investigated about the benefits that physical activity provides particularly in them, finding that it contributes to a better physical self-concept, greater body satisfaction, increase their rate of bone density and strengthening, and its positive influence on bone status in adult age (Esnaola, 2005; Lloyd et al., 2004).

But to let the benefits listed above happen, it is necessary that the practice is performed on a regular basis, both in pre-adolescence and adolescence (McMurray et al., 2005) and that aspect is neither fulfilled. This regularity will allow to acquire a healthy and active lifestyle that can be consolidated and remain throughout life (Cavill, Biddle and Sallis, 2001).

Along with the low regularity and continuity of physical activity in youth, another important aspect is the increase of abandonment, which sharpens the low levels of physical activity, being necessary to promote the practice in pupils of school age, as they are at a critical age where the neglection of the practice of physical activity is manifested the most, (Stone et al., 1998) as well as in girls based on their different forms of involvement and participation in physical activity (Navarro, Pastor and Ramírez, 2003).

The situation raised in terms of poor linkage and practice of physical activity, specially in the case of girls, is key to mention the participation status of them in the specific case of Physical Education, due to such participation influences in the total practice performed. Girls are who have less preference for Physical Education in relation to boys (Moreno, Rodriguez and Gutierrez, 2003), where the interest and liking for the subject is likewise lower (Moreno and Hellín, 2014) and being those differences manifested in the diverse courses (Douthitt, 1984).

In this indicated scenario, the approach to it plays an important role through a social-cognitive focus, analysing factors that may influence in the relationship with the practice of physical activity for girls. This approach is based on studies that have observed how internal factors influence on external factors and vice versa. Thus, the link between external and internal factors is justified by the socialization process in which everyone is involved, as this process influences, for example, on internal mediators such as the motor competence perception, expectations of success and task orientation (Jacobs and Eccles, 1992). Within this focus, and due to such work is approached from a gender perspective, it is framed as a benchmark in the Eccles' model of achievement-related choices (Eccles, 1985) which collects and organizes those psychological and social factors that influence on people when making decisions, aspirations and choices or related to their participation in an activity (Eccles et al., 1985), and being the particular case of physical activity.

In this line, studies such as those conducted by Welk (1999) and Eccles et al. (1985), have analysed that internal factors such as perceived motor competence, self-esteem, interest and utility value of the task, determine physical activity in both girls and boys. Likewise, it has been also studied how there is a positive association between physical activity in youth and external factors such as social support from family, peer group, coach and teacher (Lau, Fox and Cheung, 2006; Neumark-Sztainer et al., 2003; Sallis, Prochaska and Taylor, 2000).

Based on the mentioned panorama, a set of key factors are analysed such as personal, psychological and cognitive influence, specified in personal beliefs, attitudes and expectations of success such as interest, value-utility and perceived motor competence, and perceived support in students from immediate social environment such as family support, peer group and teachers toward physical activity. This analysis of the current reality of pupils on these factors is justified by the importance of knowing the perception of students on them, due to their influence on physical activity involvement. This knowledge can help to identify important aspects of these factors to consider in intervention strategies to promote physical activity in school, especially in girls where physical activity levels are lower.

Methods

Participants

The final sample consists of 1,642 school children, and it is formed by 434 students of Primary Education (EP) (5th and 6th) and 1,208 students of Secondary Education (ESO) (1, 2, 3 and 4th year) from the city of Madrid (Spain). In the final sample, 50.9 per cent were girls and 49.1 per cent were boys, having a very equitable participation in gender. Likewise, the distribution of the sample is very similar at different ages, as it is grouped in educational stage that represents the collective of the study, being the distribution of the sample based on the course of 13.1 per cent coursing 5th grade of EP, 13.3 per cent of students in 6th EP, 18.3 per cent coursing 1st grade of ESO, 19.8 per cent coursing 2nd of ESO, 18.9 per cent coursing 3rd of ESO and 13.1 per cent coursing 4th of ESO.

The sample was extracted from 26 schools. The selection of the participating centres was random within each layer. Similarly, for the selection of students, within each school, a group from each course was chosen randomly, obtaining each subject written consent of relatives for their participation in the study.

Instruments

Questionnaire 'Competence and Value Beliefs in Sport' by Fredricks and Eccles (2002). The questionnaire consists of 12 items designed for EP ages to ESO. Within these 12 items, three sub scales are differed: the sub scale of Competence perceived in Physical Education, formed by four items, which presents in the original study by the authors a reliability index between 0.79 and 0.95; sub scale of value utility perceived in Physical Education formed by four items and with a reliability index between 0.61 and 0.92, to which it should be marked that the authors note that the reliability index decreases when applied in the first years of primary; and sub-scale about interest in Physical Education, consisting of three items that have a reliability index between 0.79 and 0.95. The items of the three sub-scales respond to a Likert-type response with values ranging from 1 (lowest) to 7 (maximum).

Questionnaire 'Social Support Survey' from Prochaska, Rodgers and Sallis (2002) on social support for physical activity practice. The questionnaire used was composed of two scales, each one of them with five items, one focused on family support and the other one on the support of friends, with answers ranging from 1 (never) to 5 (each day). The authors collect that the questionnaire presents a test-retest value after 2 weeks of r = 0.86 and ? = 0.54, rising to ? = 0.81 when the item of derision from peers is removed and replaced with praise of partners.

For the scale of support from friends, an adaptation was performed, removing the item 'do you support your friends?' considering that it is related to social support offered and what it is needed to be valued in this study is the perceived social support. Following the recommendation from the authors, the item of 'derision/joke' was also adapted by switching to positive, so that the question was worded as follows: 'Have you been told that you stand out in physical activities or sports?'

To these two scales, it was added over one more scale adapted from the ones above, which includes the social support from the Physical Education teacher, respecting the same characteristics as in the case of the scale of support from friends.

Data Analysis

In the statistical analysis of the data, the statistical software SPSS version 17.0 (Statistical Package for Social Sciences) with alpha set at $p<0.05$ was used as a technique. A descriptive analysis of the questionnaire variables (measures of central tendency and dispersion) and an inferential analysis by calculating the difference of averages in the analysis of the variables by gender were performed, using Student's T-test for independent samples or factor variance analysis (ANOVA). Within the ANOVA, either of them were used depending on the result of the homocedasticity proven through Levene test. Also, a contrast test of multiple comparisons was performed post hoc for the analysis by educational level and gender. Parametric tests were used because the Kolmogorov-Smirnov test showed that the distribution of the variables were not significantly different from the normal distribution ($p> 0.05$).

Results

In this section, the results of the review of the boys and girls about personal beliefs, attitudes and expectations of success are reflected by the variable of interest, value-utility and perceived motor competence towards Physical Education, and the perception of support from immediate social environment, measured through the perception of students on the support of family, peer group and teachers about their participation in physical activity.

In the variables of interest, value utility and perceived motor competence, it was checked by analysis of differences in averages that in all three cases there was an association between gender and the variables studied. The test of Levene rejected the equality of variances and the T-test affirmed the existence of significant differences between boys and girls (Table 1). These differences confirm that boys show a greater interest, value utility and perceived motor competence than girls in Physical Education.

Table 1

Perception of Students about Interest, Value Utility and Perceived Motor Competence in Physical Education by Gender

		N	*Mean*	*SD*	*Mimimun*	*Maximun*	*Levene & Sig*	*T-Test & Sig*
Interest	GIRLS	832	5.10	1.579	1.00	7.00	F=32.959 P =.000	T=–7.775 P=.000
	BOYS	802	5.66	1.350	1.00	7.00		
	TOTAL	1,634	5.37	1.498	1.00	7.00		
Value Utility	GIRLS	835	4.634	1.403	1.00	7.00	F=1.944 P=.163	T=–3.630 P=.000
	BOYS	804	4.880	1.340	1.00	7.00		
	TOTAL	1,639	4.755	1.378	1.00	7.00		
Perceived Motor Competence	GIRLS	835	4.815	1.134	1.00	7.00	F=4.441 P=.035	T=–10.968 P=.000
	BOYS	805	5.408	1.052	1.00	7.00		
	TOTAL	1,640	5.106	1.134	1.00	7.00		

In the analysis by educational level and gender through ANOVA test and post hoc comparison, it was highlighted in the three variables the presence of significant differences among cycles in both girls and boys (except in boys for perceived motor competence where there is no difference in the studied educational cycles), decreasing interest, value utility and perceived motor competence when progressing from EP to ESO (Figure 1).

Figure 1

Perception of Students about Interest, Value Utility and Perceived Motor Competence in Physical Education by Education Level and Gender

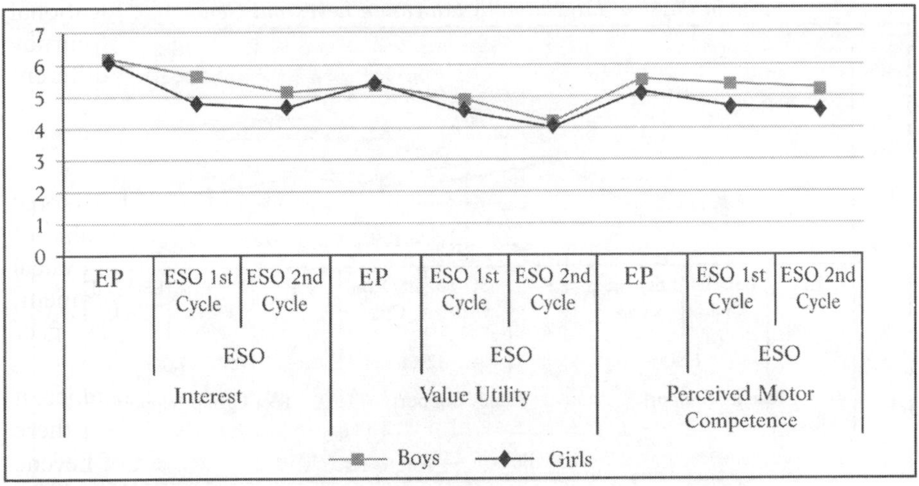

In the variables of perception of students about family support, peer group and teachers about their participation in physical activity, it was found by analysis of averages differences that in terms of teachers support, there were no differences by gender and, however, in support of the peer group and family there was an association between gender and the variables studied. In these two variables, test of Levene rejected the equality of variances and the T-test affirmed the existence of significant differences between boys and girls (Table 2). These differences confirm that boys show a greater perception of support from family and peer group than girls.

Table 2

Perception of Students about Teacher Support, Family and Peer Group and in Physical Education by Gender

		N	*Mean*	*SD*	*Minimun*	*Maximun*	*Levene & Sig*	*T-Test & Sig*
Teacher Support	GIRLS	833	1.466	0.942	0.00	4.00	F=7.428	T=–0.328
	BOYS	803	1.482	1.035	0.00	4.00	P=.006	P=.743
	TOTAL	1,636	1.474	0.989	0.00	4.00		
Family Support	GIRLS	833	2.10	0.976	0.00	4.00	F=4.133	T=–5.193
	BOYS	804	2.34	0.908	0.00	4.00	P=.042	P=.000
	TOTAL	1,637	2.222	0.951	0.00	4.00		
Peer Group Support	GIRLS	832	1.824	0.923	0.00	4.00	F=0.100	T=–6.220
	BOYS	803	2.109	0.931	0.00	4.00	P=.75	P=.000
	TOTAL	1,635	1.964	0.937	0.00	4.00		

In the analysis by educational level and gender through ANOVA test and post hoc comparison, it was highlighted in the three variables the presence of significant differences between cycles in both girls and boys, decreasing the perception of support when passing from EP to ESO (Figure 2). It should be noted also that in the case of girls, the decrease in this step from EP to ESO is more drastic, and in boys is more progressive.

Figure 2

Perception of Students about Teacher Support, Family and Peer Group and in Physical Education by Education Level and Gender

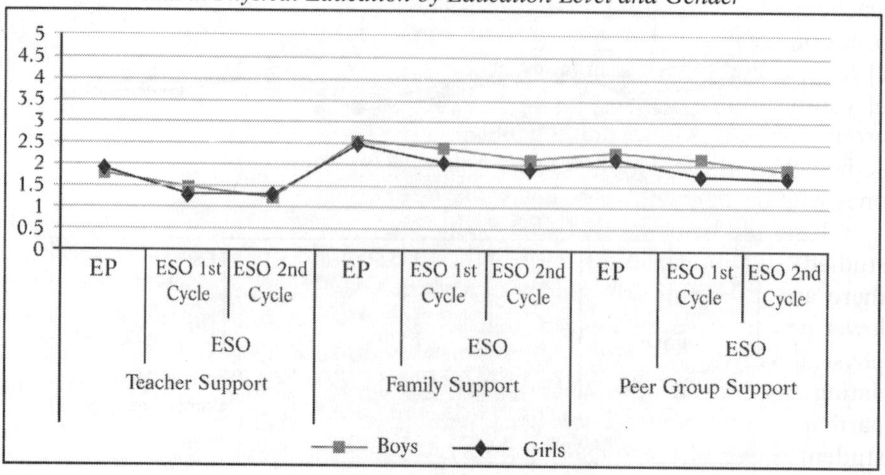

Discussion

In this study, it was found that all factors analysed, be it beliefs, attitudes and expectations of success, or the perception of the immediate social support for physical activity, show gender differences being important factors to improve since they may influence in the practice of physical activity in school, specially among girls. When deepening in the analysis of the attitude of boys and girls through interest, belief in the value and utility that they give to Physical Education and perceived motor competence, the obtained data, even though they are acceptable since their values are located above the central value range analysed, are susceptible to be situated slightly above the said central value.

Particularly, girls are who have lower values in the three factors studied, which coincides with other previous studies nationally (Vázquez, Fernandez and Ferro, 2006) and internationally scoped (Fredicks and Eccles, 2002).

The literature highlights the importance of these factors of influence on the physical activity in youth. Such is the case of the study of Chen, Darst and Pangrazi (1999) on the interest, Xiang et al. (2002) on the value and utility, and Denissen, Zarrett and Eccles, (2007) on the perceived motor competence. Based on these studies which highlight the importance of having high levels in the studied factors of influence, and depending on the results obtained in this work, it can be argued the need for the values obtained to be higher because they contribute positively to increase the practice of physical activity.

Also, these factors of influence have been analysed by educational cycle and gender, showing that both girls and boys maintain an inverse relationship with age. Thus, the interest in Physical Education, perceived motor competence and value and usefulness granted decrease when students grow older, making evident the descent from EP to ESO. Similar results have also been obtained by other authors (Fredrick and Eccles, 2002; Moreno, Hellin and Hellin Rodriguez, 2006), highlighting the critical point representing adolescence (Eccles et al., 2007; Jacobs et al., 2002).

Regarding perception about the immediate social support, for both boys and girls in the sample, none of the three areas of support studied (family, teachers and peer groups) can be considered sufficient since they appreciate it occasionally and not in a stable and consolidated basis. Greendorfer, in 1987 (1987), linked the influence of a good perception of support on physical activity of youth, noting that the social system formed by the family, school and peer group influences on young people, because those involved less in physical activity were those who had less positive influence in the social system, and the ones who participated more had more influence on the system.

It should be noted that data of this perception in the three types of support studied, show lower rates in girls than in boys (in teachers support, although there are no significant gender differences, it is slightly higher in boys). The lower perceived social support in girls can influence them to have lower levels of physical activity than boys, and we should emphasize upon the need of consolidating and increasing social support in girls to increase their involvement and participation in physical activity. Other studies show a poor perception that the students have of the social support received (Fernández et al., 2006), having identified these differences in perception of support received toward physical activity from an early age (Eccles and Harold, 1991).

Likewise, the analysis by gender and educational cycle of the results found about the perception of students in the three types of support notes that in all three cases the relationship with age is inversely proportional since as students grow older, the perception of support decreases.

Conclusion

The whole picture manifested leads to the conclusion that the social and cognitive factors of influence should be improved for the benefit of the practice of physical activity, and emphasizes that, besides being necessary to increase in all ages all influencing factors, the secondary stage deserves special attention. The lack of appreciation of the usefulness of Physical Education and the decrease of interest as they are incorporated into the adult world and the perceived motor competence makes the role of the teacher very important as enhancer and promoter of Physical Education.

In this sense, it is confirmed that the female population requires special attention because it is the group where the influence of the factors studied has been more negative. To do this, the approaches of social-cognitive genre, such as that followed in this work, are of great interest as they allow the analysis from a perspective that helps to increase the knowledge of the existing gender inequalities, promoting the understanding of the problem and providing information that promotes patterns and lines of interventions for greater equity in the field of physical activity.

References

Armstrong, N. and McManus, A. (1994). 'Children's Fitness and Physical Activity: A Challenge for Physical Education', *The British Journal of Physical Education,* 25(1): 20–25.

Calfas, K.J. and Taylor, W.C. (1994). 'Effects of Physical Activity on Psychological Variables in Adolescents', *Pediatric Exercise Science,* 6(4): 406–423.

Cavill, N., Biddle, S. and Sallis, J.F. (2001). 'Health Enhancing Physical Activity for Young People: Statement of the United Kingdom Expert Consensus Conference', *Pediatric Exercise Science,* 13(1): 12–25.

Chen. A., Darst, P.W. and Pangrazi, R.P. (1999). 'What Constitutes Situational Interest? Validating a Construct in Physical Education', *Measurement in Physical Education and Exercise Science,* 3(3): 157–180.

Crocker, P.R.E. and Faulkner, R.A. (1999). 'Self-Report of Physical Activity Intensity in Youth: Gender and Grade Level Considerations', *Avante,* 5(3): 43–51.

Denissen, J.J.A.; Zarrett, N.R. and Eccles, J.S. (2007). 'I Like to do It, I am able, am I know I am: Longitudinal Couplings between Domain-Specific Achievement, Self-concept and Interest', *Child Development,* 78(2): 430–447.

Douthitt, V.L. (1994). 'Psychological Determinants for Adolescent Exercise Adherence', *Adolescence,* 115: 711–722.

Dowda, M.; Pate, R.R.; Sallis, J.F.; Freedson, P.S.; Taylor, W.C.; Sirard, J.R. and Trost, S.G. (2007). 'Agreement between Student: Reported and Proxy-reported Physical Activity Questionnaires', *Pediatric Exercise Science,* 19(3): 310–318.

Eccles, J.S. (1985). 'Sex Differences in Achievement Patterns', in T.B. Sonderegger (ed.) *Nebraska Symposium on Motivation 1984: Psychology and Gender*, Lincoln: Nebraska University Press.

Eccles, J.S.; Adler, T.F.; Futterman, R.; Goff, S.B.; Kaczala, C.M.; Meece, J.L. and Midgley, C. (1983). 'Expectancies, Values, and Academic Behaviors', in J.T. Spence (ed.) *Achievement and Achievement Motivations,* San Francisco: W.H. Freeman and Co. 75–121.

Eccles, J.S. and Harold, R.D. (1991). 'Gender Differences in Sport Involvement: Applying the Eccles' Expectancy-Value Model', *Journal of Applied Sport Psychology,* 3(1): 7–35.

Eccles, J.S.; Wigfield, A.; Harold, R.D. and Blumenfeld, P. (1993). 'Age and Gender differences in Children's Self-and Task Perceptions during Elementary School', *Child Development,* 64(3): 830–847.

Esnaola, I. (2005). 'Autoconcepto físico y satisfacción corporal en mujeres adolescentes según el tipo de deporte practicado', *Apunts,* 80: 5–12.

Fernández, E.; Vázquez, B.; Camacho, M.J.; Sánchez, F.; Martínez de Quel, O.; Rodríguez, I.; Rubia, A. and Aznar, S. (2006). 'La inclusión de la actividad física y el deporte en el estilo de vida de las mujeres adolescentes: estudio de los factores clave y pautas de intervención', *En las mujeres jóvenes y las actividades físico-deportivas nº 46* Madrid: Consejo Superior de Deportes, 25–63.

Fredricks, J.A. and Eccles, J.S. (2002). 'Children's Competence and Value Beliefs from Childhood through Adolescence: Growth Trajectories in Two Male-Sex-Typed Domains'. *Developmental Psychology,* 38(4): 519–533.

Greendorfer, S.L. (1987). 'Gender Bias in Theoretical Perspectives the Case of Female Socialization into Sport', *Psychology of Women Quarterly,* 11: 327–340.

HBSC (2008). 'The Health Behaviors in School-age Children (HBSC) 2005/2006 Survey School Report', *Worl Health Organization,* Web, 5 Nov. 2014.

Hovell, M.F.; Sallis, J.F.; Kolody, B. and Mckenzie, T.L. (1999). 'Children's Physical Activity Choices: A Developmental Analysis of Gender, Intensity Levels and Time', *Pediatric Exercise Science,* 11: 158–168.

Jacobs, J.E. and Eccles, J.S. (1992). 'The Impact of Mothers' Gender-role Stereotypic beliefs on Mothers' ability Perception', *Journal of Personality and Social Psychology,* 63: 932–944.

Jacobs, J.E.; Lanza, S.; Osgood, D.W.; Eccles, J.S. and Wigfield, A. (2002). 'Changes in Children's Self-competence and Values: Gender and Domain Differences across Grades one through Twelve', *Child Development,* 73(2): 509–527.

Lau, P.W.C.; Fox, K.R. and Cheung, M.W.L. (2006). 'An Analysis of Sport Identity as a Predictor of Children's Participation in Sport', *Pediatric Exercise Science,* 18: 415–425.

Lloyd, T.; Petit, M.A.; Lin, H.M. and Beck, T.J. (2004). 'Lifestyle Factors and the Development of Bones Mass and Bone Strength in Young Women', *Journal of Pediatric,* 144: 776–782.

McMurray, R.G.; Harrell, J.S.; Wang, Z. and Bangdiwala, S.I. (2005). 'The Influence of Habitual Physical Activity Levels on the Change in Weight Status as Youth become Adolescents', *Pediatric Exercise Science,* 17(1): 75–76.

Ministry of Education and Science and Ministry of Health (2007). *Programa Perseo: Actividad Física y salud. Guía para familiares,* 20 Dec.

Moreno, J.A. and Hellín, M.G. (2007). 'El interés del alumnado de Educación Secundaria Obligatoria hacia la Educación Física', *Revista Electrónica de Investigación Educativa,* 9(2).

Moreno, J.A.; Hellín, P. and Hellín Rodríguez, M.G. (2006). 'Pensamiento del alumnado sobre la Educación Física según la edad', *Apunts,* 85: 28–35.

Moreno, J.A.; Rodríguez, P.L. and Gutiérrez, M. (2003). 'Intereses y actitudes hacia la Educación Física', *Revista Española de Educación Física,* 11(2): 14–28.

Navarro, C.J., Pastor, R. and Ramírez, A. (2003). *Subcultura deportiva de género y espacio público en el ámbito local (el caso del municipio de Córdoba),* Cádiz: Universidad Pablo de Olavide.

Neumark-Sztainer, D.; Story, M.; Hannan, P.J.; Tharp, T. and Rex, J. (2003). 'Factors associated with Changes in Physical Activity: A Cohort Study of Inactive adolescent Girls', *Archives of Pediatrics and Adolescent Medicine,* 157(8): 803–810.

Prochaska, J.J.; Rodgers, M.W. and Sallis, J. (2002). 'Association of Parent and Peer Support with Adolescent Physical Sctivity', *Research Quarterly for Exercise and Sport,* 73: 203–216.

Ramírez-Rico, E.; Fernández, E. and Blández, J. (2013). 'Levels of Physical Activity in Spanish adolescents Measured', *Journal of Human Sport and Exercise,* 8(2): 401–411.

Ramírez-Rico, E.; Hilland, T.A.; Foweather, L.; Fernández-García, E. and Fairclough, S.J. (2014). 'Weekday and Weekend Patterns of Physical Activity and Sedentary Time among Liverpool and Madrid Youth', *European Journal of Sport Science,* 14(3): 287–293.

Sallis, J.F.; Prochaska, J.J. and Taylor, W.C. (2000). 'A Review of Correlates of Physical Activity of Children and Adolescents', *Medicine and Science in Sport and Exercise,* 32: 963–975.

Shropshire, J. and Carroll, B. (1998). 'Final Year Primary School Children's Physical Activity Levels and Choice', *European Journal of Physical Education,* 3(2): 156–166.

Stone, E.J.; Mckenzie, T.L.; Welk, G.J. and Booth, M.L. (1998). 'Effect of Physical Activity Interventions in Youth: Review and Synthesis', *American Journal of Preventive Medicine,* 15(4): 298–315.

Vázquez, B.; Fernández, E. and Ferro, S. (2000). *Educación Física y Género,* Instituto de la Mujer, Ministerio de Educación y Asuntos Sociales, Madrid: Gymnos.

Welk, G.I. (1999). 'The Youth Physical Activity Promotion Model: A Conceptual Bridge between Theory and Practice'. *Quest,* 51: 5–23.

Xiang, P.; McBride, R.E.; Guan, J. and Solmon, M. (2003). 'Children's Motivation in Elementary Physical Education: An Expectancy-Value Model of Achievement Choice'. *Research Quarterly for Exercise and Sport.* 74: 25–35.

18

Role of Self-Help Groups in Enhancing the Capabilities of Women

A Case Study of Varanasi District

TRIPTI KUMARI

Abstract

Capabilities are the combinations of many choices and opportunities of freedom through which an individual can achieve a good life that a person deserves. 'Freedom of choices' to do something at individual's level without any obstruction is simple meaning of capability. In this field, Self-Help Groups (SHGs) are emerging as an instrument through which the most vulnerable and deprived section of the society, especially women, are organizing themselves together in a common group and collecting their own small savings and credit which help them in advancing their capabilities. Self-Help Groups is based on the principle 'of the people, by the people and with the people.' Homogeneity and self-help are the bases of the SHGs organization. Varanasi is one of the great ancient cities of India having a rich history. Many Self-Help Groups were organized and these groups are helping the members in the advancement of their life. The present paper focusses on the concept of capability approach and Self-Help Groups. The role of Self Help Groups as a key to achieving the concept of 'capability approach' is discussed in the Varanasi district.

Keywords

capability approach, self-help groups, freedom of choices

Introduction

The process of development of a country necessitates including women in the development. It has been realized that, without including women in the development path, without which the goal of the development of the nation cannot be achieved. But women, who contribute half of the population, are not in the position to even get the advantage of different welfare and development programmes started by the government especially in the rural areas. They are the major labour force in many informal sectors such as agriculture, house workers, vendors, tailors, shopkeepers, beauticians, etc. But in spite of this, they are not getting equal participation in the decision-making process inside and outside the home. Self Help Groups (SHGs) are group-based organizations which provide a system to integrate women from homogeneous socio-economic background. The major aim of the establishment of Self-Help Groups (SHGs) is to provide opportunities to the people of the lowest income group who are still denied access to welfare and development plans due to unawareness and illiteracy. It empowers women who are traditionally unable to participate in the economic activities. It provides financial support to them for starting different kinds of activities based on their tradition skills, such as stitching, pickle-making, *jari* work, *papad*-making, *moti-mala* work, etc. It also enhances the capacity of members. Capacity building is one of the major aspects of women empowerment and decision-making ability of an individual is the most important factor of measuring empowerment status of the individual. The main aim of empowerment is a woman's role and share in development and their active participation in decision-making process.

Self-Help Groups (SHGs) are small groups of an average size of 10 to 20 members which is easily operational. It encourages women to save small but regular saving on monthly basis. These groups make women economically independent, confident and make them able to participate in the decision-making inside as well as outside the home. The collective saving generates a heavy amount of money which is given to the group members at very low rate of interest on their demand. In this way these groups save them from the local money lenders who offer them money at high rate of interest. This unique quality of SHGs changes the attitude of male members in the family of the women members of the group and they also help their wives in attending meeting, record-keeping, starting business and other banking formalities outside the village. Therefore these groups enhance the capabilities of women members through income generating activities and entrepreneurship development among them. Now they are also having the decision-making ability of these women. They are taking decision about themselves, their families, their children's future, education, health, family planning, expenditures, etc. The major objectives of these groups are to organize women and provide a suitable platform for development, to enhance their capacity and active participation at family, society and group level. It also inculcates the saving and banking habits among the rural women through enhancing the mutual trust and confidence between the groups and the banks. Now women are participating in group activities and work with each other in the group for their development.

Concept of Capability Approach

The capability of a person reflects the alternative combinations of functioning that the person can achieve. This approach is based on view of living as a combination of various 'doings and beings' with the quality of life to be assessed in the terms of capability to achieve valuable functioning (Kenchaigol, 2012). Human capabilities are 'people's potential' and functioning are 'being and doings' (Robeyns, 2002). People are the real wealth of nations. Indeed, the basic purpose of development is to enlarge human freedom. The process of development can expand human capabilities by expanding the choices that people have to live full and creative lives. And people are both the beneficiaries of such development and the agents of the progress and change that bring it about. This process must benefit all individuals equitably and build on the participation of each of them. This approach to development – human development – has been advocated by every *Human Development Report* since the first in 1990 (HDR, 2004: 127). Capability denotes the person's opportunity and abilities to generate valuable outcome, taking into account relevant personal characteristics and external forces (Sen, 1992).

According to Amartya Sen's 'capability approach', capability is the freedom of choices to achieve valuable beings and doings. Therefore, the core focus of capability approach is on 'what individuals are able to do' (i.e. capable of). Capability is person's ability and opportunity of freedom to do work. It also enhances the quality of life of the individual.

Initially, Sen argued five components of assessing capabilities:

1. The importance of real freedom in the assessment of person's advantage.
2. Individual differences in the ability to transform resources into valuable activities.
3. The multi-variant nature of activities giving rise to happiness.
4. A balance of materialistic and non-materialistic factors in evaluating human welfare.
5. Concern for the distribution of opportunities within the society.

Gender equality can be achieved by providing equal opportunities for women and better access to education, health, credit and employment. It is also recognized that investing in women's capabilities and empowering them to achieve their choices is the surest way to contribute to economic growth and overall development of the nation. In Cairo Conference, it was accepted that in order to deal with development issues in a meaningful way, the emancipation and empowerment of women is required. The International Conference on Population and Development (ICPD) was also remarkable for the breadth of its focus on the human dimension of population-recognition that tackling population issues in the context requires simultaneous progress on related issues such as empowerment of women, gender equality and girl's education.

Objectives

The main objective of the present paper is to examine the impact of SHGs in enhancing capabilities of women inside and outside the family in the Varanasi district. It mainly focuses on the effect of SHGs on the life of members after joining the groups. Basically, it is an attempt to highlight the advantages of SHGs in enhancing the capacity of its members.

Methodology

Data was collected with the help of an interview schedule from personal field survey of the study area. Interview schedule contains questions related to different aspects of participation in decision-making process in the family and group both in qualitative as well as quantitative aspects. A total of 340 SHGs members were surveyed from Varanasi district. Among these, 100 from respondents are from Varanasi City area, and 30 from each blocks of the study area, namely Baragaon, Pindra, Chiraigaon, Cholapur, Sevapuri, Kashi Vidhyapeeth, Harahua and Araziline. The help of SPSS 20 software and Microsoft Office Excel 2007 were used to analyse the data. Data were tabulated into different groups to achieve the objectives set out in the study.

Study Area

Geographically, Varanasi district lies between 25°10′ North to 25° 37′ North latitudes and 82°39′ East to 83°10′ East longitudes, in the eastern part of Uttar Pradesh (Figure 1). Its major areas stretch towards the west and north of Varanasi district. The total geographical area of Varanasi district is 1,535 sq km with a total population of 3,676,841 out of which, male and female were 1,921,857 and 1,754,984, respectively as per 2011 Census. Administratively, the district comprises two tahsils, namely Pindra and Varanasi which are further divided into eight development blocks, namely Baragaon, Pindra and Cholapur in Pindra tahsil and Chiraigaon, Kashi Vidhyapeeth, Araziline and Sevapuri in Varanasi Sadar tahsil. Harahua block lies in both the tahsils. The southern and south-eastern part of Harahua block has extended in Varanasi tahsil but its major parts lies in the Pindra block. Varanasi is situated on the left bank of Ganga river, lies between Ganga river in the south and the Gomati river in the north direction, while Varuna river flowing in the central part of the district. The city occupies almost a central position in the Ganga valley.

Figure 1
Location Map

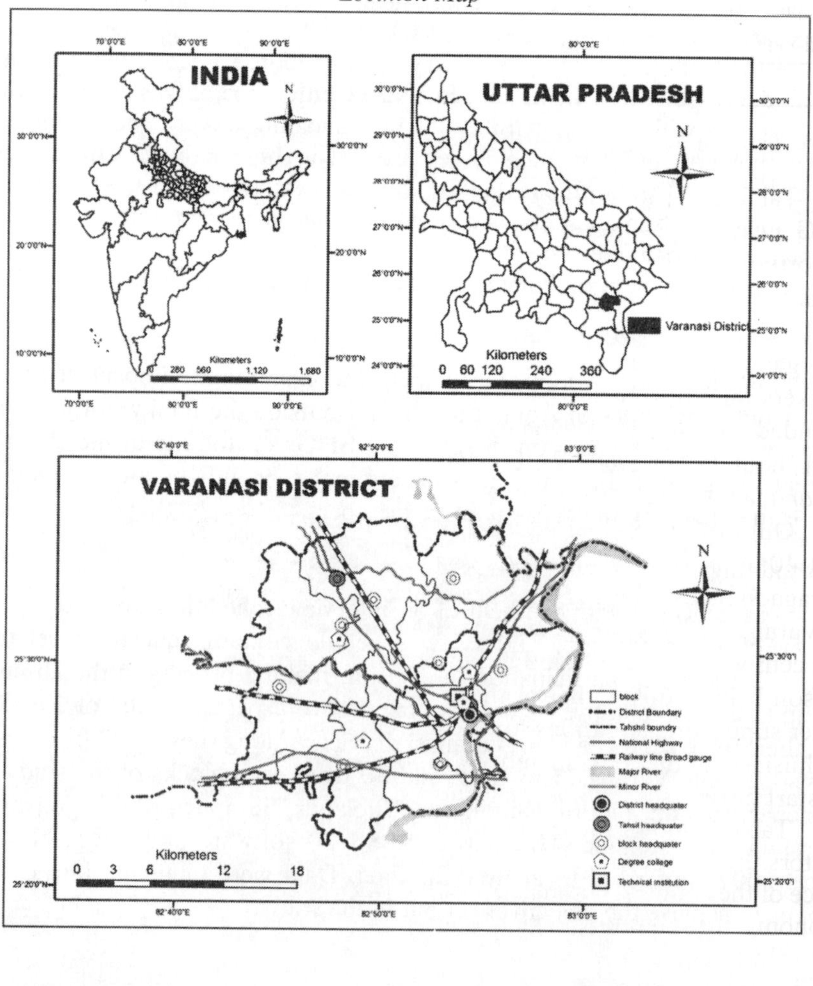

Data Analysis

Data collected on the different dimensions of the study explains the impact of Self-Help Groups (SHGs) on the life of women.

Table 1

Block-Wise Occupation Status of SHG Members

Development Block	*Total no of employed women*		*Total no of unemployed women*		*Total Workers*	
	No.	*%*	*No.*	*%*	*No.*	*%*
Varanasi City	68	68.0	32	32.0	100	100.0
Sevapuri	20	66.7	10	33.3	30	100.0
Baragaon	26	86.7	4	13.3	30	100.0
Pindra	12	40.0	18	60.0	30	100.0
Harahua	19	63.3	11	36.7	30	100.0
Araziline	17	56.7	13	43.3	30	100.0
Chiraigaon	19	63.3	11	36.7	30	100.0
Cholapur	8	26.7	22	73.3	30	100.0
Kashi Vidhyapeeth	14	46.7	16	53.3	30	100.0
Total	203	59.7	137	40.3	340	100.0

Source: Based on Personal Field Survey, 2013–2014.

Table 1 represents the block-wise distribution of employment status of SHG members in the district. Self-Help Groups (SHGs) have provided an opportunity to the members for economic development in the study area. After joining the group, women's share in the working force has been increased. In the study area, employment status of women are classified into organized and unorganized sectors. In the organized sector, MANREGA and Aanganwadi workers were included, while in unorganized sectors self-employed women are included. Self-employed women were those engaged in various activities at their own household level, such as stitching, dairy, *jari* work, *mala*-making, *achar*-making, etc.

Out of total 340 of the sample, 59.7 per cent women are workers while rest 40.3 per cent are non-workers. The percentage of workers is highest in Baragaon block which is 86.7 per cent of total women of the block. After that, in Varanasi city region, Sevapuri, Harahua, Chiraigaon blocks more than 60 per cent women were found to be working in different kinds of activities. The reason behind this is that in these regions the SHGs are providing loan and other supporting situations for the entrepreneurship development and also the enthusiasm of the SHG members, supported by their family, encouraging them to start businesses, own a small shop, a bangle shop, a vegetable shop, etc.

Table 2 shows the distribution of workers in organized and unorganized sectors. It is a known fact that women are the greatest contributors in the work force of the country, but majority of them are engaged in unorganized sectors of economy. In the study region, members of Self-Help Groups (SHGs) were engaged mainly in unorganized sectors, i.e. small shops, vegetable vendors, *mala*-making, tailoring, pickle's material-making, *jari* work, etc. and organized sectors include MANREGA and Aanganwadi workers. Data shows that out of total workers of the sampled blocks, 87.2 per cent were engaged in unorganized sector and only 12.8 per cent were engaged in organized sector. In Varanasi City and Pindra blocks, there was no one engaged in organized sectors and in Sevapuri and Baragaon blocks, 5 and 7 per cent women were engaged in organized sectors, who were MANREGA workers. Chiraigaon block ranks first where about 68 per cent women are engaged in organized sectors such as MANREGA, Aanganwadi sectors. After that, Kashi Vidhyapeeth, Cholapur, Araziline and Harahua blocks follow where, 28.6, 25, 11.8 10.5 per cent women, respectively, were working in organized sectors.

Table 2

Block-Wise Distribution of Workers in Organized and Unorganized Sectors of Economy

Development Block	*Workers employed in the Organized Sector*		*Workers employed in the Unorganized Sector*		*Total Women*	
	No.	*%*	*No.*	*%*	*No.*	*%*
Varanasi City	0	0.0	68	100.0	68	100.0
Sevapuri	1	5.0	19	95.0	20	100.0
Baragaon	2	7.7	24	92.3	26	100.0
Pindra	0	0.0	12	100.0	12	100.0
Harahua	2	10.5	17	89.5	19	100.0
Araziline	2	11.8	15	88.2	17	100.0
Chiraigaon	13	68.4	6	31.6	19	100.0
Cholapur	2	25.0	6	75.0	8	100.0
Kashi Vidhyapeeth	4	28.6	10	71.4	14	100.0
Total	26	12.8	177	87.2	203	100.0

Source: Based on Personal Field Survey, 2013–2014.

Table 3 reveals the monthly income of SHGs members in different development blocks of Varanasi district. Data shows that out of total women, about 47 per cent of women earn monthly income less than ₹ 1,000 out of which many earned ₹ 500 per month and 47 per cent earned between ₹ 1,001–3,000 per month, while only 7 per cent of women earned more than ₹ 3,001 and less than ₹ 5,000. No one earned more than ₹ 5,000. The development block-wise data in Varanasi city, Baragaon, Sevapuri, Harahua blocks showed that women whose monthly income is less than ₹ 1,000 are maximum. These women were mainly engaged in *moti-mala*-making, *jari* work, *achar*-making, stitching, etc. Women who earn monthly income more than ₹ 3,000 were engaged in milk-selling to the hotels, and some are employed in Aanganwadi works, peons in schools and in hospitals. Therefore, we can conclude that SHGs did not achieve success in enhancing the quality of life of its members in the district. The condition of women remained pathetic and that they didn't get the least minimum wage decided by the Government of India and still remain below the poverty line. There is, thus, a need to improve the quality of life of the members of SHGs in the district.

Table 3

Monthly Income of Self-Help Groups (SHGs) Members in Varanasi District

Development Blocks	*Monthly Income*			*Total*
	<1,000	*1,001–3,000*	*3,001–5,000*	
Varanasi City	34	28	7	69
	49.3%	40.6%	10.1%	100.0%
Sevapuri	15	3	–	18
	83.3%	16.7%	–	100.0%
Baragaon	22	3	1	26
	84.6%	11.5%	3.8%	100.0%
Pindra	–	10	–	10
	–	100.0%	–	100.0%
Harahua	12	6	–	18
	66.7%	33.3%	–	100.0%
Araziline	6	9	1	16
	37.5%	56.2%	6.2%	100.0%
Chiraigaon	1	16	2	19
	5.3%	84.2%	10.5%	100.0%
Cholapur	2	5	3	10
	20.0%	50.0%	30.0%	100.0%
Kashi Vidhyapeeth	1	12	–	13
	7.7%	92.3%	–	100.0%
Total	93	92	14	199
	46.7%	46.2%	7.0%	100.0%

Source: Based on Personal Field Survey, 2013–2014.

Table 4 depicts different reasons for taking loan by the women in the district. From the data, it is clear that about 42 per cent of women have taken loan from the group for medical purposes, 18.5 per cent have taken loan for their daughter's marriage and about 14 per cent have taken loan for house construction purposes. It reveals that in the district there is problem of availability of proper government medical services that forced women to take loan from the group. Another finding from the data related to 10 per cent women having taken loan from the group for the purpose of starting business at their household level and 8 per cent women have taken loan for their children's education. The data, thus, reveals that there is a positive effect of SHGs in the district as it motivates women to stand on their own feet through small and regular savings.

Table 4

Block-Wise Distribution of Reason for Loan taken by SHGs Members in Varanasi District

Development Blocks	*Reason for Taking Loan*											*Total*
	Medical Treatment	*House Construction*	*Daughter's/son's Marriage*	*Starting Business*	*Education*	*Other Work*	*Purchase Bicycle*	*Purchase Seed*	*Start Goat Rearing Business*	*Help Husband*	*Medical Treatment of Animal*	
Varanasi City	35	16	18	10	9	5	–	–	–	–	–	93
	37.6%	17.2%	19.4%	10.8%	9.7%	5.4%	–	–	–	–	–	100.0%
Sevapuri	12	2	6	2	–	–	2	2	2	2	–	30
	40.0%	6.7%	20.0%	6.7%	–	–	6.7%	6.7%	6.7%	6.7%	–	100.0%
Baragaon	11	4	7	4	1	–	3	–	–	–	–	30
	36.7%	13.3%	23.3%	13.3%	3.3%	–	10.0%	–	–	–	–	100.0%
Pindra	11	2	6	2	7	–	–	–	–	–	–	28
	39.3%	7.1%	21.4%	7.1%	25.0%	–	–	–	–	–	–	100.0%
Harahua	15	5	2	3	1	–	2	–	–	1	1	30
	50.0%	16.7%	6.7%	10.0%	3.3%	–	6.7%	–	–	3.3%	3.3%	100.0%
Araziline	14	4	6	2	3	–	1	–	–	–	–	30
	46.7%	13.3%	20.0%	6.7%	10.0%	–	3.3%	–	–	–	–	100.0%
Chiraigaon	15	3	7	2	3	–	–	–	–	–	–	30
	50.0%	10.0%	23.3%	6.7%	10.0%	–	–	–	–	–	–	100.0%
Cholapur	9	7	4	3	1	1	–	–	–	4	1	30
	30.0%	23.3%	13.3%	10.0%	3.3%	3.3%	–	–	–	13.3%	3.3%	100.0%
Kashi Vidhyapeeth	13	2	4	4	2	–	–	–	–	2	–	27
	48.1%	7.4%	14.8%	14.8%	7.4%	–	–	–	–	7.4%	–	100.0%
Total	135	45	60	32	27	6	8	2	2	9	2	328
	41.2%	13.7%	18.3%	9.8%	8.2%	1.8%	2.4%	0.6%	0.6%	2.7%	0.6%	100.0%

Source: Based on Personal Field Survey, 2013–2014

Conclusion

The study demonstrates that Varanasi is marching ahead with determination towards its goal of empowerment. From the result of analysis of data, it is clear that Self-Help Groups (SHGs) have emerged as a tool for the enhancement of knowledge, awareness, confidence, self-esteem values among women which improve the capabilities of women, thus leading to generating decision-making abilities among women. Micro-enterprises have led to starting of a range of economic activities by them and have helped the poor women to earn income on their own. SHGs have also enhanced the access to resources among the women in the study area. Their economic decision-making has been enhanced with the mobilization of women in organized collectives as SHGs and their participation in micro-enterprises. Further it helped in reducing the economic dependency of women on men. Capacity building of women in terms of saving some income and spending it on their personal items without any hesitation was encouraging. The decision-making capacity of women affects their daily lives which is one of the vital cross cultural aspects of family relations and women empowerment.

After joining the group, women understood the advantages of small savings and collective approach. They were actively participating in the group, attending the group meeting fixed by the convenience of all the members of the group, helped each other, helped in record-keeping and group-related activities. These groups have provided platform to those women who were earlier formed the most neglected section of the society and were unaware of all the opportunities of self-development. It was found that with the formation of these groups, they broke up the boundary of traditional norms and thoughts. It is very interesting to note that the husbands of these women members also understood the benefits of groups and they also helped women in attending the meeting, record-keeping and other bank-related formalities related to the group. They realized that groups were the source of loan and economic independence which will ultimately fulfil the demand of money at the time of urgent need. Women in the SHG can share their problems with the other women, which helped them solve the problems. These groups, thus, enhanced the capabilities of women and also enhanced their participation in the household decision-making. Therefore, there is a need to establish more and more SHGs so that more women can get benefits of the group. The study, thus, shows that in Varanasi district, the SHGs provided a platform to women who were otherwise still not getting the actual benefits of development plans. These are mainly from the most deprived and vulnerable sections of the society. After joining the group, these women have started saving small amount of money and have also got loan at a very low rate of interest. By using the loan, they started small business at their household level like bangle shop, vegetable shop, *kirana* shop, stitching business, *jari* work business, etc. SHGs are thus becoming a tool for the overall development of women in the district. SHGs have promoted gender equality to make women as agents of change in society and to increase women's capabilities. SHGs have provided an opportunity to improve women's social, economic and political development through active participation. Today, SHGs have emerged as an effective tool for the upliftment of women especially, from the unorganized sector who have traditional skills like weaving, *achar*-making, *papad*-making, stitching, painting, etc. and by using this skill and credit support through the group they are able to start their own enterprises. Women are becoming more independent as well as empowered by getting economic benefits through the SHGs. Members of these groups are more aware about small savings and also contribute in the family's income. They also understand the value of education and providing education to their children. They also recognize the importance of small family and adopting family planning. Family support to attend group meetings and other group level activities is yet another feature of SHGs, through which women are made aware about different government programmes for their benefit. Despite these benefits, there is still need for promoting education among women and organizing them into SHGs for the development of the district, state and the economy at the macro level.

References

Das, Baswanti and Khawas, Vimal (2009). *Gender Issues in Development: Concerns for the 21st Century*. Jaipur: Rawat Publications.

Devi, Medhabati and Upadhyay, N. (2008). 'Social Mobilization for Empowering Rural Poor Through SHGs: A Study in Assam', *Indian Journal of Public Administration*, Vol. LIV(4): 822–832.

Kenchaigol, D. Snjeev (2012). 'Assessment of Gender Equalities through Capability Approach: Proposing a Capability List', *Indian Journal of Human Development*. Vol. 6(1): 85–105.

Mohanty, Rani Sandhya; Das, Bijayalaxmi and Mohanty, Trupti (2013). 'Capacity Building and Decision-making of Rural Odisha Women through Participation in Microenterprises', *International Journal of Scientific and Research Publications*, Vol. 3(7).

Pandey, Rameshwari (2008). *Women Welfare and Empowerment in India: Vision for 21st Century*. New Delhi: New Century Publications.

Pravin, M. Razia (2005). *Empowerment of Women Strategies and System for Gender-Justice*. New Delhi: Dominant Publishers.

Rao, C. Narsimha, (2006). *Rural Development in India*. New Delhi: Serials Publications.

Sahay, Sushama (1998). *Women and Empowerment: Approaches and Strategies*. New Delhi: Discovery Publishing House.

19

Women Entrepreneurs and Empowerment

Is Micro-finance the Path for Women's Empowerment in a Changing World?

ALICIA GIRÓN

Abstract

The discourse on the empowerment of women and their necessary participation as entrepreneurs through micro-credit has been growing stronger amongst the international financial organizations. Empowerment refers to the contribution of women as economic agents in public life and in the decision-making of public policies, as well as in the reactivation of global aggregate demand. Facing the requests of international organizations such as the International Monetary Fund (IMF) and the World Bank (WB) itself to end poverty and enhance family's environment, there is still the neoliberal ideology that has prioritized the role of women as entrepreneurs through funding. In order to pose this hypothesis about the existing relationship between empowerment, women entrepreneurs, and micro-credit, it is important to maintain the changes that have happened at a macro-economic level and their effect in micro-economy. The predominance of the shadow financial system and the financialization process whose characterization is presented along deregulation and financial liberalization, has transformed women into dynamic economic agents. The latter does not mean that micro-credit is the right path for women to achieve empowerment as economic agents, microfinance obtain high profitability rates through microcredit with a feminine face.

Keywords

women entrepreneurs, empowerment, micro-finances institutions and micro-credit

Introduction

The study focused on the analysis of micro-credit from a gender point of view, the feminine face may be observed in the small loans granted by micro-finance institutions. In most countries of Latin America and Asia, international financial intermediaries have obtained great profit from micro-finance subsidiaries, which are mostly from corporate banking catalogued as 'too big to fail, too big to rescue'. These corporate banking institutions have been favoured by financial regulation from the State as well as from international financial institutions such as the IMF, the MB, and the Bank for International Settlements (BIS, 2013). To cast down poverty and to enhance family's environment are two elements of the ideological discourse that emphasizes the role of women as entrepreneurs through their access to funding. Therefore the ideal path in order to obtain funding and create small businesses is micro-credit, to such a degree that even in the Millennium Goals, concepts such as empowerment, women entrepreneurs, and micro-credit are joined to refer to women. That is, women are instruments of exchange, but they also, as Nancy Fraser would say, 'the current crisis of neoliberal capitalism is altering the landscape of feminist theory' (Fraser, 2013: 227).

The hypothesis of this paper will lie on demonstrating the existent causality between empowerment, women entrepreneurs, and micro-credit, beginning with the changes at the macro-economic level that have had an effect since the deregulation process and the financial liberalization until the predominance of the financialization process through the shadow financial system (Girón, 2012a: 63). The magnitude of that effect has been such that institutional investors, such as micro-finance institutions (MFIs), obtain large profits from micro-credits (Girón, 2012b: 89) in which the feminine face still remains. But first and foremost, and for the present analysis to begin, the definition of two concepts must be given: 'money manager capitalism' and financialization process, that which disarticulated the development banking for it to fall in a pulverization process of the major institutions of public policy of developmental funding. That is to say, public banking and development banking, which worked for the creation of employment and functioned as a source of wealth under the regulated financial institutions, blurred in order to open the way for institutional investors whose main objective is profitability. Secondly, it is said that micro-finacing works for achieving the empowerment of women, thereby a questioning arises in what refers to the role of women as small and medium entrepreneurs with their businesses funded through micro-credit. Thirdly, when performing an exercise of granted micro-credits by micro-finance institutions and when relating the amount of micro-credits hired by women, it is observed that profitability rates denounce the feminine face questioning, in this manner, micro-credit itself.

From the above, it may be concluded that the empowerment of women as entrepreneurs through micro-credit is undoubtedly untenable because, in a world of 'money manager capitalism' in which Minsky (Wray, 2011) has defined the rapacity of financial institutions and in which financialization has reached the intimate lives of society, one may hardly assert that micro-credit is the path towards the empowerment of women that live in an environment of austerity. Hence, the regulation of micro-finance institutions demands to pose for debate the legal structure of the various ways in which credit relations are established between creditors and debtors in what refers to the inside of a country as well as to the outside, that is, at an international level. The subject is of vital importance and should be posed for debate by the Parliament and by society, since very few studies who are not in favor of the traditional hegemonic way of thinking do not criticize micro-credit. Taking clue from this, the question whether micro-finance is the right tool in order to achieve the empowerment of women becomes absolutely valid.

Financialization and 'Money Manager Capitalism' and Micro-credit

In order to connect micro-credit as a part of the process of financialization it is important to define what is financialization, to achieve the objective of this paper. The financialization process consists '... of the buying and selling of assets or financial securities that can take place in orderly form in the capital markets. The new jointing of large conglomerates participated in this through off-balance sheet transactions with derivatives or financial products and services that were the consequence of technological and financial innovations' (Girón and Chapoy, 2012: 168). That is, there are major institutional investors managing, on a daily basis, enormous amounts of money and offering loans to major banks as well as to, specifically, micro-finance institutions. The offer of credits allows money to go back into financial circuits of micro-finance institutions attending the financial services demanded by small and medium enterprises so that it is able to return large profits to financial creditors, many of them anonymous. Micro-credit is part of the financialization process inserting small lenders and borrowers in a financial accumulation regimen which results in large amounts of profits.

The progress achieved by micro-credit is not casual among low-income groups of Latin American societies in countries such as Mexico, Bolivia, Ecuador, and Peru, without leaving aside the other countries within that region. This process, during several decades, has been linked to the progressive loss of development banking institutions since the 1970s until today. If the growth that Mexico had within the frame of the Mexican miracle is observed, it may be concluded that it was based on development banking, public banking, and the channeling of international credit, through the MB and the Interamerican Development Bank (IDB), towards major projects for the economic development of the country. From the blurring of development bank, the deregulation process, and the financial liberalization, the emergence of micro-finance institutions is made visible within marginalized groups when access to credit through formal procedures was inexistent. On the other side, the strengthening of the financial system provoked that the majority of institutional investors were transformed into player within the international financial circuits.

A rearrangement of the economic system towards what Minsky called at its moment 'money manager capitalism' (Wray, 2011) has provoked what the others have also called financialization process. If these two concepts were not taken into account it may be hardly settled what would be the emergence of micro-credit and the more profitable players: micro-finance institutions. Among institutional investors those that stand out are pension funds and hedge funds which, when finding support outside their countries of origin, have generated major investments that directly arrive to micro-finance institutions established in countries known as emergent, which structural changes since the 1970s triggered the disappearance of development banking. It may be asserted that there is a causal relation between micro-finance institutions, pension funds, and hedge funds in order to gran credits to marginalized groups that are part of the informal channels parallel to formal financial circuits.

While originating credit and distributing risk, the institutions of the shadow financial system not only encouraged great profits, but also set the foundations for the instability and the fragility of the whole international financial system. It is asserted the hypothesis that financialization or 'money manager capitalism' has a close relation with the generation of profits, managing liquidity, and transferring risk. The niche of funding development and the empowerment of women as entrepreneurs would be happening through micro-finance institutions, from a process given by the relation between profitability of the latter and the possibility of empowering women by changing traditional and cultural patterns of women.

Micro-Credit, Women Entrepreneurs and Women Empowerment

The break in which credit was granted, since the 1970s, was moving towards the disappearance of development banking in many countries, the processes of deregulation and financial liberalization throughout the world, under the influence of the market, and the blurring of financial structures of the public sector, acquired great strength when prioritizing the private sector. Financing now possesses a growing organization through institutional financial investors, to such an extent that micro-credit transformed into the official discourse of many governments since it works as a flag of the hegemonic thought when it comes to escaping from poverty. The necessary 'bancarization' (Conde, 2005) will work as the tool in order to grant credit to low income sectors, that is, those who have no access to credit through the formal procedures provided by commercial banking. Then micro-credit, through micro-financing, is transformed into a challenge for national development programmes. The great transformation of micro-credit is the way to ensure better income and the way to make collateral a candidate to micro-credit, which will also become an entrepreneur. Business, within the official discourse, works to cast down and get out of poverty, then it will not matter if the entrepreneur and the employer are, almost every time, the same person. Micro-credit responds then, because of the latter, to the needs of a community: the group is the collateral and, because of that, micro-credit avoids the fall into arrears or even into moratorium.

Women are the perfect candidates to transform micro-credit into the easiest way of including them into the labour market circuits as well as into the financial circuits due to the great commitment that they have toward their families and jobs. Hence, the need to be providers of the family income will be the objective to achieve, since credit granted to women changes gender roles, breaks traditional roles of money management, and faces discrimination within their families and workplace. The debate in order to get out of poverty through micro-finance was legitimated when the Nobel Prize Committee granted to Prof. Yunus the Nobel Peace Prize for the Grameen Bank. This idea may be questioned if the data of two of the larger micro-finance institutions is taken into account, that is, the Grameen Bank and the Building Resources Across Communities (BRAC) established in Bangladesh, as well as the data from two other institutions: the Proshika Human Development Centre (PROSHIKA) and the

Association for Social Advancement (ASA), which were used in order to prove the hypothesis.

Lamia (2011) mentions the fundamental axes of the micro-finance research are: first, it is said that women are the bearers of the honour of their families, NGOs operationalized this rural code of honour in order to transform it into credit collateral. Secondly, NGOs operate as a shadow state, they offer employment, and determine the production system as a quasi-sovereign shadow state. Thirdly, NGOs are a kind of occidental sponsors and a small inner circle of researchers that circumscribe to the construction of knowledge about development. Those NGOs, a shadow State, is parallel to State since almost every micro-credit loan activity, as well as those credits destined to women within rural areas, is controlled by them. Due to the fact that many of the activities of the State were privatized, they are now managed by NGOs, and the growth of the loans granted by micro-finance institutions has led to a new institutional agreement that involves NGOs and institutional investors. The latter is fuelled by two contradictory impulses: the need to generate profits and the need to help the poor. The relation between NGOs and multinational corporations looking to establish businesses is known as Socially Responsible Companies (SRC), a term coined by the Nobel prize winner professor Muhammad Yunus, since it combines profits with social objectives. These relations are presented as a win-win situation for both, corporations and marginalized consumers of the formal financial circuits. The export of the Grameen model around the world has changed developmental finances, the Grameen Bank, BRAC, and ASA, transformed into transnational microfinance institutions since they offer financial services for the poor at a global level.

This governability model is closely related to the policies of neoliberalism and the financial revolution became possible only when neoliberal structural transformations happened across nations during the decades of the 1980s and the 1990s. The crossed relation between NGOs and institutional investors through the empowerment of women has been the discourse of neoliberalism; the notions of efficiency in the discourse of development have transformed its organic process into a moving activity, social programme, war against poverty at a global scale through micro-credit, nowadays micro-finance. The powerful mantra of the developing world is micro-credit to empower women, to cast down poverty, and to expand the free enterprise; these are also the guidelines permeating the Millennium Goals.

Micro-Finance: An Obstacle for Development

During a recent talk given by the director of the International Monetary Fund (IMF) at the London School of Economics, she mentioned that there were three kinds of empowerment that should be taken into account: 'First, the empowerment of the individual – and what that means for economic policies. Second, what is needed to help individual empowerment – the empowerment of institutions. Third, what is needed in turn to help national economies flourish – the empowerment of multilateralism' (Lagarde, 2014). In the above quotation, there are two fundamental words to achieve the empowerment of women, which are: public policies and institutions through which we are able to position women, not only in what refers to making decisions for public life, but also in what refers to enhancing their conditions as citizens and transmitters of the values of society, and lastly, the access to credit in order to transform them into economic agents, as entrepreneurs without leaving aside the fact that those who consume and make decisions when it comes to purchasing corresponds to women in a 70 per cent. Therefore, there is no doubt that empowerment is not only about turning women into entrepreneurs, it is also related to the opportunities that each society offer to women. Access to education, nutrition, and better services in what refers to housing, are key elements to enhance a society through women. A scenario that involves justice implies an infrastructure that allows the best development of capacities. That is a result of the public policies of governments and of the public spending, specifically the social spending. Therefore, with austerity policies and in a recessionary environment, empowerment will hardly be achieved, as shown in The Global Gender Gap of the World Economic Forum.

From the millennium goals, the word 'advocacy' has been used to promote economic human rights and development opportunities, that is, the minimum requirements for a human being such as the right to health, to nutrition, to housing, and to education, have been quantified in the human development indicators and are the result of public policies. Hence, they are the only way to eliminate inequities as well as the gender gap in society. Another word that has been added to the latter, 'agency', refers to the influence through public policies in order to achieve the goals of economic rights. Thus, only through the sphere of mesoeconomy, in which economic policies are articulated facing the economic cycle, is possible that the policies of full employment guarantee economic rights from the reactivation of aggregate demand within an environment in which macroeconomic changes may have a minor effect on the microeconomic sphere.

In their article, 'Microfinance and the Illusion of Development: From Hubris to Nemesis in Thirty Years', Bateman and Chang (2012) mention that neoclassical economic theorists and the neoliberal policy-makers broadly agree in celebrating the microcredit model as an alternative to widen the entrepreneurial capacity to get out of poverty. This premise for sustainable growth and development of individual micro entrepreneur is accompanied by an implicit antipathy to every form of government intervention. Hulme and Mosley show that the model of financing for development promoted by the government ever since the post-war period and to the beginning of the 1970s, turned out to be a failure. Hence, within the framework of deregulation and financial liberation, the failure of development banking as a State's institution to incorporate huge development projects and overcome poverty, would have to be eliminated. The next option would be micro-finance institutions, mainly addressed to micro entrepreneur agents or micro entrepreneurs who have access to credit without having to go through the formal channels of traditional commercial banking.

The question, whether micro-financing is actually the path to achieve empowerment for women, the answer is absolutely negative since it is granted through financial institutions within the sphere of micro-economy and its relation to possible productive projects, their accomplishment depends on the capacity of consumption of those who are employed. In an environment of austerity, public policies respond to profitability interests within the financial sphere, which diminishes public spending and full employment opportunities. On the other side, funding for development of infrastructure such as the access to water, the enhancement of health centres, and education at schools becomes untenable because of the sudden reduction of public spending, since it rather responds to the interests of rentier capital (Keynes, 1961).

Profits of Micro-Finance Institutions

An analysis of micro-finance institutions (MFIs) where funding is destined at a 100 per cent to women borrowers is presented below. Further, it also shows the way in which the profit margin, the Return on Assets (ROA), and the Return on Equity (ROE) present the high profitability provided by microcredit during 2012.

First, the analysis will be focused on the profit margin, secondly on the ROA, and thirdly on the ROE:

1. The MFIs with a 100 per cent of credits granted to women and with higher margin of profit were established at Vietnam. This country owns seven of the 15 more profitable micro-finance institutions at the international level, notwithstanding that the micro-finance institution with the highest profit margin, established at India was 61 per cent. The 15 micro-finance institutions contained in this chart are characterized by having a profit margin above the 30 per cent and established at Asia.
2. The micro-finance institutions with the higher ROA are established at Vietnam. This country owns six, out of 15 micro-finance institutions, with the above-mentioned characteristics. The case of the PNN Soc Son (Vietnam) is outstanding since its ROA reached a 27 per cent, almost the double of that presented by MBK Ventura (2nd with a 14%). However, it is necessary to observe the amount of assets presented by each micro-finance institution since a low amount may take this indicator to rise. The 15 micro-finance institutions of this chart characterized by presenting a positive ROA that varies between the 8 and the 27 per cent, because they are established at the same region.
3. The MFIs with the higher ROE were established at India and Vietnam in the year 2012. The outstanding cases were those of the first microfinance institutions since they presented a ROE above the 100 per cent. Though, it is important to observe the amount of capital presented by these institutions, since a lower amount may provoke the rise of this indicator. Most of the micro-finance institutions are characterized by presenting a ROE above the 30 per cent and were established at an Asian country.

During 2012, micro-finance institutions that owned the 100 per cent of women borrowers and with higher assets were established in India. The case of Bandhan stands out since its assets exceeded the billions of dollars, and the other micro-finance institutions presented low levels of assets.

As observed, most of the micro-finance institutions that granted the 100 per cent of their credits to women, apart from the previously analysed variable, were established at Asia, but mainly at India and Vietnam. According the World Bank the indicators for these countries are as follows:

- Most of the population of these countries belongs to rural areas. Between 2007 and 2012, both countries showed percentages above the 65 per cent of rural population in comparison to their total population.
- Feminine population in these countries, as proportion of the total population, was approximately 50 per cent in Vietnam and 48 per cent in India during the same period of time.

According to the latter, it seems that the specific conditions (cultural, economic, and/or social) of Asia have propitiated micro-finance institutions to grant the 100 per cent of their credits to women. This strategy derived on profitable micro-finance institutions since they presented positive profitability indicators.

Conclusion

Micro-credit and the large amount of profits represented by women are part of the financialization process within the frame of the deregulation process and financial liberalization since the end of the decade of the 1970s until present times. The empowerment of women through micro-credit should be approached from different levels, from the macro-economic and micro-economic spheres, as well as from mesoeconomy. Innumerable micro-finance institutions grew at the same time as the disappearance of financial institutions for development, while the shadow financial system, which economic agents were institutional investors, were situated at a place in what refers to profits.

References

Bank for International Settlements (2013) (83rd Annual Report) website: http: //www.bis.org/publ/arpdf/ar2013e.htm>

Bateman, Milford y Ha-Joon Chang. (2012). 'Microfinance and the Illusion of Development: From Hubris to Nemesis in Thirty Years', *World Economic Review*. <http: //werdiscussion.worldeconomics association.org/?post=microfinance-and-theillusion-of-development- from-hubris-to-nemesis-in-thirty-years>

Conde Bonfil, Carola (2005). Instituciones e instrumentos de las microfinanzas en México. Definamos términos. México: Colegio Mexiquense, Programa Interdisciplinario de Estudios del Tercer Sector.

Fraser, Nancy (2013). *Fortunes of Feminism: From State-Managed Capitalism to Neoliberal Crisis*. London: Verso.

Girón, Alicia (2012a). 'Regulando el sistema financiero paralelo' El Reto del Siglo XXI, Regular el Sistema Financiero Global, Ed. Girón, Alicia y Eugenia Correa, Mexico: Instituto de Investigaciones Económicas, Universidad Nacional Autónoma de México, 61–78.

Girón, Alicia (2012b). 'Circuitos financieros, pequeños bancos y grandes ganancias', in Vidal, Gregorio and José Déniz (eds) *Actores del desarrollo y políticas públicas*, Spain: Fondo de Cultura Económica, 89–104.

Girón, Alicia and Alma Chapoy (2012). 'Securitization and financialization', *Journal of Post Keynesian Economics*, 171–186.

Keynes, John Maynard (1964). *The General Theory of Employment, Interest, and Money.* United States of America: Harcourt Brace edition.

Lagarde, Christine (2014). 'Empowerment: The Amartya Sen Lecture', International Monetary Fund, Online video clip, <http: //www.imf.org/ external/mmedia/ view.aspx?vid=3613602042001>

Lamia, Karim (2011). *Microfinance and its Discontents: Women in Debt in Bangladesh.* USA: University of Minnesota Press.

Wray, Randall (2011). 'Working Paper No. 661: Minsky's Money Manager Capitalism and the Global Financial Crisis', Levy Institute. < http: //www.levyinstitute.org/pubs/wp_661.pdf>

'The Global Gender Gap Report', World Economic Forum, 2013. Web. < http: //www3.weforum.org/docs/WEF_GenderGap_Report_ 2013.pdf>

Tymoigne, Eric and Randall Wray (2016). *The Rise and Fall of Money Manager Capitalism: Minsky's Half Century from World War Two to the Great Recession.* USA: Routledge.

20

Differential Effects of Social Factors Influencing Aging and Sleep Disorders in Women

ANITA JAGOTA, NAVYA JANNU AND SUCHITRA BORO

Abstract

Aging is a biological and social construct, characterized by the progressive decline in all physiological functions. It is a programmed natural process and is multidisciplinary in nature. Interestingly more than 150 million of the global aging population of 9 billion people will be from India by 2050. Although aging occurs at varying rates, it has been observed to take a greater toll on the female gender. In addition to multiple social inequalities, women experience proportionately higher rates of chronic illness and disability in later life compared to men. This often leads to depression and reduced socialization resulting in sleep disorders and early aging. We have studied here the effect of social factors influencing aging and sleep disorders in women. The aging in women was studied in variable cross sections of the society characterized by variable social structures and lifestyles. The variable age groups studied were 20–30 (adulthood), 30–40 (late adulthood), 40–50 (middle), 50–60 (late middle), 60–70 (early old), 70–80 (old) and 80–90years and above (late old). Our study demonstrates the direct relationship between sleep disorders, aging and social factors. Sleep disorders affect women differentially across variable age groups in relation to their social factors. Therefore, more effort must be put into understanding the social factors that influence aging in women. Such assimilation will prove to be a step towards healthy aging and longevity.

Keywords

aging, women, sleep disorders, social factors

Introduction

Growing old is a biological process. It occurs naturally to all living organisms with the passage of time. Aging is abiological and social construct, characterized by the progressive decline in all physiological functions with a steady decline of organ functions and body system (Estes and Carrol, 2001; Jagota, 2005; Balen and Girija, 2010). Aging is a normal part of the life span from conception through birth-infancy-childhood-adolescence-adulthood-old age to death. Each of these stages has unique characteristics and vulnerabilities that require special attention so as to ensure best health during each stage (Balen and Girija, 2010). Age depends upon genes, social and environmental influences, and lifestyle (Tinker, 1997; Sahrawat, 2010). Each individual has a unique genetic make-up and distinct social and environmental surrounding. This plays an important role in their aging process. Aging also known as 'senescence' is characterized by a complex combination of physiological, psychological and social aspects.

With the passage of time, the demographic characteristics of countries have undergone significant change. Population aging is a product of history, individual experiences and social forces (Sen, 1994; Chokrobarti, 2004). It is viewed as natural outcome of demographic transition. The rapid increase in industrialization and fast modernization has significantly affected the lives of elderly people in the society. These changes have predominantly had a negative influence on them. The conversion of traditional joint families into nuclear families together with a growing generation gap have not only made the elderly uncomfortable but also feel less important in the society. Interestingly, we note the application of different cultural values and social expectations, invariable gender and age groups (Bahura and Mohanty, 2005; Joshi, 2006; Bhawsar, 2011; Sranges and Tigbe, 2012).

It has been estimated that by 2050, the world will have more then 16 per cent of its population in the 65+ age group. More than 150 million of the global aging population of 9 billion people will be from India by 2050. This brings to the fore an urgency to meet the social security arrangements needed for these elderly persons. There is a pressing need to plan for their fiscal security, housing, health, family-care, social welfare and other needs. (Liebig and Rajan, 2005; Islam, 2010). Aging takes a greater toll on the female gender though occurs at varying rates. In addition to multiple social inequalities, women experience proportionately higher rates of chronic illness and disability in later life compared to men. The aging process in women is distinct from that in men (Karkal, 1999; Mallampalli and Carter, 2014). Aging brings about many changes on the physical, psychological and social front of a woman's life. Thus, there is a need to understand here as a prerequisite the problems of elderly. Sleep disturbances are common in older people especially among women, significantly affecting their mood, alertness, unconscious mind, etc. The change in sleeping patterns is caused by both physical and lifestyle changes, which also influence the alteration of social factors with aging. Diverse factors in addition to aging, such as physical fitness, retirement, health problems, death of family members, changes in activity or social life, as well as changes in daily rhythms play important role (Jagota, 2005) in the aging process. In addition to affecting quality of life including excessive daytime sedation, physical, psychological, cognitive problems affecting health, sleep disorders have been implicated with an increased mortality rate (Smith, 2008).

The common sleep disorders in the elderly are sleep apnea, nocturnal myoclonus and advanced sleep phase syndrome (ASPS) etc. (Jagota, 2005;

Moraes et al., 2013) These sleep disturbances have been attributed to disturbances in circadian function caused by the failure of the pineal gland to produce melatonin neurohormone which is a key molecule in regulating the timing and quality of sleep (Grad and Rozencwaig, 1993). Melatonin has also been identified as a multitasking molecule with anti-aging properties. The decrease in its levels with aging affects body physiology. Interestingly decreased melatonin levels in aging women are also accompanied by a decrease in estrogen due to menopause in this age group. This leads to multiple health problems, reduced physical activitiy, a reduced interest in socialization and thus resulting in depression and sleep disorders (Jagota, 2005; Balen and Girija, 2010; Fabbrini et al., 2015).

Aging has also been linked to the social factors like poverty, illiteracy, family, widowhood, loneliness, modern lifestyle, food habits, etc. Many of these problems are scientifically variable but have been observed to be more common among women of certain social backgrounds among ethnic profiles, etc. We, therefore, have studied here the effect of social factors influencing aging and sleep disorders in women.

Methodology

The variable age groups of women studied were – Group A: 20–30 (adulthood); Group B: 30–40 (late adulthood); Group C: 40–50 (middle); Group D: 50–60 (late middle); Group E: 60–70 (early old); Group F: 70–80 (old) and Group G: 80–90 and above years (late old) (Table 1). The survey was taken in variable age groups in variable cross sections of society characterized by variable social structures and lifestyles.

The survey was done on students, employees and residents of the University of Hyderabad as well as the surrounding *Masid Banda* locality in Hyderabad. The data was collected through surveys from the aforementioned age groups. The questionnaires were designed to focus on understanding the social factors influencing age-induced alterations in sleep patterns. The studies in the various age groups were organized as:

Case Study I: Sleep disorders in variable age groups in women (Table 1, Figure 1).

Case Study II: Social problems in variable age groups in women (Table 2, Figure 2).

The surveys for case studies II and I were done in triplicate on three different sets of people in each age group (i.e. Ia, Ib, Ic and IIa, IIb and IIc).

Limitations of the Study

The study is based on a very limited sample taken from select old age homes and individuals. But an attempt has been made for probable generalization through the results of this study of the social factors influencing aging.

Statistical Analysis

From the survey data, the social problems that induced the suffering of sleep disorders in women of various age groups were analysed. Jandel Scientific Sigma stat software was used to analyse data by one way ANOVA. This was followed by post hoc Dunkan's test for multiple comparisons of the parameters determined at variable time points within an age group. The student's test was used to compare younger age groups to older age groups for the parameters studied.

Results

The case studies were taken with a focus on identification of the social factors influencing aging and sleep disorders in women (Figure 1 and 2).

Figure 1
Sleep Problems

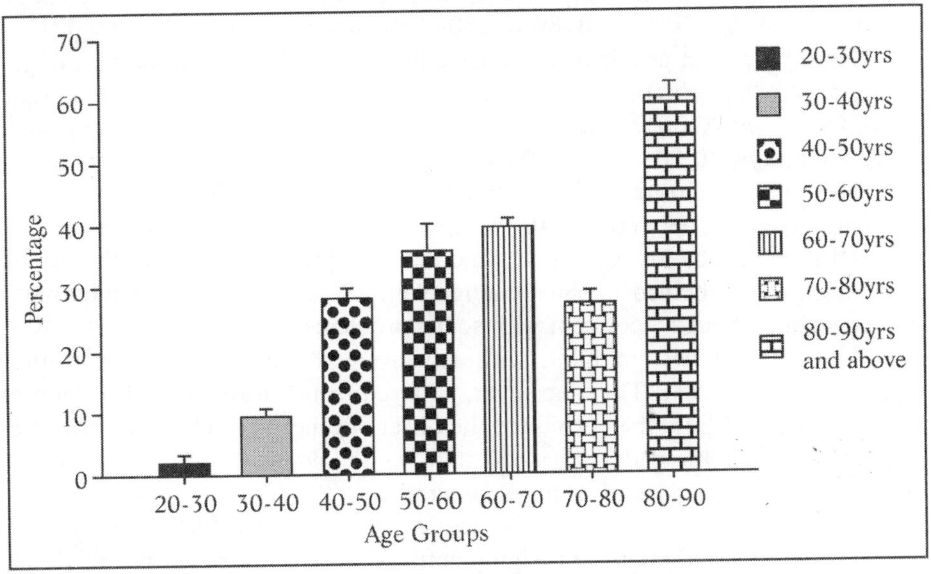

Figure 2
Social Problems

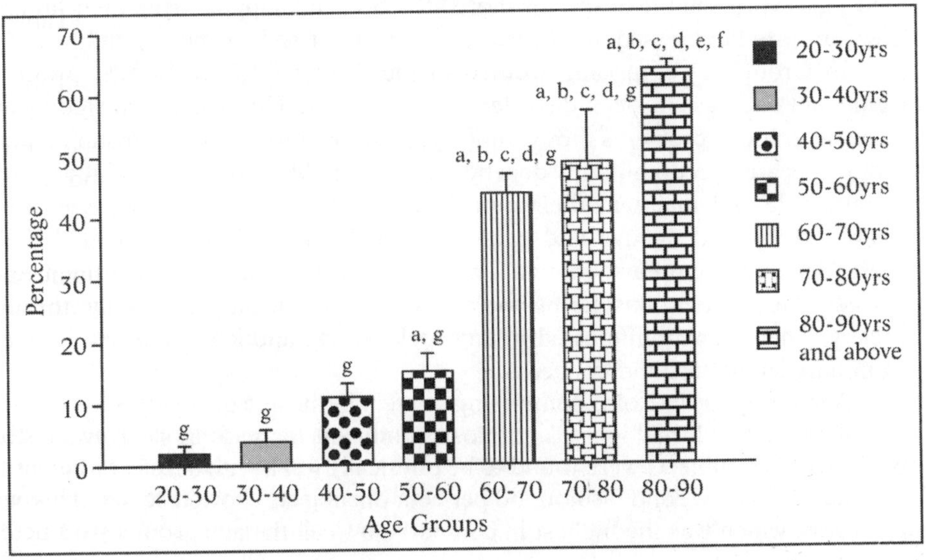

In case study – I and II (Table 1 and 2) age group A (adulthood) comprising women from 20–30 age group were found to be robustly active and healthier than other older groups. There were no social or sleep problems (Figure 1 and 2). Interestingly, most of the subjects appeared satisfied and happy with their life.

Figure Legend

Figure 1 Sleep disorders in variable age groups in women. $Pa < 0.001$, $pb < 0.001$, $pc < 0.001$, $pd < 0.001$, $pe < 0.001$, $pf < 0.001$ and $pg < 0.001$. Where a, b, c, d, e, f and g represent significantly different 20–30 (a); 30–40 (b); 40–50 (c) 50–60 (d); 60–70 (e), 70–80 (f), 80–90yrs and above (g) (P = <0.001)

Figure 2 Social problems in variable age groups in women. a, b, c, d, e, f same. $pa < 0.001$, $pb < 0.001$, $pc < 0.001$, $pd < 0.001$, $pe < 0.001$, $pf < 0.001$ and $pg < 0.001$. $pa < 0.001$, $pb < 0.001$, $pc < 0.001$, $pd < 0.001$, $pe < 0.001$, $pf < 0.001$ and $pg < 0.001$. (P = <0.001)

However, in Group B (late adulthood), comprising women in the 30–40 years age group, 9 per cent showed sleep disorders and more than 3.5 per cent showed social problems. Group C (middle), comprising women in the 40–50 years age group, showed a robust change with 28 per cent women having sleep disorders and about 13 per cent with social problems.

In Group D (late middle), with age group of 50–60 years, the women appeared independent. They, however, suffered from various kinds of sleeping problems. In addition, they exhibited the onset of other age-related disorders as joint pains, depression due to stress and household work and a difficulty in adjusting to the lifestyles of younger generations.

The 60–70 years age group E (early old) showed a further increase in social problems although not significantly different in sleep problems. In addition, problems like diabetes, joint pains, osteoporosis, etc. were also found in these groups. Those who were employed earlier but were now retired from their jobs expressed the desire for more attention and support from their family. They appeared depressed and insecure about their finances, health and future.

In Group F, comprising women in the 70–80 (old) years age group, a significant decrease in sleep disorders was observed. This was contrasted by an increase in social problems though not significantly different from group E. This group appeared predominantly dependent on their children and found it difficult to take care and maintain their nutrition and medical needs. They appeared weak and in need of love and care from their family. They associated their retirement and unemployment to a lowered status. They had low self-esteem and felt neglected, often considering themselves as burden on their family and the society. They grew uninterested in any social work, and keep themselves away from familial matters and concerns.

Age group G (late old) comprising women in the age group of 80–90 years and above showed the highest and most significant increase in sleep and social problems. The subjects were found to be physically weak with a loss of interest in maintaining lifestyle and fashion; 60 per cent of subjects showed social and sleep problems, which was the highest in comparison to all the age groups studied.

Table 1

Case Study I: Sleep Disorders in Variable Age Groups in Women

S.No.	Age Group	Age (in years)	Case Study Ia	Percentage (%)	Case Study Ib	Percentage (%)	Case Study Ic	Percentage (%)	Mean ± SE Percentage (%)
1	Group A	20–30	0/20	0	0/20	0	1/20	5.00	1.66 ± 1.66
2	Group B	30–40	2/18	11.11	2/19	10.52	1/17	5.88	9.17 ± 1.65
3	Group C	40–50	4/15	26.66	5/16	31.25	4/15	26.66	28.19 ± 1.53
4	Group D	50–60	4/10	40.00	4/12	40.00	3/11	27.27	35.75 ± 4.24
5	Group E	60–70	6/16	37.50	7/17	41.17	6/15	40.00	39.55 ± 1.08
6	Group F	70–80	5/20	25.00	5/20	25.00	6/19	31.57	27.19 ± 2.19
7	Group G	80–90 and above	5/9	55.50	5/8	62.50	5/8	62.5	60.16 ± 2.33
			108	24.07	112	25.00	105	24.76	24.61 ± 0.28

Table 2

Case Study II: Social Problems in Variable Age Groups in Women

S.No.	Age Group	Age (in years)	Case Study IIa	Percentage (%)	Case Study IIb	Percentage (%)	Case Study IIc	Percentage (%)	Mean ± SE Percentage (%)
1	Group A	20–30	0/20	0	0/20	0	1/20	5.00	1.66 ± 1.66
2	Group B	30–40	0/18	0	1/19	5.26	1/17	5.88	3.71 ± 1.86
3	Group C	40–50	1/15	6.60	2/16	12.50	2/15	13.33	10.81 ± 2.12
4	Group D	50–60	1/10	10.00	2/12	16.66	2/11	18.18	14.94 ± 2.51
5	Group E	60–70	8/16	50.00	7/17	41.17	6/15	40.00	43.72 ± 3.15
6	Group F	70–80	12/20	60.00	11/20	55.00	6/19	31.58	48.85 ± 8.76
7	Group G	80–90 and above	6/9	66.66	5/8	62.50	5/8	62.50	63.88 ± 1.38
			108	25.92	112	25.00	105	21.90	24.27 ± 1.21

Discussion

Women suffer the impact of the natural phenomenon of aging more than men. Interestingly, women in the age group of 20–30 (adulthood) years were stronger, healthier and more confident compared to other age groups. There was sudden surge in sleep disorders with more than 9 per cent in 30–40 years (late adulthood) and 28 per cent in 40–50 years (middle) of age groups with 4 and 11 per cent, respectively, having social problems. The age groups such as 50–60 years (late middle), 60–70 years (early old), 70–80 years (old), 80–90 years and above (late old) had significantly higher social and health problems in comparison to the 20–30 age groups. The onset of sleep and social problems appeared in the 30–40 years (early middle) and became more overt in the 40–50 years (middle) of age group. The later age group has been reported to be associated with natural menopause and menopausal symptoms (Vitiello et al., 2004; Li et al., 2014). The age groups of 60–80 years suffered more with sleep problems than social problems.

The present study highlights that sleep disorders in women are directly linked to social problems in all age groups but for the 70–80 years of age group. Social problems of the 60–70 years and 70–80 years of age groups were not significantly different but were three times higher than the 50–60 years of age group, i.e. more than 40 per cent of the women showed social problems. Additionally, the major symptoms of sleep disorders and problems of aging were found linked to irritation, stress, and decrease in bodily function and leading to social problems. Although sleep disorders were higher in older women, 28 per cent women in 40–50 years of age group were affected. The survey data revealed sleep disorders to have had a significant negative impact on daily functioning and quality of life. Social factors like widowhood, illiteracy, lifestyle, etc. were found to have a further influence on the aging women. Upon aging, the alterations in various physical, physiological and biochemical processes lead to a disruption of the circadian system. These alterations include the shift in the phase, reduction in the amplitude or even abolition of the rhythms (Jagota. 2005, 2012). Interestingly the sleep structure also has been reported to change with aging (Moraes et al., 2014).

Earlier in our laboratory using animal models, we reported the daily serotonin, leptin, oxidative stress indicators and clock genes to lose rhythmicity with aging and onset of such changes in middle age (Jagota and Kalyani, 2008, 2010; Manikonda and Jagota, 2012; Mattam and Jagota, 2014, 2015; Reddy and Jagota, 2014, 2015). The present observations are in agreement with our previous studies.

The findings of the above survey suggest that older people are happier and more comfortable living with their family than in old age homes. The subjects studied were in want of the love and care of their near and dear ones. Such emotional changes lead to depression and a decrease in socialization resulting in sleep disorders and early aging (Seth, 2000; Voyer et al., 2014).

Therefore, it is required to sensitize and make the society aware of the needs of the elderly. An old person should be encouraged to stay in an old age home if and only if he or she is helpless with no one to look after them in his or her old age. It is also important to improve the quality of life in old age people at physical, social and emotional levels. Socially, the problems of aging in women, must be emphasized upon so that all women will be more aware, cautious and encouraged to take care of their own health, exercise, maintain proper diet, regular sleep time and make suitable living arrangements.

Conclusion and Policy Recommendation

Aging has a significantly negative impact on the daily functioning and quality of life. From the above study, it is found that old age people prefer to be with their family rather than staying in old age homes. Here, however, old age people who lived together as couples were comparatively happier and healthier than their single counterparts. The onset of sleep and social problems were visible in the 30–40 and 40–50 years of age groups.

In 50–60 years of age group, social problems were not significant but became increasingly present and relevant in the 60–70 years of age group, leading to a marked increase in sleep disorders. Women in the age groups of 70–80 years and 80–90 years and above showed a further increase in social problems. The significant decrease in sleep problems in this age group could be linked to the sample size.

Aging and sleep disorders appeared linked as psychological disturbances lead to anger, anxiety and restlessness which in turn lead to sleep disorders which lead to physiological changes in the body resulting in social problems and, thus, early aging. Social security programmes must, therefore, be suitably adjusted and extended to cover unique interests of specific age groups. Government policies too must be made more responsive and effective in providing timely financial support and good quality free healthcare services.

Understanding the correlation between social factors influencing sleep disorders in aging women, will help design social policies and measures necessary for longevity, healthy and graceful aging.

References

Balan, S.V. and Girija, V.D. (2010). 'Health Status of the Elderly', *Indian Journal Gerontology*, 24: 194–209.

Behura, N.K. and Mohanty, P.C. (2005). *Aged in Changing Social System: Their Problems*, New Delhi: Discovery Publishing House.

Bhawsar, R.D. (2001). 'Population Ageing in India: Demographic and Health Dimension', *Indian Journal of Gerontology*. 15, 256–277.

Chokroborti, R.G.D. (2004). *Graying of India: Population Ageing in the Context of Asia.* New Delhi.

Estes, C.L. (2001). *Social Policy and Aging: A Critical Perspective.* California.

Fabbrini, M.; AricÃ, I.; Tramonti, F.; Condurso, R.; Carnicelli, L.; De Rosa, A. and Pagliarulo, M.G. (2015). 'Sleep Disorders in Menopause: Results from an Italian Multicentric Study', *Archives Italiennes de Biologie*, 153: 216–225.

Grad, B.R. and Rozencwaig, R. (1993). 'The Role of Melatonin and Serotonin in Aging: Update', *Psychoneuroendocrinology*, 18: 283–295.

Islam, M.R., Rahman, M.M. and Islam, M.R. (2010). 'Socio-Economic Condition of the Rural Aged in Bangladesh: A Logistic Regression Analysis, *Indian Journal of Gerontology,* 24: 225–236.

Jagota, A. (2005). 'Aging and Sleep Disorders', *Indian Journal Gerontology,* 19: 415–424.

Jagota, A. (2012). Age Induced Alterations in Biological Clock: Therapeutic Effects of Melatonin, in Jagota, A. *Brain Aging: Therapeutic Interventions,* New York: Springer, 111–130.

Jagota, A. and Kalyani, D. (2010). 'Effect of Melatonin on Age induced Changes in Daily Serotonin Rhythms in Suprachiasmatic Nucleus of Male Wistar Rat', *Biogerontology,* 11: 299–308.

Jagota, A. and Kalyani, D. (2008). 'Daily Serotonin Rhythms in Rat Brain during Postnatal Development and Aging', *Biogerontology,* 9: 229–234.

Karkal, M. (1999). Ageing and Women in India, *Economic and Political Weekly,* Vol. XXXIV: 1–5.

Kinsella K, He, W. (2009). An Aging World: 2008, Washington, DC: US Government Printing Office, US Census Bureau. International Population Reports, PS95/09, 1.

Li, L., Wu, J., Jiang, X.Q., Pu, D.H. and Zhao, Y. (2013). [Survey on epidemiologic factors associated with the age of natural menopause and menopausal symptoms in Jiangsu women]. Zhonghua fu chan ke za zhi, 48: 728–733.

Liebig, S.P. and Rajan, S.I. (reprint, 2005). *An Ageing India: Perspectives, Prospects and Politics*. Jaipur: Rawat Publications.

Mallampalli, M.P. and Carter, C.L. (2014). 'Exploring Sex and Gender differences in Sleep Health: A Society for Women's Health Research Report', *Journal of Women's Health,* 23: 553–562.

Manikonda, P.K. and Jagota, A. (2012). 'Melatonin Administration differentially Affects on Age induced Alterations in Daily Rhythms of Lipid Peroxidation and Antioxidant Enzymes in Male Rat Liver', *Biogerontology,* 13: 511–524.

Mattam, U. and Jagota, A. (2014). 'Therapeutic Effects of Melatonin on Age induced Alterations in Daily Rhythms of Expression of Various Clock Genes in Suprachiasmatic Nucleus of Male Wistar Rat', *Biogerontology,* 15: 245–256.

Mattam, U. and Jagota, A. (2015). 'Daily Rhythms of Serotonin Metabolism and the Expression of Clock Genes in Suprachiasmatic Nucleus of Rotenone-induced Parkinson's Disease Male Wistar Rat Model and Effect of Melatonin Administration', *Biogerontology,* 16: 109–123.

Moraes, W.; Piovezan, R.; Poyares, D.; Bittencourt, L.R.; Santos-Silva, R. and Tufik, S. (2014). 'Effects of Aging on Sleep Structure throughout Adulthood: A Population-based Study', *Sleep Medicine,* 15: 401–409.

Reddy, M.Y. and Jagota, A. (2015). 'Melatonin has Differential Effects on Age-induced Stoichiometric Changes in Daily Chronomics of Serotonin Metabolism in SCN of Male Wistar Rats', *Biogerontology*. 16: 169–123.

Reddy, V.D.K. and Jagota, A. (2014). 'Food Entrained Regulation Affects Nocturnality and Daily Leptin Rhythms in OVLT in Aged Rats', *Biogerontology,* 15: 257–268.

Sahrawat, S. (2010). 'A Tryst with Psychological Adversity in Old Age', *Indian Journal of Gerontology,* 24: 59–80.

Sen, K. (1994). *Ageing: Debates on Demographic Transition and Social Policy.* USA: Zed Books Ltd.

Seth, S. (2000). 'Ageing and Women', *Economic and Political Weekly,* Mumbai, 1.

Smith, M.W. (2008). 'Sleep and Ageing', *Web MD: Healthy Aging Guide.*

Stranges, S.; Tigbe, W.; Gómez-Olivé, F.X.; Thorogood, M. and Kandala, N.B. (2012). 'Sleep Problems: An Emerging Global Epidemic?' Findings from the INDEPTH WHO-SAGE Study among more than 40,000 older adults from eight countries across Africa and Asia. *Sleep*, 35: 1,173–1,181.

Tinker, A. (1997). The Environment of Ageing, Age Concern Institute of Gerontology, Great Britain, 1,861–1,868.

Vitiello, M.V.; Larsen, L.H. and Moe, K.E. (2004). 'Age-Related Sleep Change: Gender and Estrogen Effects on the Subjective-objective Sleep Quality Relationships of Healthy, Noncomplaining Older Men and Women', *Journal of Psychosomatic Research*, 56: 503–510.

Voyer, P.; Verreault, R.; Cappeliez, P.; Holmes, D. and Mengue, P.N. (2005). 'Symptoms of Psychological Distress among Older Adults in Canadian Long-term Care Centres', *Aging and Mental Health*, 9: 542–554.

Index